THE

PRE-ADAMITE EARTH:

CONTRIBUTIONS

TO

THEOLOGICAL SCIENCE.

BY

JOHN HARRIS, D. D.

AUTHOR OF "THE GREAT TEACHER,' ETC.

FIFTH THOUSAND.
REVISED AND ENLARGED.

BOSTON:
GOULD AND LINCOLN,
59 WASHINGTON STREET.
1854.

BOSTON,
GEO. C. RAND, PRINTER.

CONTENTS.

NOTES.

⁂ It may save the reader some trouble to be apprised, that the order in which the Principles are stated in the Second Part is not the order in which they are subsequently illustrated. The order in which they are illustrated in the Third, Fourth, and Fifth Parts, is the same.

PREFACE.

THE present volume is intended to be the first of a short series of Treatises — each complete in itself — in which the principles or laws hereafter deduced, and applied to the successive stages of the pre-Adamite earth, will be seen in their historical development as applied to individual man; to the family; to the nation; to the Son of God as "the second Adam, the Lord from heaven;" to the church which he has founded; to the revelation which he has completed; and to the future prospects of humanity. It would not be difficult to state the reasons which have induced me to adopt this particular method of exhibiting theological science; to specify the points in which it differs from those methods which may be considered most nearly to resemble it; and to enlarge on the advantages, direct and indirect, which it is proposed to secure by it. But, besides that such topics, if introduced at all, would require to be treated at considerable length, I would rather that the method adopted should, as it is gradually unfolded in the successive Treatises, be allowed to speak for itself. If any explanatory remarks respecting it are deemed necessary, they will, it appears to me, be more in place at the close of the Series than at the commencement.

This first volume consists of five parts. Of these, the first part contains those Primary Truths which Divine Revelation appears to place at the foundation of all the objective manifestations of the Deity; the second, presents the Laws or General Principles, which are regarded as logically resulting from the preceding Truths; and the third, fourth, and fifth parts, are occupied with the Exemplification and Verification of these Laws in the inorganic, the vegetable, and the animal kingdoms of the pre-Adamite earth, respectively. From this statement it will be seen that the first two parts are here as introductory, not to the present volume merely, but to the entire series; and that, as exhibiting the process by which the method has been arrived at, they will not require, except in substance, to be subsequently repeated.

As Revealed Theology is here seen in organic connection with natural science, a few remarks explanatory of that connection will not be deemed irrelevant. Of the theology itself, I will only say, at present, that it is that which I believe; but, inasmuch, as it is exhibited in mere human forms of thought and language, I can, of course, expect that others will accede to it only as far as they believe it to be in harmony with "the true sayings of God." Nor can I be insensible that the laws deduced from it will be prejudiced in some minds, by the notion that the adoption of them involves the reception of the theology. But as views deducible from the highest grounds are generally found to be inferrible also from lower and analogical premises, it should be considered, in the present instance, whether these laws might not be accepted on such inferior grounds without committing the recipient to any ulterior views. Even less than this, however, is necessary. For, if the reader should demur to adopt the Laws as they are deduced from the Primary Truths of the first Part, he has to consider whether he is not called on to admit them, as they are sustained and inductively verified by the facts adduced in the three concluding Parts. These facts, I may remark in passing, admit of almost indefinite multiplication, but it has been my aim to adduce only such and so many as appeared essential to the verification of the laws.

Of the connection between theology and natural science generally, it may be assumed that every one who admits that there is a true theology and a true science of nature, will admit also that there is a sense, whatever it may be, in which the two are related. The mind which elicits and embraces both, is one; so that, however distinct the process by which it arrives at the knowledge of each, and however different the sources and kinds of evidence on which that knowledge rests, both branches evince their inherent unison, in the unity of the knowing mind itself. On this conviction it is that men no sooner begin to think, than they next proceed to examine the laws of thought; if they collect facts, they next inquire for the causes of those facts; and when they have succeeded in developing any of the sciences, they then look for the internal bond of union which makes them all one. And for such a *nexus* they seek under the unquestioned conviction that it exists; for the conviction simply implies that, as reasoning concerning each separate science is possible, so reasoning concerning collective science must be possible.

Well had it been for theology and philosophy if the bond which unites them had been clearly ascertained, and never dissevered. But the erroneous views which some have entertained respecting the relation of the two, have originated evils only less than those flowing from their unnatural separation. The error of Descartes and his followers consisted, not in making theology the point of their philosophy, but in regarding their metaphysical deductions as adequate to explain all physical phenomena. By reasoning only, *à priori*, or proceeding continually downwards from cause to effect, they were, not questioning Nature, but answering for her; legislating, in effect, where God had legislated already; and so "building a world upon hypothesis."[1] There is, however, a wide interval between the extreme which makes everything of a prin-

[1] Introduction to Butler's Analogy, &c.

ciple, and that which seeks security from it, by abandoning the principle altogether.

As surely as the mind is one, the truth to which the mind is preconfigured is one. On this ground it is that we argue from the known to the unknown; approach a subject of inquiry under the guidance of an antecedent probability as to what we shall find in it; and employ analogy and hypothesis as instruments of scientific discovery. "How," inquires Plato, "can you expect to find unless you have a general idea of what you seek?" "The mind," says Lord Bacon, "must bring to every experiment a 'precogitation,' or antecedent idea, as the ground of that 'prudens quæstio,'" which he pronounces to be the prior half of the knowledge sought—"dimidium scientiæ." Indeed, is not the Novum Organum itself of hypothetical origin? "When Newton said, 'Hypotheses non fingo,' he did not mean that he deprived himself of the facilities of investigation afforded by assuming, in the first instance, what he hoped ultimately to be able to prove. Without such assumptions, science could never have attained its present state; they are necessary steps in the progress to something more certain; and nearly everything which is now theory was once hypothesis. Even in purely experimental science, some inducement is necessary for trying one experiment rather than another."[1] These hypotheses, as the language implies, are only provisional. They must be of a nature to admit of verification; and be actually subjected to a test which shall confirm or explode them.

In the same provisional manner might principles derived from the domain of revealed theology be advantageously carried into the province of nature. There is a true deductive method in science as well as a false; and there is a right method of employing theological principles in philosophy, as well as a wrong. Everything depends on the manner in which they are employed. The inductive conclusion must be kept distinct from the speculative assumption. However fruitful the de-

[1] Mill's System of Logic, vol. ii. p. 18.

ductive principle may be, it can be used only for suggestion, not for demnostration; the *proof* of the view suggested must be of the samenature with that of the subject investigated or discussed.

In the following pages, the principles introduced are to be regarded as employed only in this conditional manner. The reader is to view them, as far as their application to nature is concerned, as entirely tentative or provisional, until their applicability has been tested. If on a comparison of the inductive truth adduced, with these deductive principles, their applicability is apparent, let the obvious inference be accepted, that there is a theology in nature which is ultimately one with the theology of the Bible — that there are principles of varied but universal application.

The attempt which is here made to deduce such principles, and to apply them to the successive stages of creation, proceeds on the assumption that the whole process of Divine Manifestation, including nature, is to be viewed in the light of a sublime argument in which God is deductively reasoning from principles to facts, from generals to particulars. With the great synthetic Whole ever present to His mind, He is seen unfolding the parts of which it consists. In order that man may feel the force of this reasoning, his mind, equally with the Divine Mind, must pre-suppose, or be prepared to admit, the primary truths on which the reasoning depends. But besides these, the Great Argument implies (as in every case of ordinary reasoning) that there are certain ideas or truths in the mind of God, which are not yet in the mind of man, and which it is the design of the argument to convey. For example — whatever exhibits marks of design must have had an intelligent author; the world exhibits marks of design, therefore the world must have had an intelligent Author. Here, the *major* is assumed alike by God and man; the *conclusion* is, at first, in the mind of God alone, and the design of the great argument is to convey it into the mind of man also; but the attainment of this end depends on the truth of the *minor* — that the world does exhibit marks of design; and how is this proposition to be established except by induction? To the infinitely blessed God, then, the entire process of Divine Manifestation is, in its reference to man, a sublime syllogism, of which the last object and the remotest event are already included potentially in the major; the unfolding of which is destined to occupy the coming eternity. While man, appointed to find the sphere of his activity and improvement in the intermediate space between the Necessary and the Contingent, and unable to rest but in the felt junction of the two, shall derive perpetual accessions of enjoyment as he ascends from the Particular to the Infinite with whom it has originated, and in whom is it contained.

THE

PRE-ADAMITE EARTH.

FIRST PART.

CHAPTER I.

THE GREAT REASON; *or, why God is, and must be His own end from everlasting to everlasting.*

GOD is not nature; nor is nature God. Before nature, before any part or being of the objective universe existed, the God of the Bible had existed from eternity in his own self-sufficience. And the absolute perfection which that self-sufficience implies, determines that it shall be, in some sense, the chief reason and last end of everything created; so that He will continue to inhabit his self-sufficience through the eternity to come. We believe, indeed, that, while He supremely regards His own glory, He really regards the well-being of the created universe *for its own sake;* that this well-being is regarded by God as *an* end—in the sense of being an object desirable on its own account; and that He delights in it as such; but that *the* ultimate, chief, and all-comprehending end is His own glory.[1]

1. Had there ever been a period when nothing was nothing would still have been. Then the Creator of things is himself uncreated, unoriginated, *eternal.* "He i from everlasting." Far back, in thought, and beyond the

[1] See Note A.

limits of time, as we may be able occasionally, and for a single moment, to go, we are ever accompanied by the humbling conviction that we have made no approach whatever to the understanding of His eternity. The discoveries of science lead back our imagination to a period incalculably remote; but even if each of the countless stars had been formed in succession, and if the time which elapsed between the formation of each had equalled that entire period, the mind which could span the whole — which could dart back a thought to the moment in which the first star beamed on the regions of space, would feel that it had only reached the starting point for the preceding eternity. For if then it should ask, "Where dwelt the Deity before that?"—the answer of the Oracle is, "He inhabited eternity;" and that star of which it had caught a glimpse, could only be regarded as the first lamp that was lighted up to guide the way back to His dread abode.

2. Then must His mysterious existence be *necessary and independent;*[1] for as there has never been anything, ab extra, to necessitate it, had it not been necessary of and from itself only, it could neither have been, nor have continued to be. The great parent truth, therefore, which He may be regarded as silently repeating, through all the solitudes of space, and through every point of duration, is the sublime affirmation, "I AM — underived, self-existent, absolute Being; in which sense there never has been, never will be, never can be, any Being besides." All other being can only be derived and dependent.

3. In harmony with the dictates of enlightened reason, the Bible authenticates the deduction that the Being whose existence is eternal and independent, is also *absolutely perfect.* The power of God must be omnipotence; His knowledge, omniscience; His holy benevolence, unlimited by anything incompatible with perfection. No one kind of excellence can be unlimited unless it be associated with every other kind of excellence; so that the possession of any one unlimited excellence implies the existence, and involves the necessity, of absolute perfection.

4. But if the infinite nature of the Divine Being precludes the existence of another independent and unlimited Being, the existence of a second would necessarily involve mutual

---

[1] See Gillespie's Necessary Existence of God.

limitation; which would amount to a self-contradiction. In every sense, therefore, *consistent with perfection*, He has ever existed alone. Were He to break the silence of eternity, He might demand, "Is there a God besides me? yea, there is none; *I know* not any.[1] I, who know all the possibilities of being, know not of such a being; I, who at this moment am everywhere present throughout illimitable space, find such a being nowhere; I, who have thus inhabited immensity from eternity, have never, in any point of past duration, beheld the least manifestation of such a being; I, who am unlimited Being, exclude, by that very necessity of my nature, the possibility of another unlimited being."

5. But what finite mind can conceive the conditions included in Absolute Perfection! To evolve these will require eternity; for could they be evolved in less they would not be unlimited. All that we can say, therefore, or shall ever be able to say, is, that whatever the amount of mystery included in the objective universe may ever be, the probability is, that the proportion which it bears to the mystery of the Divine nature will be that of the limited to the unlimited; that if infinite perfection implies infinite mysteriousness, which it certainly does, then infinite mysteriousness must ever form one of the distinctive excellences of that perfection; that if the operation of infinite activity (either of love, of power, or of any other excellence) be essential to infinite perfection, and if such activity could not be agent and object at the same time, and in the same act, and yet no object, ad extra, existed from eternity, then must it have existed in the Divine nature itself; in other words, the Divine nature must include a plurality of distinctions, and include it as one of its necessary conditions, or essential perfections;[2] that if no exercise of the Divine efficiency, ad extra, can ever be adequate to its infinite perfection, and yet such adequate exercise, in some way, must always be necessary to infinite perfection, then must it be one of the excellences of the Divine nature, not only that it should include a plurality of distinctions, but that the adequate sphere of its infinite activity should be its own infinite perfections; that if a

---

[1] Isaiah, xliv. 6, 8.

[2] See Howe's Calm Enquiry concerning the Possibility of a Trinity in the Godhead. Professor Kidd on the Trinity. Storr and Flatt, B. ii. § 46. § 44. Ill. 8. Dr. J. P. Smith's Testimony of the Messiah, (Second Edition,) v. i. c. iv. § 35, v. iii. app. iv.

God in unity, without internal distinctions, or diversity of modes, be incapable of moral affection, because having had nothing, ad extra, from eternity to love, then such internal distinctions must ever have existed as elements of reciprocal, social, self-sufficient perfection; and that if such plurality be an excellence, and if unity be an excellence also; and if there be any respect in which this plurality of one kind can consist as an excellence with this unity of another, then it will certainly be included in absolute perfection. And further, this perfection implies not only that all the excellence which it includes is simple, uncompounded, one, but that God and it are identical: that it is not an adjunct of His being, but His being itself.

6. But for the same reason that His perfection of being and character is unlimited, it must ever have been unchangeable also. Besides which, it must be of the essence of Absolute Perfection that in everything belonging to that perfection, it can neither require nor admit of a change. Though an eternity has passed, the Deity is now what He ever was; "without the shadow of a turning." The past has stayed with Him, the future has ever been present to Him: the one could not diminish his perfection, nor the other augment it. "Who by searching can find out God!"

7. Then the Deity has existed from eternity as His own end. By supposition, nothing as yet has been brought into existence. No ground therefore exists, no occasion has yet been given, for raising the great question as to who or what can be that end. No creative fiat has yet gone forth. Time has not counted its first revolution. In imagination, we are standing in the solitudes of the past eternity. Never has this stillness been broken. No ray of created light has ever penetrated this darkness. This infinite space has never owned a world. No seraph bows before His throne. If these solitudes shall ever be peopled with finite beings, the purpose is shut up in the mind of God. Boundless as His capacity for happiness must always have been, the consciousness of His own excellence, and the contemplation of His own perfections, have ever been sufficient to fill it. Unlimited and unceasing as must have been His activity, His own nature has been sufficient to exercise and contain the whole. Dateless in His duration, the postponement of creation for ten thousand thousand ages would not increase that duration, nor would it have been diminished had the fiat gone forth ten thousand thousand ages

before it did. Unshared by anything, ab extra, as His eternity, and lonely, in the same sense, as His immensity must ever have been, His self-communion has been sufficient to occupy and replenish the whole with happiness. And inconceivably great as the end answered by this infinity and immensity of perfection must have been, His own enjoyment and glory are amply commensurate to the whole.

8. But if he has always been His own end, it follows that He must ever continue to be the same. For on the supposition of any other object becoming that end, then all that had gone before during the past eternity could only be regarded as its own end in a subordinate sense; while in reference to this other end since developed, it has been only the means. "That which exists merely as a cause, exists merely for the sake of something else — is not final in itself, but simply a means towards an end; and in the accomplishment of that end, it consummates its own perfection." From which it would follow, that, during a whole eternity, Infinite Self-sufficience stood in the subordinate relation of means to beings not yet in existence; that during that eternity Infinite Perfection was imperfect as the means without the end; and that the addition of imperfect and dependent being was necessary to give perfection to that imperfection.

9. If to be His own end be an antecedent right, antecedent to creation by an eternity; and if, after enjoying that right for an eternity, He choose to exercise another right — the right of creation — the exercise of this subsequent and inferior right cannot affect the primary eternal right. The display of Divine perfection can never impair the original prerogatives of that perfection. That He should lose his right, because of his perfection, is revolting to reason. Render his prerogatives more evident it may, but destroy them it cannot. For glorious as that display may be, and after it has been augmenting ten thousand ages, His absolute perfection will remain the same as it was before that display began. That manifestation will not have increased it; for it will be only the objective existence of that which was His subjectively from eternity. Lofty as may be the natures, and countless as may be the myriads which will encircle His throne, He must ever continue to dwell as perfectly alone, in a sense, through the eternity to come, as He did through the sublime and appalling solitude of the eternity past. On account of His incomparable greatness and excellence, never will He be able to bring himself within

their comprehension. However exalted their natures and attainments may be, the universe will still exhibit the infinite distinction of the One unlimited being, and of orders of limited beings entirely dependent on Him. Retired within the depths of his own immensity, they will never be able to approach and behold Him directly. For all they know of Him, they will ever feel that they are indebted to a medium of His own devising; and that, without that medium, the whole created universe including themselves, would only have constituted a living altar with this inscription, "To the unknown God."

10. Whatever excellence, natural or moral, the created universe may ever contain, was contained previously in the Divine Nature. Surely His impartation of it cannot give away his right in it! Rather, He will be laying the recipients under an obligation to love Him as its Giver, and to adore Him as its Source. However vast the amount of excellence may be, it will still be limited, so that they will have to remember at any given moment of their unending being, that they are still infinitely short of His excellence. However vast and various the displays of His glory may be, they will ever have to remember that the universe which displays it leaves more unevolved and undisplayed, by an infinite amount. However much they may be able to comprehend of what He is, from what He has done since they came into being, they will ever have to remember that all the eternity of His past glory remains unexplored. And unless they could exhaust the mystery of the Divine perfections during every moment since they came into being, they will ever have to remember that the mystery is every moment augmenting in their hands; that time is adding its mystery to the mystery of the past eternity; and that the mystery of both is to be carried forwards to the still greater account of the eternity to come. However various the orders of their intellect may be, here they will all find themselves on a level; here they will all and ever find that to reflect is to be lost; that the very choicest terms which they may employ to denote their knowledge of God, will be only so many tacit confessions of their ignorance, and escapes from difficulty; since to speak of Him as eternal, is only to say that His duration had not, like theirs, a beginning; and to speak of Him as infinite, that His nature is not, like theirs, bounded by limits.

11. Nor will they ever cease to be entirely dependent on Him. Suppose their creation had yet to commence, and we

may ask, How can they be ever otherwise than dependent? During the eternity past, that question has never by possibility been raised; for He has existed, and, as to anything ad extra, still remains alone. By what possibility, then, can it ever be raised in the eternity to come? The fact that God has been His own end in all the past determines the question for all the future. Whence could ever come the principle or the power which should invade, even in thought, this Divine prerogative, unquestioned and undisturbed as it has been from eternity? Surely not from any being of whom it is true that he has yet to be; and as to whom the question whether he shall ever be or not, depends entirely on the Divine pleasure; and who, even if it be the Divine pleasure that he shall be, will be as entirely dependent on the same pleasure for every successive moment of being, as he was for the first moment! The idea of such a being, or of any number of such beings, entering into, and taking possession of the place which for an eternity had been occupied by God, as constituting his own end, is revolting to reason. The necessity of their own nature will forbid it. The only relation which that necessity will sustain to Him is that of dependence more profound, universal, and absolute, than they will ever be able to comprehend; while the relation of His own nature to that end will always be, what it ever has been — that of self-sufficience.

12. And as His infinite self-sufficience necessitated that He should be His own end during the eternity past, the unchangeableness of His nature secures the same result during the eternity to come. What He was, He is, and what He was and is, He ever will be. However many worlds or systems He may create, they will never do more than display the *nature* of His perfection, they can never be the measure of its *amount*, much less limit that amount. Now, were He to make only a solitary being, that being could never think that God existed, and had existed from all eternity, for him — and why? because he would ever feel that God is infinitely above him. But no multiplication of mere finite beings will ever make an infinite being; and consequently can never affect the right of God to be the end of all things. On the contrary, the greater their multiplication, the more evident his claim, because they would feel the more vividly that the difference between them, the limited, and Him, the unlimited, is still infinite; and that after they shall have continued to advance through interminable ages from throne to throne, and shall have come nearer to

Him at every such advance, the distance between Him and them is still infinite — that God is all in all.

And thus we reach the conclusion, from the eternal self-sufficiency of God, that He must ever be His own End; or that His nature and glory form the Great Reason of the universe. For there was no reason *why* it should be, nor *what* it should be, but what existed in Himself.

CHAPTER II.

THE ULTIMATE PURPOSE; *or, the manifestation of the Divine all-sufficiency the last end of creation.*

THE preceding Chapter showed that for the great reason of His eternal self-sufficience, God will ever be, what He always has been, His own end. But if He be thus absolutely self-sufficient and infinitely perfect, it follows that He is all-sufficient. By which we mean, generally, that, from eternity, He has included in himself all that is or ever will be necessary to impart (consistently with infinite perfection) existence and ever-advancing excellence, and happiness, to a created universe. And the object of the present Chapter is to show that the manifestation of this glory, by which we mean all-sufficiency, is the great purpose or ultimate end of creation.

I. Such a manifestation appears to involve the following conditions: —

1. That the manifestation be *progressive.* For surely a system which is always in progress both in its own development, and in the powers of the beings to whom it is made known and who form a part of it, must, by the endless combinations which it involves, furnish an inconceivably severer test of Divine all-sufficiency, than one which should be in every respect stationary from the beginning.

And this anticipates and answers the plausible but inconsiderate inquiry, "If the manifestation of the Divine all-sufficiency be infinitely desirable, would it not be equally desirable that the greatest possible extent should be given to the creation, and be given at once; since, until that be done, how can it be known that God is all-sufficient?" In other words, an infinite cause should produce an infinite effect.

We reply, that an exercise of the Divine perfections properly infinite can only take place in the Divine nature itself; and possibly involves the mystery of a plurality of distinctions in the unity of the Godhead, to and by which that display is mutually made: that were such an infinite manifestation to be made, ad extra, unless the mind of the creature were adequate to its comprehension — *i. e.* were infinite — the manifestation to the creature would be limited, limited to the measure of his understanding: and that hence, for aught we know, the manifestation of God made in an atom, while to us it is extremely limited, to Him who sees the end from the beginning may be virtually and potentially infinite. So that, (if the hypothesis may be allowed,) were it possible to present such a particle to Him from the hand of another maker, He could say, "The being from whom this came is infinite, eternal, self-existent, and absolutely perfect. His titles are here all written out at full length, and his perfections embodied. He is all-sufficient. This atom-point is the type and promise of an ever-enlarging and unbounded universe. It contains potentially all that the material universe will ever exhibit actually. No additions to this atom-world could ever add to my knowledge of him. To me the manifestation is complete." We reply further; the inquirer is evidently thinking of an all-sufficiency of *power* only, whereas we are speaking of an all-sufficiency of perfection, including wisdom, holiness, and benevolence, as well as power. As to the production of an unlimited effect, ad extra, the supposition of such a thing, as far as it can be understood, is an impossibility. For, first, it would involve the contradiction of two infinities — the infinite cause and the infinite effect; in which case, the one must limit the other, so that neither would be unlimited; or, secondly, it would imply the contradiction of an unlimited something brought within limits, the limits of time; and, thirdly, it would involve the absurdity of an independent dependence — of an effect not dependent on any cause — for if dependent, in that respect, the most vital of all, it would be limited.

2. But to say what would be necessary to the full manifestation of all-sufficiency, is a task to which none but all-sufficiency itself can be competent; since it supposes a manifestation

continued through eternity. Here, then, is another condition of the manifestation, that it be *unending*. For if it should terminate at any given point in futurity, the proof of all-sufficiency for an eternal manifestation would terminate with it; and then the suspicion might be justly awakened, that if the manifestation had gone on, a crisis might have arrived for which the Deity might not have been sufficient. Besides which, all-sufficiency, from its very nature, requires infinity and eternity in which to be developed, for it implies sufficiency for nothing less than that. And it requires the same, from the very nature and constitution of those to whom the manifestation is to be made; for they are capable of interminable progression. To the objector then who should call for an unlimited effect in proof of Divine all-sufficiency, we would simply reply, that when he shall have existed for an unlimited duration, he may consistently expect to behold it.

Considering the constitution of the beings to whom the manifestation is to be made, in connection with the infinite perfection of the Being who is to make it, such a manifestation, then, would seem to require that it should be progressive and unending; in order that they might be able to go along step by step with the great development; to hang over the mighty process, and mark how the attainment of one end attains a number of inferior ones placed in a line with it; how part is linked to part; how the evolution of one part tends to the evolution of another part, contains the promise of it, leads to it, and predicts another and another yet; so that all-sufficiency is perpetually making fresh demands on itself, and illustrating itself by perpetually meeting those demands in a way demonstrative of all-sufficiency, constraining them to acknowledge that it has no limits.

The remark, then, that the manifestation, not being objectively completed at once, cannot be regarded as worthy of God, admits of the most satisfactory reply; for, to allege no other reason, it is a manifestation for a purpose — *to be understood;* and its gradual development is that which especially adapts it to this end. The objection would hold only on the supposition that the manifestation was not made rapidly enough for the rapid mental and moral progress of the beings for whom it was made — did not keep pace with their advancing powers of comprehension and appreciation. For if it does meet those demands, to them, in effect, it will be always unlimited and virtually infinite. Had such a thing been possible, then, that it could have been completed at once, man would not have known more of it ten thousand ages hence, than he will at the same distant point of time, now that it is progressive. While, at every stage of his knowledge, to him, in effect, the display will have been infinite and complete; for the limits of his comprehension will be always unspeakably within the limits of the manifestation at its every stage. We have said that, in the case supposed, he would not have known more ten thousand ages hence than he will now by a progressive manifestation. But we advance further, and remark, that one of the reasons of this progressiveness is that, in the case supposed, he would not have known so much. Nor, as we shall hereafter show, would his knowledge have equally availed him, for it would not have been the knowledge of observation and experience. Experience supposes a process, and a process requires time, and implies advance from one stage to another.

3. And a third condition of this manifestation appears to be that it be *all-comprehending* — including the revelation of everything essential to the Divine nature, and provision for every crisis in the onward history of the creature, as well as the union and coöperation of all orders of being to the one great end. If there be distinctions as well as perfections in the Godhead, and if it would be for the glory of God to reveal them, sooner or later they must be disclosed; otherwise the manifestation would not be sufficient in this infinitely important particular. Again, if this all-sufficiency implies the power of meeting every crisis; and should the creature ever come by some dreadful possibility to question the Divine all-sufficiency — which would be sin — the Deity, by the very fact of being able to meet that moral crisis, would be demonstrating the all-sufficiency called in question. And still further would this Divine perfection appear to be illustrated, if, in answering one end, it accomplished many, in sketching beforehand the great outlines of the Divine procedure; and should there be different orders of accountable beings, in including and uniting them together as voluntary and organic parts of the one great system.

II. Here, however, it may be asked, whether this does not imply that, until this all-sufficiency be made manifest, there must be something wanting to the Divine glory which that manifestation is necessary to acquire for it; and that as that all-sufficiency was not displayed for an eternity, therefore something was eternally wanting to the completion of that glory? We reply, that the display of this all-sufficiency is no actual augmentation of God's essential glory, but only the objective manifestation of excellence which existed and acted subjectively from eternity; and that the fact that He should have existed from eternity without manifesting it to the creature, arises solely from the infinite perfection of His own nature which is uncommencing, and from the unavoidable imperfection of created natures which necessarily imply a beginning. His all-sufficience was necessary to the idea of his self-sufficience, and was included in it. The objection, then, can acquire force only by erroneously supposing that, having purposed to manifest His all-sufficiency, there was yet (as is often the case with human purposes) a doubt as to whether or not it would be carried into effect: but let it be remembered that we are speaking of all-sufficiency, and the objection turns into absurdity. Further, if the objection have any force with respect to the eternity past, it has the same still, and will have the same through all the eternity to come; since the manifestation of all-sufficiency can never, from the very nature of all-sufficiency, come to an end — and herein consists its perfection. Moreover, there is not a particle of being or of excellence in existence now more than existed potentially from eternity, since the whole objective universe is the *manifestation* of the Divine being and excellence. Great and real as is the satisfaction of the Deity in the existence and happiness of his creatures, the perfection of His nature forbids that it should ever have had to begin. There can never have been a point in past duration in which His purpose has not made such existence and happiness *certain*, or in which His omniscience has not made it *present* to His mind as an object of ineffable delight. Besides which, however much of the Divine excellence be made objective, such manifestation must always fall short of the reality to an infinite amount. And, then, the infinite desirableness, of such a manifestation includes and supposes the infinite desirableness of all the conditions of the manifestation; so that any alteration would be not only infinitely undesirable, but would be so for this very reason, that it would not be a manifestation of Divine all-sufficience.

III. From the preceding section, and from what has been advanced in the preceding chapter, it is evident that if a creation take place, it can be only by the *voluntary act* of the

Godhead. To say that God creates by a natural and unavoidable necessity, is to deny His self-sufficience, and to make Him dependent for perfection on an external object; whereas we have seen that He has existed from eternity in a state of infinite perfection.

Hypotheses of fate and necessity have not been wanting, indeed, from the time of Anaximander downwards. According to him, the infinite is necessarily an ever-producing energy, and, as such, is in a constant state of incipiency. The necessary spiritualism of Leibnitz, and the necessary materialism of Spinoza, are alike hostile to the Divine free-will. Hegel and M. Cousin, have defended substantially the same tenet. According to the latter, "the distinguishing characteristic of the Deity being an absolute creative force, which cannot but pass into activity, it follows, not that the creation is possible, but that it is necessary." Now as the necessity here contended for, is not that moral necessity or determination which arises from the choice of an infinitely perfect Being, but a physical or natural necessity, it has been ably answered that "to what extent a thing exists *necessarily* as a cause, to that extent it is not all-sufficient to itself; for to that extent it is dependent on the effect, as on the condition through which alone it realizes its existence; and what exists absolutely as a cause, exists, therefore, in absolute dependence on the effect for the reality of its existence. An absolute cause, in truth, only exists in its effects; it never *is*, it always *becomes*." [1]

The God of the Bible, on the contrary, is subject neither to the necessity of acting, *ad extra*, nor to the necessity of not acting. The universe has been created for his "pleasure;" not from a necessity which He could not physically resist. And whatever takes place in it of a beneficial nature, takes place "according to the *purpose* of Him who worketh all things according to the counsel of His own will." The only necessity, therefore, which can be regarded as obliging Him in respect to a creation, is the *moral* necessity, that having freely determined to create, He should propose an adequate end, and employ the appropriate means for its attainment.

IV. Accordingly, if the Deity create, it seems infinitely desirable that the chief and ultimate design of the creation

---

[1] From a searching and masterly review of Cousin's *Cours de Philosophie*, in the Edin. Rev., vol. l. p. 213.

should be the manifestation of the Divine all-sufficiency — by which the Divine glory should appear equal to all things, even for the greatest — that of being its own end.

1. For, first, in the very nature of things, all the being, excellence, and happiness, which can ever exist, ad extra, and by which alone the Divine manifestation can be made, virtually existed from eternity, ad intra.[1] It is only in this way that they can manifest Him; and it is only so long, therefore, as they remain what they are — the means of the manifestation of Himself — that they answer their end; and the more of them there is in the creature, the more do they answer that end. All the relations which may ever bind created beings together; the laws which may prescribe the duties of these relations; the excellence which, by obedience to these laws, they may ever possess or be able to acquire; and the happiness which, as the result of this excellence, they may ever enjoy — all potentially existed from eternity in the character and mind of God, and existed there as the expression of His mind and character. His nature is the fountain of the whole. So that every authoritative announcement which He may make that such and such is His will, must be founded in the fact that such and such is His nature. From the all-comprehending perfection of the Divine nature, then, the manifestation of Divine all-sufficiency must have been the chief and ultimate design of creation.

2. But, secondly, as God does nothing which He does not purpose, and as the manifestation of a cause is necessarily the first end answered by an effect, so the *purpose* of making this manifestation must have been, in its own right, the first purpose in the mind of God. To speak, indeed, as if the purposes of God observed an order of succession in the Divine mind, is a metaphysical inconsistency; but it is one which arises from that necessary constitution of our nature by which we can conceive of but one subject at a time; and by which we conceive that that which is the first in the order of importance should be, with a perfect Being, the first in the order of intention. On this account we conclude that the Divine purpose relative to the design or end of creation must have been the first in the mind of God, since every other purpose could only

---

[1] Admirable remarks on this subject may be found in Howe's Living Temple, part i. c. iv., and part ii. c. ii.; and in Hooker's Eccles. Pol., b. 5.

relate to the means for the accomplishment of that end. What we call the various purposes of God, indeed, are, properly speaking, only parts of the same all-comprehending purpose; so that what we denominate His first purpose, included the reason of all His other purposes, and determined the order of their successive development.

When we say, therefore, that every other purpose could only relate to the means, we do not intend that God had only one end in view absolutely, or in every sense.[1] It seems to be necessary, in order to satisfy our idea of all-sufficiency, that, in accomplishing one end, it should be answering many. For instance, that the very creation of the beings to whom the manifestation should be made, should involve in itself a grand part of the manifestation; that even the globe prepared to receive them, and to be the theatre of the manifestation, should contain in itself some of the elements of that manifestation; that the well-being of the creature should furnish the chief occasion for displaying that all-sufficiency; and that the very questioning of that all-sufficiency, and the first obstruction offered to it, should bring with it the very occasion wanted to evolve and demonstrate that all-sufficiency, and to augment the happiness of the creature: so that the well-being of the creature should be as secure of attainment as if it were the chief and only end aimed at, since it is coincident with that end; — all these are designs worthy of Divine all-sufficiency. Although, then, in relation to the chief end, every other end is subordinate and a means, viewed apart from that chief end, many of the means themselves become important ends; and it seems, we repeat, worthy of Divine all-sufficiency that in answering its own great end, it should be accomplishing many subordinate ones.

3. And, thirdly, the well-being of the creature required that the manifestation of the Divine all-sufficiency should be the ultimate design of God in creation. Next in importance to this design, is that well-being itself. And hence, some would inconsiderately regard *that* as the ultimate end of creation. But if, as we have seen, the manifestation of the Divine all-sufficiency must be, in its own right, the chief end of creation, the very well-being of the creature required that no other end, not even his own well-being, should be that end. For if the creature

---

[1] See President Edwards's Treatise on God's chief End in Creation.—*Introductory Paragraphs.*

be himself a part of that manifestation, he is, in so far, a means to that end. His excellence consists in that resemblance to God by which he is constituted a part of that manifestation; and if he be an intelligent being, his happiness consists in his perceiving that resemblance, and in being conscious that he is answering that end of his existence. The character of his every act depends on its correspondence with that end. The value of every being is to be estimated by its capabilities for answering that end. And the truth of every system or theory, is to be tested by the fact whether or not it contemplates that end, and attaches to it the same importance which God does. For if that end be infinitely greater than all the subordinate ones taken together; then that theory of things which takes no note of that end, or which assigns it only an inferior place, must be faulty to a much greater degree than any arithmetical calculation which professes to give the sum total of a number of figures, but which casts up only the fractions and omits the integers.

A holy intelligence, therefore, could not be happy under an arrangement which should make his own happiness the chief end of creation, unless he were quite ignorant of the infinite perfection of God. But however happy he might be in that ignorance, it would be only necessary to disclose to him a sight of that perfection in order to render him unhappy; for he would clearly see that he could be his own end only at the expense of right, and that would render him, as a righteous being, miserable. His own happiness, then, would require that he should be subordinated to the higher end — the manifestation of the Divine glory; for he would see that his well-being consisted in it — that he was made for it. So that could the great question be referred to the arbitration of the holy universe, with one voice they would instantly exclaim, "Thou art worthy, O Lord, to receive glory, and honour, and power; for Thou hast created all things, and for Thy pleasure they are and were created. For of Him, and through Him, and to Him are all things; to Him be glory for ever, Amen." Thus the verdict of the intelligent universe coincides with the primary purpose of the Infinite Mind — that the manifestation of the Divine all-sufficiency is the ultimate end of creation. The work is dedicated to Himself: "All His works praise Him."

And thus, from the Eternal Self-sufficience, we reach the grand conclusion that God must be His own end, or that His infinitely-perfect nature is the great reason of the universe; and from a consideration of His all-sufficiency, that His glory, in creation, consists in the manifestation of His all-sufficiency, and that His display of this is His primary and all-comprehending design.

CHAPTER III.

The Fundamental Relation; *or, the manifestation of the Divine all-sufficiency, mediatorial.*

God having determined on the display of His all-sufficiency as the end of creation, the next part of His purpose related to the constitution of a medium, or system of mediation, as the only condition *on* which and *through* which the manifestation was to be made.

Let it be observed, that we do not here restrict the meaning of the term *mediation* to the principal or evangelical sense. We now employ the term as equivalent to *medial*, or that which *intervenes* between the purpose of God and its accomplishment, as the means of that accomplishment. While we regard the Atonement, therefore, as the great distinctive act of moral mediation, and as that to which all preceding acts of creation and providence were only introductory, we now employ the term in reference to these preparatory acts as well as to that great act of moral mediation.

I. And we find, first, that the constitution of the universe is mediatorial. The creation is represented in Scripture as owing its actual existence and well-being from first to last, not to the invisible and absolute God directly, but indirectly, on account of the assumed relation and voluntary agency of one who stands medially or mediatorially between Him and the dependent universe. "He created all things by Jesus Christ . . . . . according to the eternal purpose which He purposed in Christ Jesus our Lord." "By Him (the Mediator) were all things created that are in heaven and that are in earth, visible and invisible, whether they be thrones or dominions, or principalities or powers; all things were created by Him and for Him; and He is before all things, and by Him all things consist."

II. Accordingly, we find, in the second place, that the institution of the medial, or mediatorial relation, preceded the first act of creation, and was the medium of it. For, "in the beginning was the Word, (or Logos,) and the Logos was with God, and the Logos was God. This (Logos) was in the beginning with God. All things were made by Him, and without Him was not anything made that has been made." In verification of our second proposition we remark that it is here stated,

1. That the Logos is in some sense distinct from ὁ Θεὸς, for He was with ὁ Θεὸς. Besides which, His personal subsistence is manifest from the attributes of intelligence and active power which are here ascribed to Him.

2. That He sustained a relation of peculiar intimacy and union with ὁ Θεὸς, for He was πρὸς τὸν Θεὸν; πρὸς, equivalent here to παρὰ, governing the dative, and denoting rest in a place or an object. But we are by no means dependent on a single proof. Passages to the same effect are so numerous as to require selection. Such, for instance, is the language — "the glory which I had, παρὰ σοὶ, *with Thee*, before the world was." And the compound term μονογενὴς — *the only-begotten Son* — which occurs four times; and "the only-begotten Son who is *in the bosom of the Father;*" denoting a relation absolutely unique and exclusive, and a state of the most perfect conjunction of knowledge, happiness, and nature.[1]

3. That He was Himself God, for Θεὸς ἦν ὁ λόγος. The connection of this clear affirmation with the preceding clause may be expressed thus — "The Word was with God, *in such a manner, that, in fact*, the Word was God." Other proofs to the same effect might be easily adduced.

4. That of everything brought into existence, He, in distinction from ὁ Θεὸς, was the actual Maker. "All things were made by Him, and without Him was not anything made that was made." The affirmation is here followed by the negation, after the Hebrew manner, in order the more emphati-

---

[1] Authorities corroborative of these views might be cited to almost any extent; and some of them by no means unfriendly to Neologist doctrines.

cally to declare that every created thing originated with Him; and, to create, is the scriptural demonstration of Deity.

5. And therefore that the relation or office in virtue of which He created all things preceded the first act of creation. For ἐν ἀρχῇ — *in the beginning* — equivalent to the Hebrew בְּרֵאשִׁית — even then He already ἦν — was. The assertion of His pre-existence is included alike in ἀρχῇ and in ἦν. For when every created thing had yet to be, He already *was*. He comprehends every beginning in Himself.[1] As passages, parallel, in this particular, we might refer to Prov. viii. 23, where to be "from the beginning" is made equivalent with being "from everlasting, or ever the earth was," and to Isaiah xliii. 12, 13, and Hab. i. 12, where to be *from the beginning* is regarded as the peculiar prerogative of the eternal and self-existent God. And yet, this ante-beginning, or unbeginning existence is here predicated of the Logos, not once only; in the second verse it is repeated — "this (Word) was in the beginning with God." As if He had said, "This is a truth of the first importance, and I therefore repeat it, that when creation had yet to begin to be, the Divine Logos existed in a state of perfect union with the Divine Nature."[2] For, "He is before all things, and by Him all things consist." Thus Inspiration, leading us back to the beginning of all created things, points us to the existence of that medial relation which preceded creation, and was the means of its *actual* origin.

III. And, thirdly, as the primary purpose of God is the manifestation of Divine all-sufficiency, this primary official relation is represented as in coincidence with, and subservience to, that purpose. This is indicated by the very meaning of the appellation *Logos*, whether examined philologically, historically, or exegetically.

1. It might be asked, "May not ὁ λόγος stand *philologically*, as abstract for concrete, for ὁ λέγων — the speaker or teacher?" To which we reply that λέγειν does not signify directly to *teach;* and λόγος has only in an indirect manner the meaning of *doctrine.* Much more proper would it be to understand

---

[1] Qui in principio erat, intra se concludit omne principium.—*Aug. Serm.* vi. — *De Temp.*

[2] Dr. J. P. Smith's Scripture Testimony to the Messiah, v. iii. c. ii. b. iv.

λόγος according to the phraseology of Philo, who distinguishes in God the state of εἶναι — being, and that of λέγεσθαι — revealing Himself. According to which the Logos would be the Divine Revealer.[1]

2. But that which is much more important to determine, here, than its grammatical, is its *historical* sense. For the Evangelist speaks of the Logos as of a conception already known, and which he takes for granted his readers will immediately connect with the word.[2] Now, it is matter of history that by the Logos was then understood, He who is the medium of Divine manifestation. The idea of such a medium appears to have early obtained among the students of the Hebrew Scriptures; and from them to have extended to other lands, till in one form or another, the idea had become very generally incorporated with Oriental theology. Traces of it are to be found scattered, with more or less distinctness, in the Apocrypha, in Philo, in the Cabalistic Writings, and in the Chaldee Paraphrasts. In the last of these especially it is taught that God never appears acting immediately upon the world, but always through the medium of another. This medium of the Divine acts is called the Memra of Jah — the Word of Jehovah. And although the phrase is sometimes employed idiomatically, to signify merely the *Divine Voice*, at others, it can denote nothing less than a distinct personal subsistence. While in Philo the doctrine is taught that the Deity has developed His essence through His highest Revealer, the Logos, who is the express image of God — the name and the shadow of God — a representative God.

The Evangelist, aware of this familiar doctrine of Jewish theology, declares that the true Logos — He who in the capacity of Logos had made the world as a part of the Divine manifestation, has really and historically appeared with a view to a yet further manifestation.

3. To have selected so unusual a word as Logos in order to express so simple an idea as that of a teacher only, would have been, *exegetically* considered, most inappropriate. Besides, the idea conveyed is, that the Being intended had, in His capacity of Logos, or, of the Divine Revealer, created the universe; and that He who had done this had now Himself

---

[1] See Professor Tholuck, *in loc.*

[2] See Professor Burton's Bampton Lecture.

appeared to carry on the process of Divine manifestation. Thus understood — and we know no other sense in which we can understand it — how admirably descriptive is the appellation, the *Logos*, of Him who is the medium of the Divine manifestation. What speech is as a means of rational communication between one mind and another, that is the Divine Logos between the Invisible Essence and all created minds. He is the utterer of His thoughts, the discloser of His purposes, the manifestation of His character.

Now the Being who sustains this relation must in every respect be co-equal with God. To be in any sense inferior would be to be infinitely inferior; in which case, the manifestation itself would be limited to the capacity of the medium through which it came, and consequently, be infinitely inferior to the Divine original. Accordingly, we have seen, that the Divine Logos is, in perfections, as in name, co-equal with the Father; he has been with Him, and has so been with Him as to be one with Him, from eternity. To the same effect are those passages of Holy Scripture which describe Him as the Image of the Invisible God; as the Brightness of the Father's Glory, and the Express Representation of His Essence. For as the internal being and character of a man are expressed in his face, so God hath given us the knowledge of His glory in the face of Jesus Christ. The doctrine which gives to these and parallel phrases all their force is, that He to whom they relate is the great medium of Divine manifestation.

And this prepares us to expect that the manifestation will not be verbal merely. For how can the imperfect medium of speech convey an adequate idea of the invisible God? Besides, the intelligent creatures to whom the manifestation is to be made, had first to be created, and the world they should inhabit to be called into existence; and, as He performed these works in his medial capacity, it might be expected that He would begin the manifestation even in these. This is the right key to the volume of the universe. Properly understood, every material particle is impressed with His seal. Every atom is a letter, and every work a word. Every element lectures on his attributes, and each globe is a messenger ever moving in His service. Man himself was made in His image. The stars come forth nightly on their solemn embassy to "proclaim the glory of God." And the earth daily affirms with voices innumerable the "eternal power and Godhead." In harmony with this representation, the

Divine Logos is represented as having come into the world, not so much to promote the Divine manifestation by verbal instruction, as by embodying and manifesting Himself in actions. He came to *be* the manifestation of God. "He that hath seen Me," said He, "hath seen the Father also." He claimed for Himself the exclusive power of revealing the father; and affirmed that to make this revelation was the great end of His own coming. And, when about to depart from the world, He was heard to say to the Father, "Having declared unto them Thy name, and having thus glorified Thee on the earth, I have finished the work which Thou gavest to me to do." While His disciples subsequently declared, that the Life had been manifested, and that they had seen it; that that which was from the beginning they had handled and seen, even the Word of Life; that though no man had seen God at any time, the only-begotten Son had come from the bosom of the Father to declare Him, and that they had beheld His glory.

And thus, be it observed, the very means of external manifestation became itself the manifestation of a mysterious plurality of subsistencies in the Godhead. In the very first step taken to give the universe an economy *ad extra*, a mysterious economy *ad intra* was disclosed; and which became the ground and means of every subsequent disclosure.

Here, then, are the basis and the medium of the Divine Manifestation; for, in relation to God, as we shall presently evince more clearly, it is constituted the ground on which such manifestation is made; and is itself, perhaps, to His eye, the manifestation already and ever perfect. While, in respect to the subsequent creation, it is the means by which the process will be ever conducted. Thus, while the reason of this Relation is laid, proximately, at least, in the Divine Purpose, and the reason of the Divine Purpose lies in the Divine Nature, the reason of everything else will be found to be laid in this Relation.

CHAPTER IV.

The Primary Obligation; *or, Duty arising from the Mediatorial Relation.*

If the manifestation of the Divine all-sufficiency be the object for which the mediatorial relation exists, and if the Being sustaining the relation be infinitely perfect, or equal to the relation, it follows that by voluntarily assuming it, He comes under obligation to do everything which may be necessary for the full attainment of the object proposed.

I. For what is *obligation* but the necessary link which, in a moral sequence, connects the antecedent with its consequent; or, the indispensable necessity of employing the means proper to attain a requisite end? Now every relation brings with it certain appropriate obligations; and these obligations vary in character and amount according to the character of the relations. A relation may be voluntary, or involuntary, and natural. If it be voluntary, he who assumes it is bound to fulfil the obligations which it imposes; always providing that he either knew, or had the means of knowing, the nature of the relation; and that he is not physically unable to discharge its duties, and thus answer its end.

II. Now He who sustains the mediatorial relation, not only possesses, as we have seen, all the requisites for accomplishing the great purpose, but His fitness is the special reason why He sustains that relation; *the relation therefore binds or obliges Him to do everything necessary to the attainment of the end for which it exists.* That end may be immeasurably distant, but let the first creative fiat be once issued, and never can His eye be withdrawn from the process which leads to it. Vast as the theatre may be which that process may, in the course of time, come to occupy, His presence must, in some sense, pervade the entire space. Innumerable as the parts belonging to the process may speedily come to be, and receiving as they may innumerable accessions at every moment after, all of them must be known to Him in their natures, relations, and remotest effects. Various, and formidable to finite apprehension, as may be the apparent obstacles to the attainment of the end, arising from the ever-varying combinations of circumstances; from the junctures of events which had their respective causes in different ages of creation, and in different departments of the universe; and, especially, from the voluntary actions of free agents; not merely must He be prepared to meet them all, but (as an illustration of all-sufficiency) to render them all conducive, as parts of His plan, to the attainment of His ultimate end. Ever receding, and even unattainable (in an absolute sense) as that end, owing to its perfection, must necessarily be, yet as long as there are aspects of the Divine character to be manifested, new creatures must continue to be formed for the purpose of displaying and appreciating them; or, which would seem to be better still, those already formed must be placed by Him in new situations for beholding it in fresh aspects, and have their powers enlarged for appreciating such enlarged disclosures; or — that which would seem to be still more worthy of all-sufficiency — both these conditions might be made to meet in the same order of creatures; that is, besides taking up into their constitution all that is most important in the constitution of the creatures preceding them, they may be made to exhibit something more excellent of their own in addition, and be placed in circumstances favorable to the ever-advancing exercise and development of the whole. And thus the glories which creation may display at any period indefinitely distant from the first moment of the opening manifestation, and the power which the creature may at such period possess for appreciating it, will only be the means, in the hand of the Mediator, for entering on a new career of Divine manifestation as immeasurably distant, and incomparably more glorious still; and the attainment of that be only the bare preparation for another beyond, so much more glorious than the preceding that the eye which had gazed on all the splendors of the past, and the ear which had heard all the speculations and conjectures to which that past had given rise, and the heart which had been occupied ten thousand ages in putting all these together into every imaginable form of ideal glory, will yet have to confess that it had never seen, nor heard, nor even imagined, anything to be compared with it — and so on *ad infinitum*. So that as the manifestation will never have reached a point beyond which it cannot be carried further still, the mediatorial office can never, absolutely, and in every sense, cease; in other words, the relation which the Mediator sustains in the great purpose of manifestation binds or obliges Him to do everything which may be necessary to the full attainment of the great end — and therefore to continue the manifestation for ever.

This view of the mediatorial obligation harmonizes with, and is suggested by, that numerous and important class of Scriptures which appears to take such obligation for granted; and which represents even the self-denial and sufferings of the Mediator, as events which "behoved him" — and which "ought" to take place. The *proximate* obligation implied in these Scriptures, indeed, may be that which bound Him to the employment of suitable means for the attainment of a particular end. That particular end was the recovery of a race which by voluntarily obstructing the great process of manifestation, and by thus forfeiting all right to the happiness attending it, could be restored to it again only when such restoration could be made as safe to the great process, and as conducive to the great end, as their abandonment to the consequences of their sinful defection would be. And the Mediator, having undertaken to effect that restoration, had brought himself under obligation to do all that was necessary to render this particular end consistent with the attainment of the great end. The event showed that suffering and death were the necessary means — and therefore even suffering and death "became Him" and He "ought" to endure them.

But this view accounts only for the *proximate* obligation. It leaves unanswered the natural and momentus inquiry *why* such an obligation was incurred? Whereas, the right answer, I apprehend, would show that this proximate obligation, great and wonderful as it is, resolves itself into one higher and more comprehensive still; and that to this the class of Scriptures referred to *ultimately* relates — namely, the all-comprehending obligation to which His mediatorial relation binds Him, *of doing everything essential to the great end.* In virtue of that relation, He was bound from the beginning, not only to keep the great process in constant activity, but to keep it ever advancing and enlarging; and this, as we have seen, involved the requirement that He should meet every exigency which might arise, and even turn it to the account of the final result. His earthly humiliation, indeed, is, probably, on many accounts, the central wonder and most amazing part of that duty to which His mediatorial relation can ever oblige Him; but still it is only one of an unbroken series of acts, which, beginning with the first fiat of creation, can never end, unless the great manifestation itself, on account of which the relation exists, could ever arrive at completion.

III. This view seems to place us in an advantageous position for gaining an insight into the very reason of the medial relation — disclosing, not merely what it is, but partially, at least, *why* it is so. That this subject should be felt to be profound might have been expected, if for no other reason than that it appears to involve, in some degree, the very *nexus* which unites the internal economy of the Divine nature with the external economy of the dependent universe. Even in the philosophy of our own minds, the *mode* in which the thinking principle within is related to the world without — how that which is I, can come to know that which is not I, is the great, and, comparatively, the only difficulty. So that every theory on the mind derives its character from the view which is taken of this starting-point: — one denying that there is any subjective; another, that there is any objective; another affirming that they are identical; and a fourth, that they are not identical but inexplicably related. Precisely in like manner, some have denied that there is any Originating Mind, and regard the universe as eternal; others have affirmed that there is no material universe, but that God alone exists; others, that God and nature are identical; and others, that they exist distinctly, but are inexplicably related. Now Divine revelation discloses the vital *fact* that they are related, and that the relation is, properly understood, not direct but *medial.*

1. But what is the *reason* of the fact? Is it a *natural* reason merely; one, that is, arising from the disparity of nature between the created and the infinite Invisible? Such was the theory of many of the emanative systems of the East; indirectly derived, but perverted, from the Hebrew Scriptures. They taught that as the Highest Being is, in himself, incomprehensible and unapproachable, there can be no immediate transit from Him to a world of created existences; that, consequently, it became necessary that there should be found in God some transition-point to make His fulness comprehensible and communicable; and that this was found in Himself from eternity in a Being like Himself, through whom the concealed God was manifested. And this opinion, slightly modified, and reproduced in some of the early Christian creeds, has continued to

exercise a powerful influence on the theology of this subject down to the present day. That it involves *some* truths we readily admit; but, if it is to be regarded as the whole truth, the reply to it is obvious — namely, that if the supposed *medium* be infinite, the *natural* chasm intended to be filled up between God and the creature remains, for one infinite is as unapproachable as another; and that if it be *not* infinite, it no less remains, for a finite medium necessarily leaves the gulf as it was — infinite.

2. Is the reason, then, a *moral* one; and, if so, what is its specific nature? The general reply would doubtless be in the affirmative, and to this effect — that the constitution of a universe worthy of an Infinitely Perfect Being involved the existence of free agents, and therefore of a *moral* administration; that under such an administration righteously administered, forgiveness, in the event of sin, would be impossible, unless such a compensation should be provided as would render forgiveness as safe and honorable to the administration as the infliction of the merited punishment would be; and that God, therefore, foreseeing such an event, and determined on the illustration of His infinite grace, devised a system of mediation, at once safe for His government, suited to the exigency of the sinner, and glorious for His own character. Now, not only is this true — it is inestimable truth. To a sinful world it is *Gospel.* But to regard this as the whole of the reason, would be to limit the reason to a single act or class of actions; whereas, if our preceding views are correct, that reason is to be found in the *purpose* of Divine manifestation, just as the ground of that is to be found in the great Reason of all — the Divine Nature.

3. For the sake of distinguishing the original ground of the mediatorial relation, then, from that just named, and yet avoiding the employment of a term liable to misinterpretation, we would designate it simply as the *primary moral* reason, in contradistinction from the last, which we regard as the *proximate moral* reason; and this primary reason we conceive to be, *because nothing else than the institution and voluntary assumption of the subordinate office, understood by the mediatorial relation, would have adequately manifested the infinite Holiness and Love of God, or His all-sufficiency for the well-being of an intelligent and accountable universe.*

That other reasons for this amazing arrangement are deducible from Scripture, is gladly admitted. There is that great *proximate* reason, to which we have just adverted. There is also the reason, *that we might not be discouraged, by a sense of God's ineffable majesty, from approaching Him.* And there is the weighty reason of *the moral influence arising from the Mediator's example of willing subordination to the Father.* That *He* should be seen standing in the view of the universe — seen by his own creatures — in a station of obedience! Who else *can* refuse to obey? That He, of his own free-will, should consent to serve! — what creature-will but must feel constrained to yield? That He should find glory in this subordination! — does it not point the intelligent universe the only way to perfection — namely, by its coincidence with the Divine will?

But these reasons, and others which might be named, are all included in that which I have designated as the primary moral reason. And I venture to repeat, that, not only is the manifestation of the Divine all-sufficiency that primary reason, but that nothing else than the mediatorial relation can be conceived of as furnishing an adequate manifestation of that all-sufficiency. That the Divine Being might have abstained, had He so pleased, from all external manifestation, I believe to be a doctrine of Scripture; but I believe also that, having determined on the manifestation, nothing less than the voluntary subordination of one of the persons in the Godhead could adequately express the resources of all-sufficiency. Had the sufficiency of God been limited; or had He designed that the manifestation should have been of any amount of His excellence short of all-sufficiency — *i. e.*, had He himself been imperfect, or had He determined on an imperfect manifestation — an arrangement inferior to that of the system of mediation might have sufficed; but if God all-sufficient is to be revealed, this would appear to be the adequate and only exponent. And still farther, so effectually does the mediatorial arrangement provide for the purposed manifestation, that *the mere* WILLINGNESS *of the Mediator to sustain the relation*, apart from all that He has done in consequence, and, hypothetically speaking, even short of His *actually* sustaining it at all — His mere *willingness* to sustain it, could that have been signified to the universe, would have given us a deeper insight into the character of God, and have furnished a brighter illustration of His all-sufficiency, than it could ever have entered into the mind of man or angel to conceive. The wonder is, then, not so much that He should fulfil every condition to which His mediatorial relation obliges Him, as that He should be found sustaining the relation at all from which that obligation takes its rise. To say that He foresaw these conditions, is only saying that He is equal to the relation which He sustains. And to say that He yet voluntarily undertook that office, is only saying that He who is at the head of a system of free agency is Himself a free agent. But that He *should have done this*, I repeat, that He who had known no necessity but that of being, and of being what He was, should have brought himself under obligation; that He who had known no relation but that of the ineffable union of the Godhead, should oblige Himself to sustain a relation to a created universe — to become the centre of an ever-enlarging system of such relations; and to do everything necessary to the well-being of such relations; that the cause of all things, ad extra, should have voluntarily assumed that office as an effect of a previous purpose; that "the Beginning of Creation" should range Himself in a line with His own creatures — subjecting Himself to His own laws — as the first term in a series of means, for the accomplishment of the end which that purpose contemplated; — this can be accounted for only by supposing that the end is the illustration of the Divine all-sufficiency.

Nor is this final reason unfrequently or obscurely adverted to in the word of God. To this effect, ultimately, are those passages to which reference has been made already. So also is the inspired declaration, that in the most self-denying acts of the Mediator, the eternal Father was allowing or appointing that which "became Him;" but, then, the capacity or relation in which it became Him is distinctly stated, as "Him, by whom are all things, and for whom are all things,"— as Him who is His own end, and the end of everything else, even of the system of mediation, with all that it includes. And to this view the Mediator Himself sets His seal in all those passages, cited in the last chapter, in which He declares, that whatever He said, did, or suffered, the whole was for the disclosure of the Divine glory.

(1.) Then, it is to be inferred, that the character of the Father is perfectly free from that unlovely and invidious light which some views of mediation are charged with unjustly casting on it. The object of the Father in *appointing*, and of the Son in voluntarily *assuming* the relation, is one — the fulfilment of the great purpose. So that the arrangement is required by a principle rather than by a person; is rendered, on the one hand, for the very same reason that it is required on the other—namely, that the full manifestation of the Divine glory to the universe might be made possible.

(2.) That as the appointment of such an arrangement argues no deficiency of benevolence on the one hand, but the reverse, so the *accession* to it, on the other, argues no absolute loss of original prerogatives, or entire renunciation of antecedent rights. These, as they belong to the Divine nature, can never be detached or diminished, but are as unchangeable as the nature to which they belong. Besides, these prerogatives constitute the fitness of the Mediator, or His infinite adequacy, for the mediatorial office, and enable Him to discharge it; and surely His rights are not to be regarded as annulled because of His perfections. And it is because of His retaining these original prerogatives, as well as on account of His manifestation of God, that He is often spoken of in Scripture, interchangeably, as acting both in His original and in His official capacity.

(3.) That the mediatorial obligation will never terminate. As its sole design is the manifestation of God, its duration must run parallel with the manifestation; so that unless the universe were to be blotted out, or the perfections of Deity to be exhausted, it can know no end. Commencing prior to the introduction of sin, it will continue, in some sense, after all the probationary perturbations of the moral system have ceased, as the indispensable and everlasting *proof* of the Divine all-sufficiency. And what a view does this wonderful economy afford us of the all-comprehending glory of that end which could justify the adoption of such means in order to fulfil it!

(4.) And how inevitably does the arrangement suggest that if the primary relation gives rise to obligation, every subordinate relation will do the same; that the Creator will not be the only being under obligation; that all His creatures, in proportion to their relation to Him and to each other, will be under obligation also.

CHAPTER V.

THE SUPREME RIGHT; *or, Mediatorial Authority and Happiness commensurate with the discharge of Obligation.*

IF the primary obligation be commensurate with the mediatorial relation, it may be expected that the discharge of that obligation will be associated with corresponding *rights*, so that if the Being discharging it, do everything necessary to a constant approximation towards the great end, it will follow that he should meantime enjoy, or possess a right consistently with that end, both to whatever is necessary to the prosecution of his object, and to whatever flows from it. Here is a two-fold right; the first part, presupposing obligation, and the second, presupposing its discharge.

I. Independently of His original and unalienable rights, the nature of the Great End invests Him with a right of the highest order in relation to whatever may be included in the mystery of the Godhead. For example, if there be a distinction or subsistency in the Divine nature, designated the Holy Spirit; if the attainment of the end require the disclosure of this mysterious fact; and if this disclosure can be only effected, consistently with the end, by His employment of the agency of this Divine subsistency, His office entitles Him to avail Himself of that agency. His right is commensurate with His obligation. The end at which He aims being unlimited, all limitation must be removed from the means; so that all the resources of the Divine nature are to be considered as at His disposal.

II. 1. If He call any order of intelligent creatures into existence, with a view to their subordination to the great end, (and for no other purpose can they exist,) He has a right to their proper activity and service. If He Himself be under obligation to attain a certain end; and if that obligation include the production and employment of appropriate means, the same obligation rests on the means, provided they are capable of obligation, as necessary steps to the attainment of the end; for without them, the end cannot be attained. This is the very condition of their existence; for had it not been for that end they would not have been called into being; had it not been for the mediatorial constitution on which that end is pursued, they could not have existed; and were it not that they are intended to serve as means to that end, they would not have been constituted what they are. They hold existence, therefore, and their particular constitution of existence, on the prime condition that they answer the great end for which they have received both; and to do this is at once their excellence and their happiness. He who has imparted both, has in no sense parted with His right in either. The excellence and happiness now found in the creature, existed potentially in the Creator before they came into the creature; but in imparting them to the creature, the Creator intended, not that His own glory should be thereby left unaffected, but that they should answer an end by which both they should be increased, and the Divine glory be thereby augmented.

2. If, then, any of the creatures are so constituted that their activity increases their power of subserving the great end of their existence, He has a right to the whole of that increase; for it is owing entirely to His having constituted them as they are, that they are capable of such increase; and the great reason why He did so, is the same as that for which He constituted them at all — to subserve the great end of the Divine manifestation.

3. If, again, owing to the providence or plan on which the end will be sought, and the consequent relationships in which successive creatures will stand to each other, their power of subserving that end should be augmented, He will, for the same reason, have a right to the whole of that augmentation. For, as the great system of means advances from one stage of development to another, it will be only the gradual unfolding of a plan which had always existed in His infinite mind. And as it existed there only with a view to the end, so whatever may be gained by the accomplishment of a preceding part of the plan, is so much gained for the part succeeding, and so on to the end.

4. If, again, owing to any of the free agents, which the plan contemplates, abusing their free agency, and withholding their power, and thus violating the condition of their existence, the progress of the plan and the attainment of the great end should be thwarted, or, in any sense, endangered; and if, then, owing to his interposition in any way, the derangement of the system should be remedied, and be even turned to the account of the great end, He would have a right to all the advantage which

that gracious interposition would give Him. Absolute as His right to their activity and devotedness was before, He has now established a new right of peculiar cogency. Before, He had called them from *nothingness* into happy existence, now he has called them from *misery* to happiness. But for the first act, they would never have been; but for the second, they would never have been ought but miserable. Whatever may be the amount of their new obligation, therefore, He is entitled to the result of it; — of all the additional moral influence which it gives him over their minds, of all the new motives to obedience which it should call into existence, and of all the increase of power arising from the stimulating influence thus shed over the great system of means.

III. The Mediator has a right also to whatever satisfaction can arise from the contemplation of His own conduct in its respective relations to God and to the creature.

1. There is the happiness of beholding His ideas or designs *objectively* realized — He has a right to that. Accordingly, He is represented as having contemplated the first objects even of the material world, as they came forth from His hand, with Divine complacency. He looked on them as visible realizations of eternal types. On comparing them, so to speak, with the archetypes in His own infinite mind, He beheld the perfect resemblance, and was satisfied. He regarded them as exponents or signs of certain corresponding qualities, infinitely greater in the Divine nature. And He beheld them in their prospective application; serving as indexes or memorials of that infinite greatness to myriads of minds which He purposed to create, and so to constitute that each of all these things should operate on them suggestively. He knew, therefore, all the lofty thoughts which these objects would ever suggest, and all the exquisite delight those thoughts would occasion, and all the holy admiration which the perception of this relation between things that differ would ever produce.

He looked on those objects also as the first in an endless series yet to come. In His first acts of creation, the great architect was laying the foundation of an all-comprehending and eternal temple; and His infinite mind is to be regarded as having embraced, by anticipation, all the sublime results. The worshippers, the homage, the temple filled with the glory of the Divine manifestation — all were present to His mind — and He rejoiced in the glorious prospect.

2. There is the happiness of prospectively beholding the activity, enlargement, and progress of the whole system of creation and providence — He has a right to the enjoyment of that. Not more certainly is the earth perpetually speeding on its destined course through space, and carrying with it all the momentous interests of humanity, than His plan, freighted with an eternal weight of glory for the creature, and with a weightier revenue of glory to God, is in constant progress. Never for a moment does it retrograde — never pause — never linger. Look on it when He will, He beholds it arrived at that stage where, a thousand ages ago, He foresaw it would be; and look forward to what distant age He will, He beholds it, in anticipation, already there arrived. Hence, He is often represented in Scripture as foretasting the happiness arising from the contemplation of this progress. Out of the depths of eternity, He looked onward to the period when creation should commence. "From everlasting, from the beginning, or ever the earth was, when there were no depths, no fountains abounding with water, when as yet he had not made the earth, nor the fields, nor the highest part of the dust of the world,"[1] He anticipated the period when all these would be. Beyond this, He looked on to the remote period when the earth should be prepared for the reception and sustenance of animal life. He saw its forests wave; its waters roll; its surface clothed with verdure; and the whole replenished with various orders of sentient beings. Ages beyond, and when, by successive creations and mighty intervals of change, the earth should have been slowly prepared for the reception of a being such as man, His eye fixed on the time when, in order to that event, He should "prepare the heavens, and set a compass upon the face of the deep; when He should establish the clouds above; and when he should give to the sea His decree that the waters should not pass His commandment." Already, in His prescient view, the sun had received its final commission to shine, and earth had received its general outline of Alp and Apennine, and Himalaya — of Atlantic, Pacific, and Mediterranean. Already Eden bloomed, and "a river went out of it to water the garden." Man's mansion was prepared, but where was the great inhabitant? The theatre was ready — where was the being on whose introduction the mighty drama should begin? Already, in intention, He saw that creature come,

---

[1] רֹאשׁ עַפְרוֹת תֵּבֵל — *Prov.* vii. 26. Rendered by Gesenius *the first* (earliest) *clod of the earth* — i. e. which was the first formed.

radiant in his own image — the crown of creation: and, as He saw, He already heard "the morning stars sing together;" saw earth's first sabbath dawn; beheld man's earliest act of adoration; and pronounced the whole to be "good." Even then, though existing only in His Divine purpose, "He rejoiced in the habitable parts of the earth, and His delights were with the sons of men." He foresaw His blessing enlarging Japheth, and causing him to dwell in the tents of Shem. His purpose had formed the great continents of the earth, had smoothed the valleys where nations should be cradled, and given direction to the course of the rivers whose banks should become the seat of empire. The actual distribution of Canaan among the tribes of Israel was only the transcription of an eternal plan. "Remember the days of old, consider the years of many generations; ask thy father, and he will show thee; thy elders, and they will tell thee. When the Most High divided to the nations their inheritance; when He separated the sons of Adam, He set the bounds of the people according to the number of the children of Israel." Before Moses — before Pisgah itself, from which Moses looked down on the promised land, existed — His eye had looked down from the height of His sanctuary, and had beheld prospectively that Sinai whence His law should be given; that Zion which should be crowned with His temple; that Calvary which should sustain the mystery of the cross.

Now that the prospect of the development of His great plan affords him profound satisfaction is evident, not only from the Scriptures already quoted, but from the fact that he has sought, at times, to inspire His church with an ecstasy of delight by affording them glimpses of its onward course. All the sublime disclosures of prophecy are merely revelations of that future on which His eye is perpetually fixed; and by the prospect of which He would fain admit the faithful to a fellowship in His own delight. And all the satisfaction those disclosures have ever yielded to an Abraham, who "saw His day, and was glad;" to a David, an Isaiah, an Ezekiel, a Paul, a John, entranced with the vision — to the whole church, which "having seen them afar off, were persuaded of them, and embraced them," and died in exulting faith — all this is only a particle of the boundless "joy which they have ever set before him."

3. To Him also belongs the happiness of prospectively beholding the effects of His gratuitous interposition for human salvation. If, owing to no defect in the original constitution

of the great plan of Providence, any part of that plan be violated by man; and if, owing to no original defect in man, but owing to an abuse of his necessary free-agency, that violation take place; and if, therefore, without any claim on the interposition of the Mediator, He yet determined to remedy the evil, to take advantage of it in a way which shall accrue to the infinite good of the very beings who had introduced the evil, and to the furtherance of the great end of Divine manifestation — surely He has a right to the happiness arising from a view of the effects of His own interposition. Accordingly, there is a class of Scriptures which represents Him as rejoicing in the prospect of this interposition. And the satisfaction which He derives from the contemplation of that prospect, is heightened by the vivid contrast in which it ever stands before his view with what must have been the dreadful alternative if He had not interposed. And when He anticipates the day in which "He shall come to be glorified in His saints, and admired in all them that believe," He "sees of the travail of His soul, and is satisfied."

4. Then He is entitled to the grateful homage of all who share the effects of His gracious interposition. Hence His own language, "that all men should honor the Son even as they honor the Father."

5. The happiness flowing from the fact that on account of His mediatorial work, He is the object of the Father's infinite delight, is greater still. For He estimates that complacency at its proper worth, which is infinite, absolutely infinite; and therefore greater than the intelligent creation, though its capacity be always enlarging, will ever be able to experience.

6. And then there is the happiness derivable from knowing that He is attaining the greatest of all ends — the manifestation of the Divine all-sufficiency. Now, if this end be so great, that every other stands to it only in the relation of means; if this is infinitely greater than all other ends combined, the happiness arising from the attainment of it must be infinitely greater also. The happiness flowing from the spectacle of a redeemed and happy creation must be great; for He knew not only what would be the exact measure of its happiness at this moment, but how happy it will be ten thousand ages hence, when its capacity for happiness will be increased ten thousandfold — with all the happiness it will have enjoyed in the interval, and so on for ever. But inconceivably high as He values that complacency, more highly still does He value that glory

on account of the manifestation of which that complacency is accorded to Him. He estimates everything as the eternal Father does; so that if the manifestation of the Divine glory be so dear to the Father that He pours His complacency on the Son for undertaking it, the Mediator Himself regarding it in the same light, must derive from the contemplation of its attainment His highest delight. The prospect of beholding a universe of dependent beings hanging on independent all-sufficience; every heart a channel through which a fulness of delight is constantly streaming from the great central source, and every moment enlarging to receive more; every sin forgiven, every evil remedied, every want supplied; the whole reflecting, and replenished with, the Divine glory — this is the consummation of that glory which is set before Him. Much as He may delight in the *favor* of Deity, He rates *the glory* of the Deity higher still: for it is that which gives even to His *favor* all its value; so that to be the means of manifesting it to the universe is the crown of His mediatorial happiness, as it is the end of creation.

And thus by a circularity in the nature of the mediatorial constitution we are brought back to the point from which we set out — that the glory of God is the chief end of creation. It must necessarily have been so independently of all appointment; and even had there been (supposing an impossibility,) an appointment to the contrary. For even if a decree had appointed that the ultimate end of all things should be the well-being of the creature, the infinite capacity for enjoyment of the Divine Being would not have allowed it to be the greatest end; since God in beholding, that well-being and the manifestation of the Divine glory which it carried along with it, would by right and necessity of nature, enjoy more than all the creatures together — infinitely more. And if God, and not the creature, would thus have been, by necessity of nature, the great end of all things, we are to suppose that He is so by *choice;* or that He approves of, and proposes to himself, as an end, that which the infinite excellence of His nature conditionally necessitates. The great *reason*, then, accounts for the primary *purpose;* the purpose originates the medial *relation;* the relation imposes the great *obligation;* and the obligation is followed by the *right* of the being discharging it; that is, the last ensues on the attainment, or, in proportion to the attainment of the first: and thus the Mediator, as such, finds His own end in attaining the great end.

SECOND PART.

Principles deducible from the preceding Lectures; or, Laws of the Manifestation.

FROM the preceding scriptural views of that which is predicable of the Deity, considered as prior to the manifestation of the divine all-sufficiency, and in order to it, the following general deductions seem logically to result. Certain other intermediate principles, indeed, might with equal clearness, be inferred; but, for the present, it is proposed to deal only with general truths.

I.

That every divinely originated object and event is a result, of which the supreme and ultimate reason is in the Divine Nature.

By which we mean that, not only is *a* reason *for* it to be found there, — this would only acquit the Maker from a charge of folly — but, that the ultimate and adequate reason *why* it is, and *what* it is, is to be found there. For, if the origin of everything which may exist must be traced to him as the great first cause, everything will, in some sense, be like him; i. e., it will *be*, and will *be what it is*, when it proceeds from him, because he is what he is; for before it was produced, it was potentially included in him. Additional reasons *may* be found in itself, and in other parts of creation, to account for its existence. And of vast significance may many of these reasons be to the creature. Yet all these will be found subordinate and traceable to that infinite reason which includes, but is independent of them all, as belonging to the infinite nature of God. These subordinate reasons may be only coëxistent with the respective natures in which they are found, — beginning and ending, therefore, in some cases, within the space of a few short hours — soon, and perhaps forever, to be forgotten by all the rest of creation: but the infinite reason of their being at all existed from eternity in the nature of God, and can never cease to exist. However insignificant, comparatively, any given creature may be, not only is the reason of its existence to be sought in God, as prior to, in the order of time, and causative of, that existence; but as a reason which approved itself to, and, in some sense, expressed a property of the divine nature. So that even if there were no purpose of manifesting Divine all-sufficiency, — but the creation were to be limited to the production of a single creature — still, as every effect must be in some sense like its cause, that single effect would be, (not *formally* but *virtually*,) a manifestation, *pro tanto*, of the Divine Nature: in other words, its ultimate reason would be found in God.

And on the same ground, every expression of His will, however it may be made, whether by word or act, will be a manifestation of something anterior, viz. of the Divine Nature.

II.

That everything sustains a relation to the great purpose, and is made subservient to it.

If our view of the Divine purpose be correct, it will follow, that besides the former law of the creature's existence, by which it is what it is, because God is what he is, and which law can never be superseded; there is another law, arising from the Divine purpose, which makes it a primary condition of the creature's existence that it should contribute in some measure to the Great Manifestation. We can conceive, then, of a two-fold reason for everything, *ad extra:* — the one, arising from what God *is*, the other from what he *purposes* — the former a *natural reason*, the latter a *moral necessity* or reason of Divine appointment — the former looking back to its origin, the latter looking onward to its end. For if the design of the whole be to manifest the Divine All-sufficiency, every part of the whole must of course combine to the same end. And as nothing which may exist, can have a separate, exclusive, and independent end of its own, everything will find its own end, in answering His.

III.

That the Manifestation will be carried on by a system of means, or medial relations.

If our view of the great relation be correct, we may expect, that *that relation*, as constituting the *medium* of the Divine Manifestation, will itself be manifested; or that, in harmony with that primary relation, the whole manifestation will consist of, or be carried on by, a system of corresponding medial relations, (relations rising with the rising nature of the being sustaining them;) otherwise, that great relation itself will be but partially disclosed, if it be not even entirely, and for ever unknown.

Another reason for the medial constitution of the Creation, is, that the Great Relation is not merely the *medium* of the manifestation, but an *important part of* it; just as the sun, besides being the medium of vision, is also the most glorious object of creation. Now as everything exists for the Divine Manifestation, of which that relation itself is a vital part, everything may be expected to manifest that Relation by itself sustaining a medial relation.

And, as everything is to express something of the Divine nature, and the Great Relation involves an infinite disclosure of that nature, everything may be reasonably expected to bear, in some respects, the stamp of that Relation.

And further, — if, as we have shown in a previous chapter, the Great Purpose requires that the Manifestation should be progressive, it follows that it must consist of a succession of events, in which each part will necessarily hold a relation to all the parts preceding, and following; just as the Primary relation is medial between the purpose and the end. For we can neither conceive of an event which must not be conceived of, as being, in some sense, an effect; nor of a succession of events which must not be conceived of as medially dependent and related. So that viewed in connection with the second law, which determines that everything shall subserve the great end, this determines the *mode or form* in which that subserviency shall be rendered — by everything sustaining a relation, not merely to that end, but to everything else contributing to that end — a relation of mutual dependence and influence.

IV.

That everything will be found either promoting, or under an obligation to promote, the great end commensurate with its means and relations.

If our view of the Great Relation be correct — that it brings him who sustains it under obligation commensurate with his means of answering the great end — we may expect to find, that every subordinate relation will be accompanied by obligations corresponding in their number and amount with its power of promoting the end.

For, according to the *first* law, it will necessarily express something of the Divine nature; and according to the *second* law, it receives existence on the condition of manifesting that resemblance, and of contributing towards the Great End; and according to the *third*, it is placed in a system of Medial Relations, in order that such manifestation may be made possible.

V.

That everything will be entitled to an amount of good, or of well-being, or will be found in the enjoyment of it, proportionate to the discharge of its obligations, or, to the degree of its conformity to the laws of its being.

For as, according to the *first* law, everything will necessarily express something of the Divine nature; and according to the *second*, will come into existence in order to express it; and according to the *third*, will receive and sustain a relation in which to fulfil this law of its being; and according to the *fourth*, will be held under obligation to this effect; it will follow, according to the *fifth*, that it cannot fulfil this law of its being without enjoying well-being. For, to manifest whatever its nature is calculated to exhibit of God, is to stand related on one side to the greatest of beings, and on the other to the greatest of ends; so that to fulfil the law of its being, or to find its own highest end, is to answer the Great end; nor could it be supposed to be in any way deprived of its right, while thus fulfilling the law of its being, without the great end itself being, in so far, defeated. And here is the coincidence of the creature's happiness with the Creator's glory.

For example; if the intelligent creature can do the same thing in obedience to different laws, his happiness can never rise above the law which he fulfils; and if that law be a lower one, when it might, and therefore ought to be a higher one — i. e. if the higher be sacrificed to the lower, — though obedience to the lower may not be unattended with reward or gratification, — the painful sense of having violated, or disregarded the higher, will more than counterbalance the gratification.

According to these five laws, then, everything may be viewed, in its origin; its ultimate design; the way in which it answers that design; its obligation to do this as the necessary means to an end; its consequent share in the great end. Or, in itself, as a separate and isolated product of the Divine Being; in its intended subserviency to the great end; in the nature of that subserviency, or the relations which it sustains in the great system of mutual dependencies; in the obligatory fulfilment of this great conditional law of its existence; in the natural and necessary results of such fulfilment, in its own well-being. The *first* law determines that it shall *be* — bear a resemblance to God. The *second, why* it shall be — as a manifestation of that resemblance, in subserviency to the Great End. The *third, how* it shall do this — as a part of a great system of means. The *fourth,* the indispensable necessity of doing it — as means to an end. And the *fifth,* what shall result to it from answering that End.

According to the *first* law, it may be said, that everything looks *back* to its origin. — According to the *second, forwards* to its ultimate end. — According to the *third, around,* to its medial relations. — According to the *fourth, on* the duty consequent on these relations. — And according to the *fifth, within,* on its own well-being, or particular end, as the result of answering the Ultimate End.

VI.

That everything will be found to involve the existence of necessary truth.

By *necessary* truth is meant *that* of which the proposition not only *is,* but *must* be true, and of which, therefore, the negation is not only *false* but *impossible;* so that it exists necessarily, and therefore universally, independently of the existence of the individual intellect which contemplates it. The *origin* of our knowledge of it, whether by induction, or otherwise, is a question for separate consideration.

The *possibility* of the manifestation, for example, pre-supposes the existence of certain *necessary* truths. It pre-supposes the existence of *space and duration* in which this manifestation is to be made — pre-supposes them as *conditions* of the manifestation. For, as nothing outward can be conceived of, without space — and nothing existing, without time in which to exist, it follows that everything *must* be, in some sense, related to space and time, or be included in them; and therefore space and duration must have existed prior to, and independently of, the manifestation. It pre-supposes also the possibility of *causation*, for it involves the necessity that every event shall be, in some sense, an effect; and this proposition, therefore, would have been truo, even if the manifestation had never taken place. It pre-supposes, then, the existence of the Great First Cause or Being to be manifested, whose absolutely unlimited perfection, suppose infinite space and infinite duration; and, consequently, whose existence would have been a truth even if the manifestation had never been made. And thus as the purpose refers us to the Great Reason of which it is simply and necessarily the expression, and as the Great Reason is all that it is necessarily, or independently of everything *ad extra*, so every event included in that purpose, being an effect or expression of that reason, will sustain some relation to the necessary and the independent.

VII.

That everything will be found to involve the existence of contingent truth.

By contingent truth is meant that of which the existence is not necessary, but conditional — true, because something else is true; or dependent for its truth on something else.

As the possibility of the manifestation pre-supposes the existence of *necessary* truth, so the *purpose* of the manifestation implies the existence of *contingent* truth — contingent, that is, in the sense already explained, as opposed to absolutely necessary. For had the manifestation been *necessary* in any other sense than that of being infinitely desirable, or *morally* necessary, no *purpose* of manifestation needed to have been formed. And then, as the great purpose itself was contingent on the Sovereign will of God, so every part of the *internal arrangements* of the plan (*provided they secure the fulfilment of the purpose, or the manifestation of divine all-sufficiency,*) must be contingent also, or dependent on "the good pleasure" of that will in which the purpose itself originated. For if, in the sense described, the whole be contingent, the parts must be also; nor could such contingency remain unknown, without defeating the ultimate end of the manifestation.

VIII.

That everything will be found, by necessity of nature, and as a relative perfection essential to the manifestation of Divine all-sufficiency, to involve truth surpassing the perfect comprehension of the finite mind—i. e. *there will be ultimate facts.*

For if it were absolutely and in every sense comprehensible, it could be only, to created minds, the representation of something absolutely finite and limited. But such a thing is inconceivable. For as everything must be *related*, in some respect, to time, space, and causation, as well as to every other thing included in the plan,—in consequence of these relations, if in no other respects, it will stand connected with the infinite, and incomprehensible. So that while the Great Purpose requires that it should manifest something of God, its relation to the Great Reason will leave it involved, in some respects, in the necessary and the universal.

And thus it will at once proclaim its *origin* and answer its *end.*

IX.

That the manifestation be progressive; or, that the production of new effects, or the introduction of new laws, be itself a Law of Manifestation.

For were it to terminate at any given point, the proof of all-sufficiency for unlimited manifestation would terminate with it. Besides which, all-sufficiency, from its very nature, requires infinity and eternity in which to be developed, for it implies sufficiency for nothing less than these. But if the development of the Great Purpose, or the attainment of the Great End, be in its very nature *progressive,* this is only saying that the process must ever be kept open to receive the addition of new effects, or the superinduction of new laws. So that the law of uniformity itself will always be subject to, or bounded by, this more general law of Progression: just as this more general law itself will always be subject to the law of the end, to which all particular laws owe their existence, and from which they derive their authority. And this again is only saying that the end shall not be subject to the means: but that the Great Purpose shall be carried into effect.

So that, that which is commonly regarded as miraculous interposition may be itself a law of the manifestation — not the exception, but the rule — or if the exception to *us* who view things only on the scale of a few days, to Him who views them on an *unlimited* scale it may be the rule.

X.

That the manifestation, besides being progressive, will be continuous; or will be progressive by being continuous — leaving no intervals of time, or of degree, but such as the modifying influence of other laws may require or account for.

For were it to leave such intervals, except on such conditions, the proof of all-sufficiency for filling them up would be wanting. Besides which, if all-sufficiency requires infinity, and eternity, in which to be developed, intervals in the manifestation of time and of degree are inadmissible; unless on the supposition that such intervals or pauses in the manifestation would themselves contribute to the manifestation of all-sufficiency.

It may be expected that it will be impossible to lay one's finger on the line which separates any one province of knowledge from that which lies next. To complain of a theory, therefore, that it combines and synthesizes, is to complain that it treats of things as they are; or, as God has made them. Since it belongs to the perfection of these things, that they should not admit of isolation; if they did, they would not and could not belong to a system of progressive and continuous manifestation.

XI.

That the Continuity of the manifestation requires that all the laws and results of the past should in some sense, be carried forwards; and that all that is characteristic in the lower steps of the process should be carried up into the higher — as far as it may subserve the great end; or unless it should be superseded by something analogous and superior in the higher, and the future.

For if it were not, the manifestation would be neither progressive, nor continuous, but would be every moment beginning *de novo.* Everything would be isolated. After the manifestation had continued for untold ages, all the past would be unknown and lost to the present, and to all the future. And the proof of all-sufficiency, for such a continuity of manifestation as that expressed in the proposition, would be forever wanting.

XII.

That everything will be found to manifest all that it is calculated to exhibit of the Divine Nature, by developing, or working out its own nature.

For as, according to the *First* law, we are to expect that everything, *per se*, and separately considered, will exhibit something of God from mere necessity of nature — just as the purpose of manifesting Divine all-sufficiency brought to light necessarily, and independently of all intention, the Divine self-sufficiency, so, according to the *Second* law, we are apt to expect, that as it is only by the activity of the Divine Nature, that that nature is made manifest, every being will be found to manifest all that is calculated to exhibit of God's nature, by properly manifesting, or, working out its own. The mere formation of the purpose implies the acting of the Divine Mind; the accomplishment of that purpose, especially as it is a purpose of self-manifestation, clearly supposes self-activity also; — the manifestation of Divine all-sufficiency evidently requires that that activity should be constant, unending, and all-comprehensive. A creation, then, devoid of regulated activity, could be no manifestation of an everliving and ever-active God. Such a creation (were its existence possible) would less represent him than would the absence of all external objects; for, as a Divine manifestation, it would essentially misrepresent him. For how could that which neither moved nor was moved — which evinced no adaptation of means to an end — no capacity of enjoyment — that which could receive nothing from without, and which involved nothing from within — that, therefore, which knew nothing, did nothing, and, in effect, was nothing — do anything but misrepresent Him who is All in All? The existence of such a universe is inconceivable. It is only by a universe of activity, then, that He can be manifested to whose activity the universe owes its existence.

Still more may an active nature be expected in that order of creatures whose distinction it is to be, that not only *by* them, but *to* them, the manifestation will be made. For such activity may be looked for in them if only to help them to understand, by *sympathy*, the same property in the Divine Nature. And still more complete would this resemblance to their Maker be, if certain possibilities of active excellence could be stored up in them, and if these could in some way be put at their disposal, or under the power of their will; so that, as the Divine activity, *ad extra*, has been voluntary, their activity might resemble his in this essential respect — that it be voluntary also.

The grounds which the other laws afford for the same expectation of activity in the intelligent creature are too obvious to require extended notice. For if the *first* provides for it by imparting to him a measure of Divine resemblance, and the *second* by making his manifestation of that resemblance the condition of his existence, the *third* enables him to fulfil that condition, by placing him in a constitution of medial relations, where his activity will be felt, the *fourth* makes such activity obligatory, and the *fifth* rewards it in his own well being, or attainment of the Great End.

XIII.

That the same property or characteristic which existed in the preceding and inferior stage of the manifestation, be superior in the succeeding and higher stages, or else be applied to additional or higher purposes, (if it be not altogether superseded by something superior;) *or, that it be in the power of the succeeding, and the higher, so to render or to apply it.*

For as, by the great law of the Manifestation, everything is in alliance and dependence; and as everything looks on to an end beyond itself, its nature, or its relations and results, may be expected to advance, the further it proceeds from its original starting-point towards the distant end, for the sake of which it exists.

XIV.

That as every law will have an origin or date, it will come into operation on each individual subject of it, according to its priority of date in the great system of manifestation.

For as, by the law of continuity with progression, every law has come into operation in orderly succession, that order of succession is itself a law: and as laws operate uniformly for the same reason that they operate at all — viz., for the purpose of manifestation — the order of their introduction at first into the general system, could not be dispensed with in any of the subsequent stages or parts of the manifestation, without defeating the design of their introduction at all.

XV.

That everything will occupy a relation in the great system of means, and possess a right in relation to everything else, according to its power of subserving the end; or, *everything will bring in it and with it, in its own capability of subserving the end, a reason why all other things should be influenced by it — a reason for the degree in which they should be influenced — and for the degree in which it, in its turn, should be influenced by everything else.*

For if, according to the first law, everything, by necessity of nature, expresses some property of the Divine Nature: — if, according to the second, it possesses that resemblance on the sole condition of manifesting it in subserviency to the Great End: — if, according to the third, it is medially related to everything else, that it may be able to make the manifestation: — and if, according to the fourth, it is bound to fulfil the Great Purpose, *according to its means and relations*, then everything will sustain an active and a passive relation, or will have a right to influence everything of inferior, and a susceptibility of being influenced by everything of superior, subserviency to the Great End.

So that (according to the all-connecting purpose) co-existence implies co-relation, co-relation involves mutual obligation or subserviency, determinable as to kind and degree, in every instance, by the subserviency of the subjects of it to the Great End.

XVI.

That every law subordinate in rank, though it may have been prior in date, be subject to each higher law of the Manifestation, as it comes into operation.

This, indeed, is a corollary from the preceding, and is only saying, in effect, that in no case shall the means be put in the place of the end. But if the means are to be always subordinate to the end, then, as everything is related, every inferior law must sustain a relation of subordination to every higher law of the Manifestation.

XVII.

That the whole process of manifestation be conducted uniformly, as far as the end requires, or according to the operation of laws.

(By law is meant a constant relation, or an order of sequence, according to which, if one event occur, another will follow.) This, the great reason requires, for it supposes that every event will be, in some sense, an effect, (which is itself a law): and that divinely originated effect will, when traced back to its origin, be found to express something in the Divine nature.

The Great Purpose requires it: for it is only by the uniformity supposed that the immutability of the Divine nature, or even the Divine existence, could be evinced; or indeed, that *proof* of any kind could be made possible. Farther, the Great Purpose necessarily supposes a series of effects: and that as often as God should will, the same effect would follow from the same volition; otherwise He could not be certain that the end would ever be attained. Besides which, as the purpose of an infinitely perfect being, it is pursued on a plan, and a plan supposes the orderly arrangement and concurrent operation of distinct sequences of events, for the attainment of a certain end. It was only on the same supposition, of the operation of general laws, as far as the end requires, that the Mediator could assume the great *Relation*, or undertake to discharge the *Obligation*, or calculate on the enjoyment of his exalted *Right*. Indeed, the proposition that the manifestation will be conducted by general laws, is involved in the statement of all the preceding laws; for each of these statements is an attempt to define them.

XVIII.

That every part of the manifestation be analogous to every other part, or according to a plan.

(By analogy is here meant, generally, a similarity of relation between things in *some* characteristic respects, when in other respects, the things are different.)

The truth of this proposition may be inferred from the *per-*

vading operation of general laws: from the *primary relation,* according to which he who is to conduct the great process sustains his office expressly as the Logos or manifestation of God; so that everything else can answer the end of manifestation only as it is analogous, according to, or, in some respect, resembling the Logos: from the *Great Purpose;* for, if the whole creation is to be, in some sense, an analogue of the Divine nature, (and in no other way can it manifest God) then, every separate portion of it must be similarly related to every other part, otherwise the *whole* will not resemble Him. If the first act be an act of manifestation, and every subsequent act be a counterpart to all that has gone before, then the last of any given series will, to some extent, correspond to the first — each will be a measured resemblance of all, that the whole may be a manifestation of God. If the whole is to be a manifestation, it must be known; if known, classed; (for only a very few things could be known if each were isolated and unlike everything else) and if classed, possessing similarity of relation.

XIX.

That the law of ever-enlarging manifestation be itself regulated by a law determining the time for each successive stage and addition in the great process.

The time for the change in any given department of the Divine manifestation, will of course be determined *in a manner, and for a reason,* differing with the particular *nature and design* of the department: — by each existing stage passing through all the combinations and changes of which it admits, before another begins; or, by its existing long enough to show that it involves all the necessary possibilities for answering such and such ends, if its continuance be permitted; or, until it has sufficiently taught the specific truth, and attained the proximate and particular end, for which it was originated.

But, whatever the *particular* reason for determining the period of change may be, it is evident that the law of the time and the occasion for every change must harmonize with the Great End of the whole — the manifestation of the Divine All-sufficiency. For, were a stage of the manifestation to be recalled or replaced a moment before it had, *in some way,* demonstrated the all-sufficiency of God for that particular stage, the Great Purpose would not be answered.

From which it follows that no such change or interposition takes place arbitrarily; but, as the laws of progression, and of the end, require it.

And that the *length* of the time which may be allowed to elapse, after the introduction of one law or change, before the introduction of another, so far from growing into an objection against any further addition or change, becomes, in a progressive system, an ever-increasing ground for expecting it.

XX.

That the beings to whom this Manifestation is to be made, and by whom it is to be understood, appreciated, and voluntarily promoted, must be constituted in harmony with these laws; or, *these laws of the objective universe will be found to have been established in prospective harmony with the designed constitution and the destiny of the subjective mind which is to expound and to profit by them.*

The truth of this proposition, if not *self-evident*, will receive abundant illustration when, in a subsequent volume, it comes under consideration.

THIRD PART.

ORGANIC NATURE.

The First Stage of the Manifestation.

POWER.

1. *Order of the Manifestation.*— The great end of creation, then, is supposed to be the gradual manifestation of Divine all-sufficiency. Now, travelling back, in thought, to the eve of creation, "Here," we might say, "here is an infinite expanse of unoccupied space in which the great end is to be realized; what will be the first step? or with what will the manifestation commence? In what order, and at what rate, will it proceed? What extent of space will it occupy? What possibilities will it involve? Of how many parts or stages will it consist? Will it, or will it not, have any special scene or scenes of operation?"

That these are subjects which occupied the Divine mind — not, indeed, as questions which admitted of hesitation — but as parts of His one great purpose, is evident; for they are actually suggested by the fact of what He has done; and He does nothing which He has not purposed to do. Now, imagining ourselves in the situation supposed, and taking along with us the laws which we have derived from the Scriptural view of the Nature and Purpose of God, we might have justly reasoned that if the Divine purpose requires that the creation be progressive, it might be expected to determine also the order of the progression, or what perfection of the Deity shall be first displayed, as well as the act or means by which the display shall be made. In the nature of the case, there is nothing, *ab extra*, to determine either with what the manifestation shall begin, or how it shall proceed. Even if there were, inasmuch as the great object of creation is the manifestation of the Divine perfections, the order of the process must be regulated by the order prescribed by the object of the Divine purpose — the means must be made subservient to the end. But there is nothing *ab extra*, so that there is a necessity as well as a reason, why the order of the manifestation should take the order best adapted for the attainment of the Divine purpose, and prescribed by it.

Whether there is any order, then, in the Divine purpose, and, if so, what that order is, are among the very things to be manifested. Now, according to the constitution of the human mind, we are led to the conclusion that such order exists; and that the earliest display of the Divine Nature will be that of a perfection fundamental to all the rest, namely, Power. It may here be proper to observe, though it is only, in effect, the repetition of a remark in our first Part, that by the Divine perfections we do not understand "a congeries of separate and separable attributes, like the members of an organized body," one of which may be exercised at one time and another at another; but the same one unitive perfection, exhibiting itself in a variety of phases and aspects with a view to entire manifestation. And according to the constitution of our minds, there is a certain order in which these different aspects may be viewed; by which we gain sight of an additional characteristic or perfection at each view; and are prepared by each foregoing perfection for the contemplation of each succeeding one.

Now the first and the only simple attribute of whose manifestation we can conceive is that of Power. The display of every other attribute supposes the co-existence and *manifest* co-operation of this in order to its display. But the exercise of this does not necessarily suppose the manifest co-operation of any other. For although, in the case of an infinitely perfect Being, we can never conceive of power exercised apart from intelligence, we can conceive (and the case before us is one in which we are conscious of the conception) of an act of combined intelligence and power,[1] of which, while the power should be so self-evident and awful as suddenly to fill us with

[1] Indeed, if this were the place, it might be shown that even the inference of design, is subsequent to the observation of the adjustments and adaptations of nature, as that again must necessarily be subsequent to the production of the things adjusted.

amazement, the intelligence which it involved, owing to its very depth, should be completely hidden from our view, and require the lapse of ages for its development. In this case we should contemplate power in its simplest form — that of causation; — a mighty moral cause producing a stupendous effect.[1]

2. *Antiquity of the Earth.* — *If, according to our first law, every divinely-originated event is a result of which the supreme and ultimate reason is in the Divine Nature*, it might have been expected that the order of the Divine perfections, or else the nature of the Divine Purpose, would determine the order of the creative process, and that the opening act would be a display of power. But if, by one law, we arrive at the conclusion that the first act of manifestation will be a display of power, the law of progression suggests that that display will be made by an act to which we can conceive no act antecedent; one which is not merely introductory to every other, but preparatory to the whole — first in the order of nature as well as of time.

Now revelation and science harmonize with reason, and are decisive on the subject that, as far as *the visible universe* is concerned, the formation of its material preceded the formation of everything else. Turning first to the inspired record to ascertain the origin of things as they now are, we learn, of our earth, that it assumed its *present* state a few thousands of years ago, in consequence of a creative process, or of a series of creative acts concluding with the creation of man, which extended through a period of six ordinary or natural days. Possessed of this fact respecting the date of man's introduction on the earth, we proceed to examine the globe itself. And here we find that the mere shell of the earth takes us back through an unknown series of ages, in which creation appears to have followed creation at the distance of vast intervals between.

But though in the progress of our inquiries we soon find that we have cleared the bounds of *historic* time, and are mov-

---

[1] I believe that we derive the idea of causation — *voluntary* or *efficient* causation — from consciousness; that besides the constant connection which we observe between physical causes and effects, we are conscious of exerting a power in the effects which we ourselves produce on matter subject to us; that this consciousness awakens the idea of voluntary causation; and that this idea leads to the belief in the existence of a First cause. But the psychological views to which the discussion of this question would lead, belong to another treatise.

ing far back among the periods of an unmeasured and immeasurable antiquity, the geologist can demonstrate that the crust of the earth has a *natural* history. That he cannot determine the *chronology* of its successive strata is quite immaterial. We only ask him to prove the *order* of their position from the newest deposit to the lowest step of the series; and this he can do. For nature itself — by a force calculable only by the God of nature — lifting up in places the whole of the stupendous series in a slanting, ladder-like, direction to the surface, has revealed to him the order in which they were originally laid, and invites him to descend step by step to its awful foundations.

Let us descend with him, and traverse an ideal section of a portion of the earth's crust. Quitting the living surface of the green earth, and entering on our downward path, our first step may take us below the dust of Adam, and beyond the limits of recorded time. From the moment we leave the mere surface-soil, and touch even the nearest of the *tertiary* beds, all traces of human remains disappear, so that let our grave be as shallow as it may in even the latest stratified bed, we have to make it in the dust of a departed world. Formation now follows formation, composed chiefly of sand, and clay, and lime, and presenting a thickness of more than a thousand feet each. As we descend through these, one of the most sublime fictions of mythology becomes sober truth, for at our every step an age flies past. We find ourselves on a road where the lapse of duration is marked — not by the succession of seasons and of years, — but by the slow excavation, by water, of deep valleys in rock marble; by the return of a continent to the bosom of an ocean in which ages before it had been slowly formed; or by the departure of one world and the formation of another. And, accordingly, if our first step took us below the line which is consecrated by human dust, we have to take but a few steps more, before we begin to find that the fossil remains of all those forms of animal life with which we are most familiar, are diminishing, and that their places are gradually supplied by strange and yet stranger forms; till, in the last fossiliferous formation of this division, traces of existing species become extremely rare, and extinct species everywhere predominate.

The *secondary* rocks receive us as into a new fossiliferous world, or into a new series of worlds. Taking the chalk formation as the first member of this series, we find a stratification upwards of a thousand feet thick. Who shall compute the tracts of time necessary for its slow sedimentary deposition! So vast was it, and so widely different were its physical conditions from those which followed, that scarcely a trace of animal species still living is to be found in it. Crowded as it is with conchological remains, for example not more than a shell or two of all the seven thousand existing species are discoverable. Types of organic life, before unknown, arrest our attention, and prepare us for still more surprising forms. Descending to the system next in order — the oolitic — with its many subdivisions, and its thickness of about half a mile, we recognise new proofs of the dateless antiquity of the earth. For, enormous as this bed is, it was obviously formed by deposition from sea and river water. And so gradual and tranquil was the operation, that, in some places, the organic remains of the successive strata are arranged with a shelf-like regularity, reminding us of the well-ordered cabinet of the naturalist. Here, too, the last trace of animal species still living, has vanished. Even this link is gone. We have reached a point when the earth was in the possession of the gigantic forms of Saurian reptiles, — monsters more appalling than the poet's fancy ever feigned; and these are their catacombs. Descending through the later red sandstone and saliferous marls of two thousand feet in thickness, and which exhibit, in their very variegated strata, a succession of numerous physical changes, our subterranean path brings us to the carboniferous system, or coal formations. These coal strata, many thousands of feet thick, consist entirely of the spoils of successive ancient vegetable worlds. But in the rank jungles and luxuriant wildernesses which are here accumulated and compressed, we recognise no plant of any existing species. Nor is there a single convincing indication that these primeval forests ever echoed to the voice of birds. But between these strata, beds of limestone of enormous thickness are interposed; each proclaiming the prolonged existence and final extinction of a creation. For these limestone beds are not so much the charnel-houses of fossil organisms, as the remains of the organisms themselves.[1]

The mountain masses of stone which now surround us, extending for miles in length and breadth, were once sentient

[1] See a memoir "On some of the Microscopical Objects found in the Mud of the Levant, and other deposits: with Remarks on the Mode of Formation of Calcareous and Infusorial Siliceous Rocks." By W. C. Williamson, Esq.

existences — testaceous and coralline, — living at the bottom of ancient seas and lakes. How countless the ages necessary for their accumulation; when the formation of only a few inches of the strata required the life and death of many generations. Here, the mind is not merely carried back through immeasurable periods, but, while standing amidst the petrified remains of this succession of primeval forests and extinct races of animals piled up into sepulchral mountains, we seem to be encompassed by the thickest shadow of the valley of death.

On quitting these stupendous monuments of death, we leave behind us the last vestige of land-plants, and pass down to the old red sandstone. Here, too, we have passed below the last trace of reptile life. The speaking foot-prints impressed on the carboniferous strata, are absent here. The geological character of this vast formation, again, tells of ages innumerable. For, though many a thousand feet in depth, it is obviously derived from the materials of more ancient rocks, fractured, decomposed, and slowly deposited in water. The gradual and quiet nature of the process, and therefore its immense duration, are evident from the numerous "platforms of death,"[1] which mark its formation, each crowded with organic structures which lived and died where they now are seen; and which, consequently, must have perished by some destructive agency, too sudden to allow of their dispersion, and yet so subtle and quiet as to leave the place of their habitation undisturbed.

Immeasurably far behind us as we have already left the fair face of the extant creation, while travelling into the night of ancient time, we yet feel, as we stand on the threshold of the next, or Silurian, system, and look down towards "the foundations of the earth," that we are not half way on our course. Here, on surveying the fossil structures, we are first struck with the total change in the petrified inhabitants of the sea, as compared with what we found in the mountain limestone; implying the lapse of long periods of time, during the formation of the intervening old red sandstone which we have just left. But still more are we impressed with the lapse of duration, while descending the long succession of strata, of which this *primary* fossiliferous formation is composed, when we think of their slow derivation from the more ancient rocks;

---

[1] Mr. Hugh Miller's "Old Red Sandstone," (1841,) p. 234; a work of peculiar interest.

of their oft repeated elevation and depression; of the long periods of repose, during which hundreds of animal species ran through their cycle of generations, and became extinct; and of the continuance of this stratifying process, until these thin beds had acquired, by union, the immense thickness of a mile and a half. Next below this, we reach the Cambrian system, of almost equal thickness, and formed by the same slow process. Here the gradual decrease of animal remains admonishes us that even the vast and dreary empire of death has its limits, and that we are now in its outskirts. But there is a solitude greater than that of the boundless desert, and a dreariness more impressive than that which reigns in a world entombed. On leaving the slate-rocks of the Cambrian and Cumbrian formations, we find that the worlds of organic remains are past, and that we have reached a region older than death, because older than life itself. Here, at least, if life ever existed, all trace of it is obliterated by the fusing power of the heat below. But we have not even yet reached a resting-place. Passing down through the beds of mica schist, many thousand feet in depth, to the great gneiss formation, we find that we have reached the limits of stratification itself. The granitic masses below, of a depth which man can never explore, are not only crystallized themselves, but the igneous power acting through them, has partially crystallized the rocks above. Not only life, but the conditions of life, are here at an end.

Now, is it possible for us to look from our ideal position, backwards and upwards to the ten miles height — supposing the strata to be piled regularly — from which we have descended, without feeling that we have reached a point of immeasurable remoteness in terrestrial antiquity? Can we think of the thin soil of man's few thousand years, in contrast with the succession of worlds we have passed through; of the slow form a tion of each of these worlds on worlds, by the disintegration of more ancient materials and their subsidence in water; of the leaf-like thinness of a great proportion of the strata; of the consequent flow of time necessary to form only a few perpendicular inches of all these miles; or of the long periods of alternate elevation and depression, action and repose, which mark their formation, without acknowledging that the days and years of geology are ages and cycles of ages! Let us conceive, if we can, that the atoms of one of these strata have formed the sands of an hour-glass, and that each grain counted a moment, and we may then make some approximation to the past periods of geology; periods in the computation of which the longest human dynasty, and even the date of the pyramids, would form only an insignificant fraction. Or, remembering that only two or three species of animals have, so far as we know, died out during the sixty or seventy centuries of man's historic existence upon earth, can we think of the thousands, not of generations, but of species, of races, which we have passed in our downward track, and which have all run through their ages of existence and ceased; of the recurrence of this change again and again, even in the same strata; and of the many times over these strata must be repeated in order to equal the vast sum of the entire series, without feeling that we are standing, in idea, on ground so immeasurably far back in the night of time, as to fill the mind with awe? "How dreadful is this place!" Here, at as incalculable a secular distance, probably, from the first creation of organic life, as that is from the last creation — here, silence once reigned: the only sound which occasionally broke the intense stillness being the voice of subterranean thunder; the only motion (not felt, for there was none to feel it) an earthquake; the only phenomenon, a molten sea, shot up from the fiery gulph below, to form the mighty framework of some future continent. And still that ancient silence seems to impose its quelling influence, and to allow in its presence the activity of nothing but thought. And that thought — what direction more natural for it to take than to plunge still farther back into the dark abyss of departed time, till it has reached a First, or Efficient Cause?

3. *The earth not eternal.* — But, although we seem to be thus conducted almost into the frontiers of eternity, the moment we glance our eye in that direction, all the cycles of geology dwindle to a point. In the presence of Him, with whom a thousand years are as one day, we recover ourselves to perceive that these cycles are immense only in relation to ourselves. Accordingly, every step of our downward path has been suggestive of a beginning; for everything speaks of derivation. Each rock, for example, points downwards to its source. We can trace the lineal extraction of each successive stratum. And even now, having reached the crypt of nature, and standing at the bases of her gneissic columns, should the question be asked, — "Whence their derivation?" geology points to the older granitic masses, of whose water-worn crys-

talline particles they are evidently composed. "But whence that granite?" Mineralogy shows that it is composed of three very distinct mineral substances. Crystallography demonstrates, next, by cleavage, or mechanical division, that each of these three substances is compounded of atoms or molecules inexpressibly minute, and each of these again of others still more minute, and so on to an indefinite extent; yet that each of these possesses a determinate geometrical figure, and combines in fixed and definite proportions. Chemical analysis now takes up the process of reduction, and shows — taking the carbonate of lime, for example — that each of these integrant molecules is divisible into two compound substances. And, still farther, it shows that even each of these is a compound body. But here the process of decomposition ends. The elementary molecules thus obtained — of calcium, carbon, and oxygen, — are three of the fifty-four or fifty-five substances which, to us, are indivisible and ultimate; and which, as it has been beautifully expressed by Daubeny, deserve to be regarded as the alphabet, composing the great volume which records the wisdom and goodness of the Creator.[1]

The ancient atheistic theory of a *fortuitous* concourse of atoms is thus exploded; since it is demonstrable, as we have seen, that all crystalline mineral substances exist only under fixed geometrical forms, and unite only in unchangeably definite proportions. Fortuity has no existence here. We are in the region of law; and law implies a lawgiver.

Here, too, the sceptical theory which would substitute an eternal nature for an eternal God of nature, stands exposed and condemned. To say nothing of the logical absurdity which the theory involves, in professing to account for the existence of a vast magazine of exquisite contrivances without a contriver; we have only to recall the fact, that in our subterranean descent we passed the actual beginning of species after species, down to a state of the globe in which life was impossible. Thus Nature herself, disclaiming the honor thrust upon her at the expense of her Maker, emphatically declares, "It is not in me." The compounded state of the inorganic masses, down to the crystalline granite, joins also in affirming the same truth; and it is with the argument from inorganic matter that we have, at present, to do. Now, it cannot be affirmed that matter has always existed in a compounded state; for, unless

1 See Dr. Buckland's Bridgewater Treatise, vol. i., c. xxiii.

it could be proved that its compound is its necessary state, it would follow that, at some period or other in past duration, it must have been in a simple state. But chemical analysis demonstrates that a compounded state is not a necessary condition of its existence; for it can be analyzed and exhibited in its elements. From which it follows, either that there was a period when matter existed in its uncompounded simple elements — and then the questions arise, whence the existence of these mysterious substances? and whence the multiplied laws by which they began to combine in so varied, definite, and complex a manner, that, to bring one of them to light, immortalizes the discoverer for his sagacity and wisdom? or else, that matter has never existed otherwise than in a compounded state, and has thus always confessed itself a made, originated thing.

Indeed, the non-eternity of the planetary system, or the fact that the present order of things had a commencement, might be argued from the admitted existence of a resisting medium in space. The argument is mathematical, and may be regarded as the continuous summation of infinitely small quantities. For, only admit that planetary motion encounters resistance; and though it be so small as to be inappreciable within a thousand millions of years, still, if it had been from eternity, the motion resisted must have come to an end. Now, the motion of Encke's comet, as well as that of the comet discovered by M. Biela renders the existence of such a medium almost certain. True, its effect even on the wisp-like vapor of a comet may be so small as to require between twenty and thirty thousand years to reduce the cometary motion to one-half its present value. To reduce the present velocity of Jupiter by one-half might require a period of four hundred and ninety millions of years. Still, as that reduction has not taken place, the planet cannot have existed from eternity. Its motion must have had a beginning. The chronometer of the heavens must have been wound up within a limited time, for it has not yet run down.

The object of the *nebular hypothesis* of Laplace — which supposes the earth, and the system to which it belongs, to have arisen from the gradual condensation of a diffused, vaporous, nebula — professes to take us back to a beginning, but only a beginning of existing *motions*. Its immediate design was merely to suggest analogically the possible origin of the motions of the solar system. It says nothing whatever — it can say nothing — in disproof of the Divine origination of matter. It may trace back the mass to an anterior state, which "was itself preceded by other states, in which the nebulous matter was more and more diffuse. And in this manner we arrive," says Laplace, "at a nebulosity so diffuse, that its existence could scarcely be suspected. Such is, in fact, the first state of the nebulæ, which Herschel carefully observed by means of his powerful telescopes." Superior telescopic power, indeed, has recently thrown discredit on the hypothesis, by resolving many of the supposed nebulæ into clusters of stars; a fact suggesting the probability tnat a still superior telescopic power would resolve other nebulous appearances and bring new ones to light; and so on without end. So on at least, until we possess that which we have not at present, nor are likely to obtain, a *telescope* — an instrument for viewing the *end* or *limit*.

But even allowing the hypothesis to become a demonstration, it has only removed the *origination* of matter to an epoch farther back in past duration. Having professedly conducted us back to its earliest nebulous condition, the hypothesis leaves us. This is the ultimatum of physical science. Respecting the anterior, the primitive, state of matter, we are still left in ignorance. Transferring our inquiries into those depths of past time to which the hypothesis would conduct us, we still have to inquire, whence came that nebula? Why is it where it is? Whence the cause of its condensation, separation, collocation, and motions? — processes which, under the circumstances, no laws we are acquainted with are sufficient to explain. Having traced the history of the earth back through numerous changes to its supposed nebulous state, we ask, with the confidence that we are so much the nearer to the beginning, what was the primary change — the first effect? The very fact, that our examination has disclosed to us the proximate beginnings of previous states of the earth, suggests the idea of a primary beginning, and prepares us to hear of it.

We do not expect, be it remarked, that science will ever be able to conduct us knowingly to such a commencement.[1] Even if permitted to gaze on the primordial elements of things, science could not of itself be certain of the fact. If, while the astronomer was searching the depths of space with his instruments, a nebulous body were to be strictly originated under his gaze, his science could not assure him that the body has come wan-

[1] See Dr Whewell's excellent Treatise on the Indications of the Creator, pp. 150 — 171.

dering thither from some distant quarter, where it had existed under other conditions. The fact that it must sometime have had a beginning, might be *instinctively felt* by him as a truth of reason; but, in the nature of things, the fact could be made *known* to him only as an authoritative announcement, and that announcement could come to him only from another and a higher source — from the Divine Originator himself. All that we look for at the hands of science is, to admit the analogical evidence which the natural history of the earth affords of a true and real beginning; and to satisfy the intellectual necessity, the imperative requirements, of reason, by admitting that such a commencement there must have been preparatory to the due reception of the sublime and inspired affirmation, *In the beginning, God created the heavens and the earth.*

4. From a careful consideration of the subject, my full conviction is, that the verse just quoted was placed by the hand of Inspiration at the opening of the Bible as a distinct and independent sentence; that it was the Divine intention to affirm by it, that the material universe was primarily originated by God from elements not previously existing; and that this originating act was quite distinct from the acts included in the six natural days of the Adamic creation.[1]

5. Before leaving this part of the subject, it may be proper to notice two objections to the great antiquity of the earth, although they are not of a directly Biblical nature. The first relates to the geological *evidence* of that antiquity, and may be expressed thus: Why might not God have created the crust of the earth just as it is, with all its numberless stratifications and diversified formations, complete? And the analogy for such an exercise of creative power is supposed to be found in the creation of Adam, not as an infant, but *an adult;* and in the production of the *full-sized* trees of Eden. To which the reply is direct: the maturity of the first man, and of the objects around him, *could not* deceive him by implying that they had slowly grown to that state. His first knowledge was the knowledge of the contrary. He lived, partly, in order to proclaim the fact of his creation. And, could his own body, or any of the objects created at the same time, have been subjected to a physiological examination, they would no doubt have been found to indicate their miraculous production in their very destitution of all the traces of an early growth;

[1] See Note B.

whereas the shell of the earth is a crowded storehouse of *evidence* of its gradual formation. So that the question, expressed in other language, amounts to this: Might not the God of infinite truth have enclosed in the earth, at its creation, evidence of its having existed ages before its actual production? Of course, the Objector would disavow such a sentiment. But such appears to be the real import of the objection; and, as such, it involves its own refutation.

6. The second relates to the long period during which the earth was, according to geological disclosures, comparatively unoccupied, and amounts to this: Is it likely that so long a period would have been allowed by the Almighty to elapse, after the creation of the earth, before the production of the human race? Now, if this be said from a regard to the relative importance of man, as if all created time were lost till he appeared, it is sufficient to reply, that he has still an eternity before him; and that had he been created a myriad of ages earlier than he was, there would yet have been an eternity behind him. If it be said, in the spirit of homage to the Creator, it should be remembered that to Him "who inhabiteth eternity," there can be neither early nor late; that to Him "a thousand years are as one day, and one day as a thousand years." Besides which, the pre-Adamite antiquity of the earth is not, as the objection seems to imply, useless to man. On the contrary, he is indebted to the processes which were then taking place, for all the principal means of his material civilization. And, then, as a creature in whose mind ideas succeed each other, how eminently calculated is the mere attempt of opening his imagination to let a procession of ten thousand ages pass through, or of the events of such a period, to subserve his highest interests, by elevating his conceptions of the Being who has superintended the whole. Other beneficial results might easily be specified. And unless the objector knew all the ends which were answered by the long periods of the earth's existence, prior to the Creation of man; and all which will be derived from it in the eternity to come, he is not in a situation to pronounce on the subject. For aught he knows, a disclosure of all those ends would convert his present scepticism respecting the antiquity of the earth, into a feeling of wonder that the periods of geology had not been of longer duration than they were.

I.

The First Effect.— Assuming, on the grounds stated, then, the great antiquity of the earth, let us go back in thought to that "beginning" when God created the material universe. Up to the moment of its origination there had been only one substance; for "God is a Spirit." Not more amazing, therefore, as a display of power, would the origination of a third substance now be, differing from the two already existing as much as these two differ from each other, than was the origination of matter as the opening act of the visible creation. Here, according to our first law, was *an effect of which the supreme and ultimate reason must be in the Divine Nature.*

1. It is by no means important for us to inquire, whether or not the Being who spake this immensity of matter into existence and activity, separated it from the first into masses, and distributed those masses into the places and proportions and harmonious relations which prevail at present; or, whether he merely produced a vast central and aggregate chaos, as the material from which stars and systems should subsequently issue, by a series of distinct creative acts. If it should appear that the first was the fact, it might indeed be considered that the collocation and adjustment of the celestial mechanism, by furnishing a grand display of the *knowledge* of God, impeached our general proposition that the primary act of creation was chiefly a manifestation of *power*. But to this it would be sufficient to reply, that the knowledge which such a distribution of matter would have displayed from the first, would only show that the power was intelligent and not a blind fate; that it was a knowledge distinct from the wisdom displayed in the second or organic stage of creation;[1] that it would not the less, but the more, illustrate the power which effected it — "knowledge," in this instance, would be "power;" that we do not claim for the first stage of the manifestation a display of power exclusively, since every act of an infinitely perfect Being must virtually include the effect of every attribute of which that perfection consists; that such a virtual inclusion of wisdom and goodness in power, as well as of power in wisdom and goodness, is essential to that continuity of divine manifestation which it is our aim to illustrate; but that we claim for it the exhibition of power principally and supremely; and that God himself is

---

[1] See Note C.

often found to appeal to the work of creation as his own chosen proof of power.

2. According to the nebular hypothesis, however, such a distribution of matter was not simultaneous with its origination. Now, whatever may be the merits of this hypothesis in relation to the whole universe of matter, it is certain that the shape of our own planet — that of an oblate spheroid, or a sphere flattened at the poles — is precisely that which a fluid body would assume by rotation about an axis. And, on examining the constitution of the primary rocks, it is, as we have seen, found to be the result of a state of fusion. They are all crystallized; and many of the series above them are found to be almost as crystalline in their texture.

3. Now, let us suppose that we had been admitted, not only to contemplate the first act of the Divine manifestation, but to study that display in the whole of this first stage, distinguished as it must have been by elemental conflicts and volcanic explosions beyond all human conception, in what other light could we have regarded the phenomena than as signs or expressions of unknown power? We are not now to speak of the extent of the power to be inferred from the supposed scene — whether it be limited or unlimited. This view belongs to a subsequent part of the subject. At present we have to do only with the origination of matter and its planetary formation, as an expression of power. Every property, indeed, which was now brought to light, and every idea which can be supposed to have been truly suggested and represented, expressed a spiritual correspondence in the Divine Creator. Thus, the bare existence of the dependent substance, matter, pre-supposed the existence of the Independent and Infinite Substance. The laws which the planetary motions exhibited were His laws; and proclaimed him to be "the God of order." For, no being can impart that which he does not, in some sense, possess. But even the origination of the substance, and the prescription and maintenance of the laws, were preëminently demonstrations of power. Here was the first objective effect — the origination of matter; irresistibly awakening the conviction of the First Cause: the solemn utterance of the Deity on the subject of causation. Here was the universe of matter in motion, awakening the idea of force; it was the great practical lesson of the Deity on dynamics — the doctrine of force producing motion. Every property of matter, every process by which its properties were developed, every law which regulated these pro-

cesses, every elementary particle and every revolving planet, was lecturing on the power which imparted that force. Nor could we have looked on the geological, planetary, and astral motions — the systems of motion — the complicated and boundless whirl of motion, in its multitude, variety, velocity and extent, and have referred the whole to its origin and support, without feeling the deep emphasis of the declaration, "Power belongeth unto God."

II.

The past brought forward.— One of our principles requires that the laws and results of the past be carried forwards; and that all that is characteristic in the lower steps of the process be carried up into the higher as far as it may subserve the ultimate end; or unless it be superseded by something analogous and superior in the higher and the future. (As we are only, at present, in the first stage of creation, it is obvious that our means of illustrating this law can be derived from nothing antecedent; but are restricted to the earlier operations of this opening stage, as related to its later periods.)

Thus the law of attraction had collected matter around a centre. But it knows nothing of selection; holding the most heterogeneous masses together by the one common bond of gravitation. But having brought the particles of which the masses are composed so near together, another law — that of chemical affinity — appears. Two of the leading principles of chemical affinity are, that it is *elective* — passing by one particle to coalesce with another; and *definite* or *constant*, — each element uniting only with a certain fixed proportion of the element elected.

And, then, as chemical affinity is an advance on attraction, crystallization is an advance on chemical affinity; and to this we are indebted for the granitic foundations of the earth, and all the ten thousand symmetrical forms which matter assumes. The first of these laws does not more prepare the way for the second, than the second for the third. For "bodies never crystallize but when their elements combine chemically; and solid bodies which combine, when they do it most completely and exactly, also crystallize."[1] The matter which was merely

[1] Professor Whewell's Philosophy of the Inductive Sciences, vol. i. p. 353.

held together by attraction — is sorted by chemical affinity — and, in crystallization, according to Berzelius,[1] it assumes its definite forms by a presupposed effort of the particles, not simply to unite, but to unite at certain points. But when the perfect crystal is formed, be it remarked, no law is repealed. It is no less in the all-grasping hand of attraction than it was at first.

III.

Progression. — One of our principles is, that the production of new effects, or the introduction of new laws, will be itself a law of the manifestation; in other words, that the system will be progressive. Accordingly, when we reach the second stage of the process, we shall be able to show its advance as compared with the first. But as we are now merely entering on that first stage, we have nothing prior with which to compare it. We can only regard inorganic matter as something, an existence; and, as such, an advance on nothing, or on non-existence. In this light, we have simply to speak, *first*, of its *constitution.* But if, then, taking our stand at a period towards the close of this stage, we look back on the succession of changes which the material system is supposed to exhibit; we may speak also of *progression in relation to these changes.*

1. Over the physical constitution of every planet except our own, there hangs a deep obscurity. We may be able to weigh them, and to measure their volumes; but this is nearly the sum of our knowledge concerning them. Here, however, we find ourselves in contact with matter; it courts and compels our attention. To the observant mind the earth is a vast laboratory, in which the great processes of chemistry are in constant operation. Accordingly, the researches of science have brought to light between fifty and sixty forms or modifications of matter. Each of these, having hitherto resisted all endeavors to resolve them into any others, is termed a *simple* or *undecompounded* body. It is deemed probable that these bodies exist ultimately as atoms or *indivisible* particles. And easy as it may be to change, in any given instance, their state and appearance, they are, as far as we know, *indestructible.*

2. The properties of matter have been divided into the primary and secondary. The first, including extension, impen-

[1] Essay on the Theory of Chemical Properties, p. 113.

etrability, and inertia, are such as belong to all kinds of matter, and without which we cannot conceive of its existence. The second, are those by which one kind of matter is distinguished from another. To this class belong light, heat, electricity, magnetism, molecular attraction, crystallization, and gravitation.

3. These properties are developed, and operate according to laws. Viewed as merely existent, or in relation to space, matter presupposes a cause; viewed in its fixed relations, and its uniform successions, it exhibits laws, and therefore presupposes a lawgiver also. Thus, the most general law, with which we are at present acquainted, in the chemistry of Nature, is, that all the elementary bodies of which we have spoken, besides exhibiting what may be called preferences, enter into combination with each other, not arbitrarily, but only in *fixed and definite proportions*, by weight. So that having discovered a new elementary substance, and ascertained its chemical properties, we can foretel all the proportions in which it can enter into combination with all the others. Into some of these combinations, it may have never yet entered. But our knowledge of the law respecting it enables us to foresee what the Author of Nature has ordained that it shall do in such circumstances. The law governs our anticipations. "This use of the word *law*, has relation to us as understanding, rather than to the materials of which the universe consists as obeying, certain rules." Our mind discovers the mind of the Creator on the subject, even before the thing created has been made, in the particular case, to illustrate His will. And thus we obtain a view of the constitution of matter which effectually destroys the idea of its eternal and self-existent nature, "by giving to each of its atoms the essential characters, at once, of a *manufactured article*, and *a subordinate agent*."[1]

4. The laws which regulate the changes and combinations of matter are brought to light by those changes themselves; such as solution, evaporation, rarefaction, decomposition, and combustion. The combinations of which the elementary substances are susceptible are endless. The principal forms, indeed, in which matter is found at the surface of the globe, are, the solid, the liquid, and the gaseous. Into the composition of the solid earth there enter but eight or ten of the elementary substances in any *large* quantities. The water, which covers

[1] Sir J. Herschel on the Study of Nat. Phil., §§ 27, 28.

about three-fourtns of the earth, is made up chiefly of two of these substances. And the atmosphere, which envelops both the earth and the water, is composed principally of two also. Indeed, there are grounds to believe that all inorganic substances unite by what is called the *binary* principle of combination; so that, however numerous the inorganic elements in union, in any instance, may be, they will be found to exhibit a progressive combination of pairs of substances, simple and compound. But, we repeat, the combinations of which the fifty or sixty elementary bodies admit, are inconceivable; like the letters of the alphabet, whose union in words and sentences admit of a diversity which no speaking or writing can ever exhaust. In the great laboratories of Nature, every description of chemical process is doubtless in activity, by which compounds of every kind are continually forming. By far the greater part of the rocky crust of the globe is made up of the fragments and powder of an incalculable variety of substances, mingled together in all degrees of proportion, and in such a manner as to defy separation. Nor can it be doubted that this round of change has been going on from the beginning.

6. This brings us to remark, *secondly*, on that *progression* in the state of the primitive earth, indicated by its mineral and chemical changes. If, for the sake of illustration, we adopt the nebular hypothesis, we shall admit that there was a time when the original planetary material was yet circulating in diffused and undetached masses around the sun. Then came the period when the planets, aggregating into separate bodies, occupied their respective orbits, and received their appropriate impulses; impulses involving phenomena so traceable to the hand of the Creator, that Laplace has said, respecting a certain class of them, "It is infinity to unity that this is not the effect of chance."[1]

7. Or if, dispensing with the nebular hypothesis, we suppose the planetary bodies to have existed in their assigned orbits from the first, our imagination will yet take us back to the dateless period when the earth was passing from its vaporous form to that of incipient consolidation. The phenomena exhibited by certain comets — especially by that of 1744, and by Halley's comet, on its last appearance in 1835 — have been supposed to justify the inference, that they are passing through

[1] Syst., vol. ii. p. 366.

a rapid succession of formative processes. The secular cooling down of the insufferably high temperature of the earth was followed by the formation of its shell, or the crystallization of its rocks; and this again by their decomposition by mechanical and chemical means. Then came the period when, as the process of consolidation went on, the volcanic forces began the transformation of the older strata, and produced new and strange admixtures — gneiss, and mica slate, and granular limestone. — Every repetition of the process was followed by new combinations of old materials. The vast rifts and chasms in the crust of the earth closed up, or gave room for the elevation of mountain chains. The external signs of volcanic activity, if they did not contract in range, diminished in intensity. The central heat given off from the surface of the earth was greatly reduced; life became possible; and the earth approached nearer and nearer to its present configuration. And thus, on each imaginary visit we make to the ancient earth, we find it in progress. The activity we behold is not in reality chaotic. Every change is only the result of a new chemical combination, or the evolution of a new law, or the effect of a force newly come into operation.

IV.

Continuity. — According to another of our hypothetical laws, it may be expected that the manifestation, besides being progressive, will be continuous, or will be progressive by being continuous, leaving no intervals of time, or of degree, but such as the modifying influence of other laws may require or account for.

1. I am well aware of the metaphysical, as well as mathematical, universality which has been ascribed to the law of continuity; and of the errors and evils arising from such an unqualified extension of its application. It was first applied to motion. Galileo[1] — referring the idea to Plato — affirmed that a body cannot pass from a state of rest to a certain degree of velocity without passing through all the intermediate degrees of motion. Leibnitz not only asserted the law in a more general form,[2] but carried it on from matter into the domain of mind; adducing it to demonstrate that the mind never ceases to think, even in sleep; and that death, in an

[1] Dialog. iii. 150; iv. 32.

[2] Opera, i. 366.

absolute sense, is an impossibility.[1] Bonnet, in harmony with the maxim, *Natura non operatur per saltum*, deduced from the law of continuity the conclusion — not indeed entirely unknown to philosophy before — that creation must consist of a scale of being, graduated downwards, without any *saltus*, or leap, from the Creator to the unorganized atom. And, subsequently, Helvetius applied the law to the progress of human improvement.[2] Nor have writers since been wanting to press it still farther — to the illustration of that doctrine of necessity, which regards all the phenomena of human life as concatenated in a chain of iron mechanism. And even beyond this, it has been made to countenance a theory of development, according to which, an unbroken chain of gradually advanced organization has been evolved, from the crystal to the globule, and thence, through the successive stages of the polypus, the mollux, the insect, the fish, the reptile, the bird, and the beast, up to the monkey and the man.[3]

2. But while, on the one hand, we avoid being led away by a dazzling generality, or being offended by a wild speculation, reckless alike of inductive facts and of moral consequences, let us not, on the other, reject a principle which, when viewed in subservient relation to other principles, may prove to exist, and to have a place in the reality of things. Such a view I have expressed generally in the announcement at the head of this section. The actual modifications to which I believe it to be subjected will become apparent as we advance, from stage to stage, in our examination of its history. For the present, we have only to do with its application to unorganized matter.

3. What was the primordial constitution or condition of the material universe? That it existed, at first, in a gaseous, diffused, and nebulous state, is only an hypothesis; and an hypothesis, as has been remarked already, employed by Laplace, chiefly for the purpose of accounting for the motions of the solar system. And the fact that the space-penetrating power of Lord Rosse's telescope has resolved many of the supposed nebulæ into starry systems, requires us to keep the hypothesis still at a wide distance from the realities of science. Indeed, it awakens the conviction that, in the present life, we can never arrive at certainty respecting the nebulous formation of systems; for were our telescopic power to be multiplied a

[1] Ib. ii. 51. [2] De l'Esprit, dis. iv. c. i.

[3] Among such speculators may be named the author of the "Vestiges of the Natural History of Creation."

thousand-fold, so that we could resolve all the nebulæ within the extended range of our present observation, we could not be sure that nebulous bodies did not exist beyond; and were our power of observation to be then doubled, we should probably still behold in the horizon of space other nebulous appearances — realms of apparent star-dust — defying our utmost powers of resolution. All that we can hope for is an approximation to the truth.

Now such an approximation, however far it may be from the actual attainment of the truth, does appear to be made by the nebular hypothesis. It harmonizes with what appears to be the formative processes, going on at present in certain cometary bodies. It hypothetically accounts for the motions of the planetary bodies, as masses thrown off from the central body. It agrees with the geometrical form of the earth; its oblateness seeming to reveal the pristine fluidity of the body; for such is the figure which it would assume as the consequence of a centrifugal force operating on a soft rotating mass. So that "its figure is its history;" for it indicates the mode of its origin as formed, under the conditions supposed, by gradual condensation. And "surely the vision of these unfathomable changes, of the solemn march of these majestic heavens from phase to phase, obediently fulfilling their awful destiny, will be lost on the heart of the adorer, unless it swells with that humility which is the best homage to the SUPREME! Between us and the HIGHEST there is still vastness and mystery. To take wing beyond terrestrial precincts, perhaps, is not wholly forbidden, provided we go with unsandaled feet, as if on holy ground. An order hanging tremblingly over nothingness, and of which every constituent fails not to beseech incessantly for a substance and substratum, in the idea of ONE WHO LIVETH FOR EVER!"[1]

It has been affirmed, indeed, that the planets show "a progressive diminution in density from the one nearest the sun to that which is most distant;" that the motions of the solar system are "all *in one direction* — from west to east;" and that "the distances of the planets are curiously relative."[2] But

---

[1] Nichol's Architecture of the Heavens.

[2] Vestiges of Creation, pp. 9, 10. The period of the newly-discovered planet *Neptune* is now ascertained to be 166 years, and its mean distance 30 terrestrial radii, instead of 38. So that Bode's empirical law of the "curiously relative" distances of the planets, has failed with regard to *Neptune*.

such continuity has no existence in nature. The *density* of the sun itself is only about a fourth of that of the earth. The densities of Venus, Earth, and Mars, are nearly equal. While the density of Uranus is greater than that of Saturn, which is nearer the sun. The *motion* of the satellites of Uranus is retrograde — from east to west. And the relative *distances* of Mercury and Venus, and of the only satellites which admit of comparison, — those of Jupiter, Saturn, and Uranus, — from their primaries, exhibit no such uniform disposition as the statement implies. The collocation and motions of the system cannot be referred to chance, because of its calculated uniformity; nor to natural law, owing to its departures from uniformity.

4. The law of continuity, in a modified form, has been applied, not only to the formation of material systems by passing from a fluid state through all the intermediate stages to that of the separation and solidification of their parts, but also to the subsequent history of the earth as one of these parts. Thus, Macculloch and others employed it to show that the rocks called *trap* rocks were not of sedimentary origin, but that, as they were found in all the intermediate stages between the igneous and that most nearly resembling the sedimentary form, they constitute a connecting link between these two extremes, and form a *transition* series. Lyell has employed this principle of gradation, in opposition to the *catastrophists*, who suppose that the present state of the earth has been rapidly attained by violent changes and paroxysms, to show that all geological phenomena have been produced slowly, by causes which are still acting on the surface of the earth. According to this view, the present condition of our planet has been reached, not by the wide leaps of geological causes, but by their continuous and gradational operation.

5. The true view, probably, is that which reconciles both methods; and which sees alike in the steady operation of laws leading, in the lapse of ages, to a geological catastrophe, and in the catastrophe preparing the way for the resumed and steady operation of these laws, the uninterrupted progress of the great design. Thus interpreted, science joins with Inspiration in asking, "Hast thou not known, hast thou not heard, that the everlasting God, the Lord, the Creator of the ends of the earth, fainteth not, neither is weary?" No pause occurred through all the unmeasured periods of the geological process; no revolution, which rendered it necessary to begin the work again.

6. Descending even to the chemical properties of matter, we find a gradation in the nature of its elementary substances. For convenience, indeed, these fifty or sixty substances are divided into the metallic and the non-metallic. But there is no such a break in their characteristics as to justify this division. Arsenic, antimony, phosphorus, selenium, sulphur, constitute a connecting chain between the two series.

V.

Activity.— Another of our laws prepares us to find the universe of matter in a state of activity.

1. Accordingly, even the present repose of nature is only apparent. Not an atom, not a world is at rest. The simplest and minutest body is the subject of *internal* movements among the particles composing it. The interior of the earth is incessantly reacting on the exterior. Waves of motion pass through it. The bursting forth of hot springs, jets of steam, mud volcanoes, the up-heaval of dome-shaped mountains, the appearance of new eruptive islands, the processes of rock formation, and the steady rising in its level of Sweden and other portions of the earth's surface, proclaim the constant action of an elastic vapor within. "Could we obtain daily news of the state of the whole of the earth's crust, we should, in all probability, become convinced that some point or another of its surface is ceaselessly shaken; that there is uninterrupted reaction of the interior upon the exterior going on."[1]

By the operation of the various forces and modifications of the law of *attraction*, everything is changing its relations or its place; the granite itself yields; and nature is kept in mutual action and reaction. "Electricity, as a chemical agent, may be considered not only as directly producing an infinite variety of changes, but, likewise, as influencing almost all which take place. There are not two substances on the surface of the globe, that are not in different electrical relations to each other; and chemical attraction itself seems to be a peculiar form of the exhibition of electrical attraction; and wherever the atmosphere, or water, or any part of the surface of the earth, gains accumulated electricity of a different kind from the contiguous surfaces, the tendency of this electricity is to produce new arrangements of the parts of the surfaces."[2]

---

[1] Humboldt's Cosmos, p.221.

[2] Sir Humphrey Davy's *Consolations in Travel*, p. 271.

All is in motion around and beyond the earth. Climate is the aggregate result of an unknown variety of agents and laws in constant play. The comparative repose of the complicated atmosphere depends on the incessant activity of its elements. The northern light is a magnetic storm — "a terrestrial activity raised to the pitch of a luminous phenomenon," — as lightning is evolved by an electrical storm. The fall of meteoric stones indicates the forces which are at work in the regions beyond our planet. A solitary star shooting across the blue vault of heaven tells us that the realms of space, calm and dreamless though they look, are realms of all-pervading, burning activity. But, at times, these "fiery tears" of the sky are seen to fall in showers, and even streams; awakening the idea of an ever-circulating ring composed of myriads of luminous meteoric bodies, intersecting the orbit of the earth. The zodiacal light circles round the sun. The pulsations which tremble through the tail of a comet millions of miles in length, are probably only apparent, and produced by our atmosphere; but the nuclei of those comets "bind, by their attractive power, the very outermost particles of the tail that is streaming away at the distance of millions of miles from them." The motions of the double stars reveal the presence of the gravitating force, in the remotest regions of space. The solar system changes its place in the universe. Stars appear and disappear. The astral universe moves. "If we imagine, as in a vision of the fancy," says Humboldt, "the acuteness of our sense preternaturally sharpened even to the extreme limit of telescopic vision, and incidents, which are separated by vast intervals of time, compressed into a day or an hour, everything like rest in spacial existence will forthwith disappear. We shall find the innumerable hosts of the fixed stars commoved in groups in different directions; nebulæ drawing hither and thither, like cosmic clouds; the milky way breaking up in particular parts, and its veil rent; motion in every part of the vault of heaven."

2. Now this ideal picture may help us to conceive of scenes which actually existed in the earlier stages of the material universe. If matter first appeared at the Omnipotent call, in nebulous masses, or if the heavenly bodies generally have passed through changes similar to those of our own planet, space must have been the theatre of dynamic activity and conflict beyond all our present powers of illustration. The crust of the earth tells its own eventful history. Time was when that solid but still thin crust ever quivered and undulated with the concussive

forces within. Earthquakes shattered and rifted it, and opened, in all directions, volcanic communication between the molten interior and the surface. Through the yawning and abyss-like fissures which traversed it, mountain chains were uplifted; or else eruptive matters were poured forth from unknown depths — granite, porphyry, and basalt — an ocean of rock. Sedimentary formations took place, through mechanical and chemical action of an intensity incomparably greater than that which obtained in later eras. Subterraneous forces repeatedly lifted these ever-thickening strata from the beds of the primitive waters, and allowed them to sink back again. But besides unheaving these masses, dislocating and rending them asunder, the eruptive rocks chemically transformed them into new species of rocks. In the great subterranean laboratory, the metamorphic process was ever proceeding on a scale immeasurable. And while this mighty action from within was penetrating outwardly and changing the nature of the older strata, causes of equal potency without were maintaining the antagonist process of stratification. Vast beds of alluvium or drift were formed; and inland lakes and pent-up seas, displaced by the upheaval of some new range of Alps or Apennines, rushed tumultuously down, displacing, in their turn, the mountain masses which obstructed their course, and hastened to resume their office of chemical deposition.

The history of all these changes, we say, is legibly incribed in the earth itself. It is only by beholding the effects of such activity, as preserved from the morning of time, and still continued in our presence, that we know anything of the laws and properties of matter. A dead, motionless expanse of matter — if such a thing were possible — would be a petrifying blank. It would reveal nothing of itself, and could say nothing of its Maker. But such an anomaly is unknown. Matter is full of the life of motion. Geology admits us into the laboratory of the past; and we behold, laid up for our inspection, the results of activities and powers, which fills the mind with awe to imagine. We see that the great antagonist processes of sedimentation and crystallization have never paused. The endless admixtures of matter have maintained its forces in ever-varying play. And still its multifarious chemical diversity evokes the spirit of change and motion. Its particles essay to arrange themselves in regular forms. In its ever-shifting restlessness, it discloses relations to light, to heat, and to the phenomena of electro-magnetism. In a word, its activity reveals its laws and develops its properties; and the record of these is the record of the Power which originated and keeps them all in motion.

VI.

Development.— Here, also, according to another law, the same property which existed in the preceding, or inferior part of the stage, is not only carried up to the higher, but is there applied to a new and a higher purpose. Cohesion finds its complement in affinity; and affinity finds its perfection in crystallization. This appears to be the highest state of mere inorganic matter. It involves the idea of numerical and developed symmetry. A body perfectly crystallized, and exhibiting not merely geometrical symmetry of outward shape, but showing, by its cleavage, its transparency, its uniform and determinate optical properties, that the same regularity pervades every portion of the mass, is an object for the production of which every great physical law and element of nature appears to have combined — suggesting to the imagination a beautiful pre-intimation of the coming flower.

VII.

Relations.— Another of our laws warrants us to expect that every object and event in the material universe will be found to be variously related. Accordingly, not an atom floats apart in isolation; no change, however slight, is self-originated, or terminates with itself.

1. Matter has relations internal and coexistent; — by the attraction of cohesion, for example, the particles of masses are kept together even when in violent motion. It has also relations external and coexistent; for, by gravitation, these masses themselves are bound to each other. "When we contemplate," says Sir John Herschel, "the constituents of the planetary system from the point of view which this relation affords us, it is no longer mere analogy which strikes us — no longer a general resemblance among them, as individuals independent of each other, and circulating about the sun, each according to its own peculiar nature, and connected with it by its own peculiar tie. The resemblance is now perceived to be a true *family* likeness; they are bound up in one chain — interwoven in one web of mutual relation and harmonious agreement — subjected

to one pervading influence, which extends from the centre to the farthest limits of that great system, of which all of them, the earth included, must henceforth be regarded as members."[1]

2. Matter has relations internal and successively existent; chemical changes which take place in all inorganic bodies by motions which are not sensible, or at least not measurable. And it has relations external and successively existent; and which proclaim themselves in the sensible and measurable motions of bodies. If, instead of confining myself to the bare illustration of the law now under consideration, it were my object to enlarge on the relations of inorganic nature scientifically regarded,[2] this would be the place for their introduction and methodical distribution; for the coexistent phenomena of matter belong to natural history, or are related to space; and its successively existent phenomena to natural philosophy, or are related to time.

3. Among the relations more obvious and interesting to a dweller on the earth, I would merely advert to the relative quantities of land and sea, a relation which, as it was often changed in the early geological periods, must have produced corresponding changes upon the distribution of temperature; to the relation between the velocity of the earth's rotation on its axis, and the degree of its mean temperature; and, to the geological relations between the interior and exterior of the earth — between the aqueous formations without, and the igneous processes within, by which rocky masses, granitic, porphyritic, and serpentine, forcing up their way from below, have burst through the sedimentary strata, hardening, changing, or variously commingling them.

4. In fine, every object and event in the material universe is all-related. Action and reaction, relations of coexistence and of sequence, are everywhere. In the process of generalization, science discovers that the relations of physical cause and effect are only secondary, or phenomenal; that they are properly *medial*, referring it back to something higher, more general and comprehensive still. The discovery of the law of attraction, enabled man to generalize many inferior laws, and to point out their subordinate place and their relations. But does not attraction itself sustain a relation to something prior and more general still? To ascertain this is the office, and

[1] Astronomy, Cabinet Cyclopedia.
[2] See Mrs. Somerville's Connection of the Physical Sciences, *passim*.

the present occupation of science. Man only knows — as a fact of reason — that, generalize the relations of matter as he may, there must be a point at which the whole coexistent series merges in the will of the great Originating Cause; and that, of the whole series of sequent relations, there is no point from which that agency is absent. The most absolute, comprehensive, and profound, of all the relations of matter, is that of the dependence on the will of God.

VIII.

Order.— As each of the physical laws to which we have adverted may be supposed to have come into operation, in the opening stage of creation, in succession; so, according to another of our laws, *in the same order of succession they operate still.* The crystalline state of the body may be destroyed, and yet the affinity and the gravitation remain; the affinity may next be destroyed, and yet the gravitation remain. Each prior law acts, in so far, independently of that which succeeds it; each subsequent law is dependent on pre-existing laws, or is generated by them, and yet harmonizes with them, or subordinates them to itself. This is seen alike in the formation of the crystal, in the laboratory of the chemist, and in the granite masses which we find thrust up from the subterranean laboratory, through the crust of the earth.

IX.

Influence.—We may expect also that everything will bring in it, and with it, in its own capability of subserving the end, a reason why all other things should be influenced by it; a reason for the degree in which they should be influenced by it; and for the degree in which it, in its turn, should be influenced by everything else. The manner in which one law may be said to wait on another, we have seen. And the way (taking our example from gravitation) in which the lighter mass may be said to be subordinated to the heavier, is equally evident; for matter attracts directly as the mass, and inversely as the squares of the distance. So that it does not follow, from the superior gravity of the earth, that the mote floating near the surface has no weight. The earth and a gossamer mutually attract each other, in the proportion of the mass of the earth to the mass of the gossamer, but only in that proportion.

Every mass finds a place, and every action produces reaction; but, for the same reason that the one is related to space at all, and the other to motion and time, the relation of each is proportioned, definite, regulated by law.

X.

Subordination.— In harmony with the last named law, we are led by another of our principles to expect that everything subordinate in rank, though it may have been prior in its origin, will be subject to each higher object or law of creation. The facts adduced under the two laws immediately preceding will, it is presumed, sufficiently exemplify this principle. Illustrations of it, as applied to organic nature, will be found in their proper places, in the subsequent part of this treatise.

XI.

Uniformity.— According to another of our principles, natural laws, though originally contingent, as opposed to absolutely necessary, are, as far as we know them, uniform and universal. "Not one faileth."

1. The same law which forms the tear into a globule, produces the spherical form of the vast masses which people space. All the phenomena of the material system, as far as we know them, are reducible to mathematical laws. The rotation of the earth in twenty-four hours has not varied by the one-hundredth part of a second, since the age of Hipparchus — full two thousand years ago. Newton, indeed, inferred that the irregularities arising "from the mutual actions of comets and planets upon one another will be apt to increase, till the system wants a reformation."[1] He left these perturbations to be calculated by his successors. And Lagrange and Laplace, by a profound analysis, established the great principle that these variations are limited within certain periods, and that they alternate with periods of restoration. This has been called "the stability of the planetary system." And thus laws, originally contingent on the will of God, are made, by the same will, permanent and universal.

2. In affirming the invariableness of the laws of nature, then, it is to be distinctly understood; first, that this constancy

---

[1] Optics, Query 31.

involves no idea of eternal or independent existence, but the contrary. "The question,—what are the laws of nature? may be stated thus: what are the fewest and simplest assumptions, which, being granted, the whole existing order of nature would result? . . . When Kepler expressed the regularity which exists in the observed motions of the heavenly bodies, by the three general propositions called his laws, he, in so doing, pointed out three simple volitions, by which, instead of a much greater number, it appeared that the whole scheme of the heavenly motions, so far as yet observed, might be conceived to have been produced."[1] *Laws of nature*, then, strictly speaking, is a phrase denoting only the *uniformities* existing among natural phenomena. To speak of these uniformities as if they were producing or regulating powers, is obviously absurd. They simply presuppose such powers or volitions, and are their manifestations. The first sequence was a thing produced, and proclaimed a producer. Secondly, the regularity of the laws of nature is quite compatible with the numerical increase of their manifestations, and even, conditionally, with the numerical increase of the volitions which they manifest. Unless the universe was flashed into existence, entire and complete, at once, the phenomena of nature must have become more complex and multiform, as time has advanced. Nor, thirdly, is the stability of nature inconsistent with apparent derangements and partial perturbations; for these very perturbations are only manifestations of other created laws. Still, however, it must be admitted that they are of a kind to intimate, that all which is now understood as included in the stability of creation, may prove to be included in a still more comprehensive law of change. And hence, fourthly, the regularity of nature for unnumbered ages, is quite compatible with subsequent changes in its constitution. As its laws were originally contingent on the Divine appointment, so may be their continuance. Its present stability may be only provisional. And they who would abandon its phenomena to caprice, are but little more blameworthy than they who deem its laws for ever unalterable. The laws of nature are uniform and universal, but only conditionally so.

---

[1] Mill's System of Logic, vol. i. p. 384.

XII.

Obligation.— One of our laws prepares us to expect that everything belonging to the great system of creation will be found, either promoting, or existing under an obligation to promote, the great end, commensurate with its means, and relations.

1. Of course, *obligation* can be predicated of inanimate matter only in a metaphorical sense, similar to that in which the same material nature is said to be governed by *laws*. Now laws, strictly speaking, are *moral* rules ; "rules for the conscious actions of a person ; rules which, as a matter of possibility, we may obey or transgress ; the latter event being combined, not with an impossibility, but with a penalty. But the *Laws of Nature* are something different from this ; they are rules for that which *things* are to do and suffer ; and this by no consciousness or will of theirs. They are rules describing the mode in which things *do* act ; they are invariably obeyed ; their trangression is not punished, it is excluded. The language of a moral law is, man *shall* not kill ; the language of a Law of Nature is, a stone *will* fall to the earth." Here "all things are ordered by number, and weight, and measure. 'God,' as was said by the ancients, 'works by geometry ;' the legislation of the material universe is necessarily delivered in the language of mathematics ; the stars in their courses are regulated by the properties of conic sections, and the winds depend on arithmetical and geometrical progressions of elasticity and pressure." [1]

2. As "the laws of nature," then, can only properly denote those rules by which God is pleased to regulate the phenomena of nature — rules revealed by the mode of His own working in nature ; so, if obligation be predicated of nature, it can only denote the necessity which He is pleased to incur to operate uniformly in harmony with those rules, in order to the attainment of a proposed end. Thus, if the planetary system is to be maintained as it is, certain conditions must be fulfilled. With a perpetual tendency to fly off in a straight line from its solar centre, the physical well-being or continuance of the system depends on its mechanical obedience to an opposite law. The stability and physical progress of the whole depend on the perfect balance of laws apparently opposed to each other ;

[1] Professor Whewell's B. Treatise, chap. ii.

and accordingly the balance is allowed to know no material disturbance. "For ever, O Lord, thy word is settled in heaven: Thou hast established the earth, and it abideth. They continue this day according to thine ordinances: for all are thy servants."[1]

XIII.

Well-being.— By another of our laws we are led to expect that everything will enjoy an amount of good, or exhibit a degree of well-being, proportionate to the degree of its conformity to the laws of its being. Here, again, our language, in its present application, must be understood metaphorically. We are still in a domain in which obedience is only mechanical, and from which the possibility of transgression is excluded.

It might, indeed, be remarked, that even here we meet with many things which are at once suggestive of an ideal physical perfection, and which yet exhibit departures from it — orbits elliptical, motions with perturbations, spheres bulging, depressed, and even the surface of such a sphere rising and sinking with Himalayan irregularities. But all this is according to prescribed law; and, as such, is a part of the material system. As far, therefore, as the principle now under consideration has any application here, it can relate only to the necessary changes and apparent conflicts which the material phenomena exhibit. The composition of a chemical body, for example, depends on the presence of certain conditions, a mechanical force disturbs or destroys one or more of these conditions, and the composition is at an end. Certain stars have disappeared from the firmament; a fact, proclaiming, at least, that the laws on which their visibility depended are no longer in operation in relation to them, but have been overborne by some counteracting power. Certain changes have been going on in the motions of the heavenly bodies from the first records of science; — the eccentricity of the earth's orbit has been diminishing; the moon has been moving quicker and quicker; and the obliquity of the ecliptic becoming less. But, according to Laplace, the disturbance never passes a certain limit. The system contains a provision for complete restoration, so that the continuance of

---

[1] Ps. cxix. 89—91.

the system depends on the certainty of that provision, and on its mechanical conformity thereto.[1]

XIV.

Analogy.—We may expect that the whole creation, as it is to answer a purpose, is arranged on a plan, and is therefore analogous in all its parts. Accordingly, relations of resemblance form the subject of the science of physical induction. "These are a grammar for the understanding of nature;"[2] the perception of such resemblances, and the conviction of their infinite extension, form the ground of that antecedent probability of success which encourages the inductive inquirer to advance from the known to the unknown. Induction is not a random aggregation of instances, it involves the idea that nature is at unity with itself, and thus suggests the direction of his inquiries. Every addition to his knowledge is an additional clue to future discovery; "for nature is very consonant and conformable to herself."[3] Now, here, in this opening stage of creation, analogies already abound; numerical analogies, glimpses of which, from Pythagoras to Kepler, have disposed the loftiest minds to indulge in mysticism; and analogies, which, by the scientific use of general symbols, or algebraic formulæ, have led to discoveries[4] at which the discoverer himself was not aiming. Here, analogies of motion exist; suggesting to a Newton, a relation between the falling of a stone to the earth and the circulation of the moon around the earth; the periodical return of comets; the union of the planetary system. Here are remarkable points of resemblance, if nothing more, between electricity, galvanism, and magnetism; striking parallels between light and sound; and, indeed, such resemblances as have not merely ever been the only legitimate guide of man in his interpretations of nature, but have enabled him to theorise in advance of his facts — to announce the existence of a law afterwards to be discovered. Often, too, have they forced

[1] Hence the apostrophe of the philosophic poet of nature in his Ode to Duty:

"Stern lawgiver! ——
Thou dost preserve the stars from wrong;
And the most ancient heavens through thee are fresh and strong."

[2] Bishop Berkely's Siris, p. 120.

[3] Newton; 31st Query at the end of Optics.

[4] Professor Forbes on Polarization of Heat; Edinb. Trans., vol. xiii.

him from the arbitrary distributions of facts in which he had taken refuge, and have conducted him, as by a clue, to the natural classifications of the Creator himself.

2. Here, in this primitive stage of the Divine Manifestation, the Deity appears casting the moulds, sketching the outlines, and constituting the relations of future things. As the laws as yet in operation are few and simple, hints and shadows of the nobler things to come are all that can be expected. But, like a hieroglyphic language in its early state, every color is a symbol, every form expressive of an idea, and, as in such a language too, to be subsequently employed to represent loftier truths not yet disclosed. Here — could we have looked on the scene with a prophetic eye — here, we might have said, the poet will find many of his most impressive images; the reasoner his comparisons; and hence the scientific theorist will derive his prolific suggestions. To these mountains Divine Faithfulness will point and say, "It is like the great mountains, and it reacheth to the heavens." Divine Immutability, pointing to this firmament as an image of its own stability, will declare, "If the heavens can pass away, then my covenant shall fail." And creating power, deriving a proof of omnipotence from the magnitude of the material universe, will simply affirm, "I the Lord made all these things." God is here sowing the seeds of things for all the future.

3. *Classification.*— Laplace has said that "an intelligence, which, at a given instant, should know all the forces by which nature is urged, and the respective situation of the beings of which nature is composed; if, moreover, it were sufficiently comprehensive to subject these data to calculation, would include in the same *formula*, the movements of the largest bodies of the universe and those of the slightest atom. Nothing would be uncertain to such an intelligence, and the future, no less than the past, would be present to its eyes." And Leibnitz, before him, had gone still farther, representing the Eternal Mind as incessantly occupied in the solution of this problem — The state of one monad, or elementary atom, being given, to determine the state, past, present and future, of the whole universe. Now, to conceive of truths physical and moral as being linked together mathematically, changes ethics into physics, and is alike repugnant to philosophy and religion. Nor is it less so to conceive even of the laws of mechanical force and motion as if they were superior to the Will which produced them, and were as necessarily binding on Him as on

the phenomena of matter. We freely admit that all mechanical actions are thus open to the calculation of the Supreme Intelligence, for they are only the expressions of His own laws; but we would always accompany the admission with the remarks that His knowledge of material phenomena is independent of such calculations, and that the phenomena themselves never pass from His control.

4. Such a knowledge of the material universe is the unattainable ideal of human science; and every new discovery, however minute, seems to bring us a step nearer to it. But a perfect physical science would require a knowledge of all the properties of matter; the processes which develop these properties; the laws of these processes; the number of elementary or undecompoundable substances; the combinations of which they admit; together with the original quantities and relative positions of each. Now, were we possessed of such knowledge, the principles of our theory would enable us to classify inorganic phenomena according to the method in which they have been arranged and employed in nature. For we should place them according to *the order in which they come into operation*; and according to *their relative value, or to the nature and number of the properties which they include, and of the changes which they are capable of producing upon others; so that no property would be regarded as absolutely valueless.*

5. According to this method, 1. No inorganic characteristic is to be regarded as absolutely valueless. If minerals are to be classified, their external characters of hardness, specific gravity, color, lustre, and crystalline forms, as well as their chemical constitution, are to be taken into the account. 2. That property, or union of properties, is to be held as the most important which contributes most to distinguish and individualise the body to which it belongs, and is most capable of affecting naturally other things. 3. Such property cannot be arbitrarily assigned, but must be determined by observation or experiment; for it may be the most unobvious and antecedently unexpected property. 4. As even inorganic elements exhibit a great system of relations, an arrangement formed on one true principle will not be found at variance with an arrangement formed on another true principle.

True, much of the knowledge essential for such a classification, is still wanting; knowledge as essential as that of the laws of mechanics, and of the law of definite proportions, which we do possess. But not the less important is it that material phenomena should meantime be arranged, *as far as we know them*, according to the principles suggested; that a supposed elementary body, for example, should be regarded as such until it can be proved to be otherwise, since its power of resisting attempts to decompose it shows that it is a body of primary importance in the economy of nature. For, if our method of classification be correct, it cannot fail, by calling attention to those leading properties on which it is founded, to bring before us the effects resulting from their operation, and thus to increase our knowledge; which increase of knowledge again would enable us to test and improve our classification.

XV.

Contingent.—In harmony with another of our Laws, the constitution of the material system may be expected to be found contingent—i. e., *resolvable into the sovereign will of the Divine Creator; and, as such, to be ascertainable by observation and experiment alone.*

1. For example, under the present collocation and motion of the solar system, or of any similar system, the simultaneous existence of every mass of matter composing it was mathematically necessary; but this does not prove that the existing balance of motions might not be a change from some previous arrangement; or that it might not have been an originally selected balance. The laws of motion cannot be shown to have been inevitable. No reason can be assigned why they *must* obtain. Gravitation, as it is, does not exist necessarily; in many respects it is a unique law, characterized by peculiar properties; and, for aught we can see, it might have been variously modified. "Its being found everywhere is necessary for its uses; but this is so far from being a sufficient explanation of its existence, that it is an additional fact to be explained." That peculiarity of the satellites, by which their motion of rotation is exactly equal to their motion of revolution, being calculated, by Laplace, according to the laws of probability, it was found that there is more than 2000 to 1 that this is not the effect of chance.[1]

2. That the sun, which is the centre of attraction to our system, should be also the grand centre of illumination and of heat, cannot, as Newton pointed out,[2] be shown to be a neces-

[1] Syst. vol. ii. p. 327.

[2] Letter I. to Bentley; Works, vol. iv. p. 430.

sary arrangement. There is no apparent connection between its mass and its luminousness, its central position and its diffusion of heat. The direction of the satellites and of their primaries from west to east is not necessary; the satellites of Uranus move from east to west. The molecular constitution of matter, with all its admirable and complicated adaptations to the economy of nature, is by no means a necessary condition of its existence.[1] Leaving to it, for example, hardness, and weight, and motion, we can yet conceive of the laws of these properties being very different from what they now are, and can specify some of the consequences which would result from such difference.[2]

3. Why such and such natural agents were originated, and no others, "or why they are commingled in such and such a manner throughout space, is a question we cannot answer,"[3] by any study of the things themselves. As to the precise amount of matter which should exist, or the space which the whole should occupy — what but the Sovereign will of the Creator was to determine? In a word, both the internal and external constitution of the material universe, the properties of its particles, and the distribution of its masses, the nature of its laws and the magnitudes (sometimes called arbitrary) which those laws regulate, were alike contingent on the Divine appointment. No being existed to challenge His right. As He was the absolute originator, so He was the sole Disposer of the whole.

4. Here, then, was scope for the exercise of the same "good pleasure" on which the whole purpose of the Divine manifestation had depended. And thus the creation, while it presupposes those necessary truths which are the condition of its existence, exhibits the Creator meting out all its internal arrangements with the line and balance of His Sovereign appointment.

XVI.

Ultimata. — The mention of the dependence of matter introduces another law — *the law of ultimate facts.*

1. By an ultimate fact is meant a truth, or an event, not

[1] Prout's Bridgewater T., c. iii.
[2] Whewell's Bridgewater T., b. ii. pp. 20, 223.
[3] Mill's Logic, vol. i. p. 417.

derivative from anything of the same kind, and which, by necessity of nature, admits of no physical solution. And the difference between necessary truths and ultimate facts is, that the former exist independently of any external manifestation, and, therefore, antecedently to creation; the latter are the facts which, to our view, touch that necessary truth, or stand next to it, being immediately related to it, and dependent on it. The former is unconditional; the latter are conditional on the former: for, as we have seen already, we cannot conceive of body without space; of succession or motion without time; nor of either body or motion without a causal Power. Space, is the condition of body; time, of motion; while Power is not only the condition, but also the cause, of both. And the ultimate truths belonging to this first stage of creation respect the relation of the Divine power to matter as connected both with space and with time. Here all *objective* mystery begins.

2. In the order of nature, matter is to be viewed, first, contemporaneously in its relation to space: — how came it really and objectively to be? what relation did the Divine power bear to its creation? We may, or may not, be able to resolve it all into its primordial elements; — but how came these elements themselves to exist, and what is their nature? Having found, for instance, that a salt is composed of an acid and an alkali, and having decomposed the alkali into oxygen and a metallic base, we seem to have reached an impassable barrier — an ultimate fact. Beyond these elements we cannot go. They include nothing in themselves to account for their own origination. Could we have looked on them in the first moment of their existence, we should have seen intuitively, that the only ground of their existence must be the will of God.

3. But if the first moment of the existence of the material universe would have awakened the question, how comes it to be? — the second moment would have brought the corresponding question, how comes it to continue in being? The first moment revealed a creation; the second moment revealed a providence, or the causing of the created material to continue. If the first exhibited it in relation to space, as coexistent, the second exhibited it in relation to time, as successively existent — for all its parts are in motion. Attraction, repulsion, transformation, change of physical relations, are constant and universal. What is the relation of the Divine power to the forces employed in all this motion? Here we come to ultimate laws. When we have traced back the order in which the sequences

in any particular class of natural phenomena occur, till we have reached the highest and the last of the series — that which, in the order of time, is presupposed by all the rest — we have reached our physical ultimatum. And we are conscious of the instinctive conviction that the continuance of the world, no less than its origination, has its ground in the will of God.

4. But does the Divine will act in this case by a primary appointment only, or does it act also by an ever-present agency? Is motion only the prolonged result of an original impulse: or is the power which was put forth in the great original act, directly operative still? There are those who entertain the former opinion. And although they may sometimes have been charged with thus magnifying second causes to the oblivion of the First Cause — and often, it is to be deplored, with justice —not only is the opinion in question not incompatible with true piety, no doubt piety has, in some instances, erroneously led to its adoption. I speak not now, of course, of any theory such as that propounded in the " Vestiges of the Natural History of Creation;" and which represents the universe in its present state as the result of a gradual unfolding of an original germ, or the natural development of a principle, without any subsequent creative interposition. This is to render creation an independent existence. After the primary act, according to this view, the Creator might have ceased to be — as far as the created universe was concerned. Rejoicing in its own independence, it could proceed, *ad eternitatem*, without Him.[1]

5. Now, not only in opposition to such a theory, but even to that qualified view which, while it admits of creative interpositions, yet regards the sequences of nature as ascribable only to the action of matter upon matter, according to a primary appointment — in opposition to such a view, we regard these sequences as owing to the constant concurrence of the Divine will. We believe that the same power which originated matter with all its properties, its selected quantities, and combinations, maintains it in operation, not indeed by separate acts of power in each particular case, but by a constant regular volition acting according to conditionally established laws. And we believe that this ever-present concurrence of the physical agency of the Deity with material phenomena differs, accord-

---

[1] And as Newton affirms in his Scholium, at the end of the Principia: "DEUS sine dominio, providentia, et causis, finalibus, nihil aliud est quam FATUM et NATURA."

ing to the differing nature of the properties and laws which they have, from the first, exhibited.

6. With any of the moral objections which may be supposed to lie against this view, we have not now to do; except to remark that *any hypothesis which essays to remove them from pressing against Providence, only transfers and leaves them to press equally against an original creation.* As to the physical objections, it cannot be justly alleged that the *regularity* of the mechanism of nature is opposed to our view:[1] we recognise that regularity as much as the other party; we even rely on it in evidence of the truth of our views. Order is natural to Him; He needs not to aim at it. The only question between us is, does the power which that regularity evinces, belong, at present, to the machine or to its Maker?

Nor does our view affect the instrumentality of what is properly meant by second causes. The *subordination of the parts* of the great mechanism, is still supposable to any extent: but their orderly operation is viewed as always in dependence on the continuance of the Divine will to that effect. The sequences of nature, however derivative and particular; and the laws of nature, however general; are the laws which He, in His wisdom, is pleased to prescribe to His own agency.[2]

7. But, is it worthy of God — it is sometimes asked — to

---

[1] It may be worth the consideration of those who regard the universe as a self-acting machine — of which we have no true analogy — whether they are not misled by confounding *regularity* with *explanation* — *law* with *cause* — a perceived uniformity of sequence with the manner or principle of the sequence. "What is called explaining one law of nature by another, is but substituting one mystery for another; and does nothing to render the general course of nature other than mysterious: we can no more assign a *why* for the more extensive laws than for the partial ones. The explanation may substitute a mystery which has become familiar, and has grown to *seem* not mysterious, for one which is still strange. And this is the meaning of explanation in common parlance. . . . . The laws thus explained or resolved, are sometimes said to be *accounted for;* but the expression is incorrect, if taken to mean anything more than what has been already stated." — *Mill's Logic*, vol. i. pp. 559, 560. Yet the ordinary fallacy is, that to discover the law of a sequence is to discover its cause; and that having discovered the natural or proximate cause, no other cause need be thought of; that the discoverer has taken it out of the hand of God and of mystery at the same time; whereas, not only is the law where it was before in relation to the Lawgiver, but the mystery is often numerically doubled — the discovery being the unveiling of a new mystery.

[2] Sir John Herschel's Discourse on the Study of Natural Philosophy, p. 37.

perform certain creating and sustaining acts of an inferior description? Is it not beneath the Divine *dignity?* Thus, the author before alluded to, represents it as "a most inconceivably paltry exercise"[1] of the power of God to create one of the lower species. But, to account for the existence of the said species by ascribing it to the evolution of a natural law, is only an adjournment of the difficulty. For, unless it be supposed that in originating that natural law, the Deity was putting a power into operation of which He knew not the effects, the production of that species must have been originally contemplated by Him as one of its effects; so that the charge of paltriness would be only carried back from the creation of the animal, to the prior origination of the supposed law which produced it.[2] Besides, who shall undertake to graduate a scale of great and little things for the Deity? *This* is to "anthropomorphize"[3] God; to assimilate Him to a poor earthly potentate who has to save his artificial dignity by a constant compliance with etiquette; who retains caste not so much by doing, as by not doing. In comparison with infinite greatness, everything is little; the entire creation — not any of its parts merely — infinitely little. It is only as those parts belong to an all-comprehending plan, that their existence is to be accounted for. Apart from that plan, the noblest parts of the universe, and even the universe as a whole, is utterly insignificant. But viewed as an integral part of that plan, nothing is insignificant. It is an all-related part of a system which hallows all which it encloses, and ennobles all that it employs.

8. The preceding objection belongs to an anthropomorphizing view of the Divine dignity. There is another, which springs from a similar view of the Divine *ability,* viewed in

[1] Vestiges, etc., p. 164. Third Edit.

[2] So when others, instead of dispassionately arguing the question, aim to stigmatise the doctrine of creative interpositions by affirming that it represents the Creator as "mending" His own work, they forget that the atheist may fasten the same epithet on their own view of the subject. For if the creation exhibits change and progress, it matters not to him whether the change aud progress, (and this is all that is meant by the "mending,") be said to be effected by the natural operation of a law originally appointed by the Creator, or by the direct agency of the Lawgiver; whether it be mended, or be self-mending. "Why," he will ask, "should *any* mending, change, or progress be necessary? Even if it take place according to natural law, still, as you profess to believe that law to have been of Divine appointment, you only remove the difficulty involved, from the God of providence to the God of creation."

[3] Vestiges, etc., p. 147.

analogy with the powers of a human artist. It expresses itself thus — the theory of God's perpetual agency does not appear to afford such exalted views of the Divine power and skill as that which represents him as originating a law, or creating a vast mechanism, capable of self-activity and development, for as long a period as he might choose to keep aloof from it. Hence, we are assured that "it is the narrowest of all views of the Deity, and characteristic of a humble class of intellects, to suppose him constantly acting in particular ways for particular occasions."[1] We reply, that such a supposition is a figment of the author's own, if (as it would appear) he imagines, that there is no alternative between it and his own theory. Our own view expressly provides against both. We will add, that to suppose the Deity *not capable* of acting in the manner described, if He please, and of acting thus without distraction, "is the narrowest of all views respecting Him, and characteristic of a humble class of intellects." And yet the only ground which is generally assigned for the theory which exempts Him from such action is that of exonerating Omnipotence from labor. Hence, it is thought to be a very unfitting "mode of exercise for creative intelligence, that it should be constantly moving from one sphere to another."[2] Here the anthropomorphism of the reasoning comes out. When man has constructed a, so-called,[3] self-acting machine, that which constitutes the triumph of his powers is, that he should have so built it as to be himself left at liberty to be absent from it,

---

[1] Vestiges, etc., p 160. [2] Ibid. p. 165.

[4] There is an inconsistency, "with which all those philosophers are justly chargeable, who imagine that, by likening the universe to a machine, they get rid of the necessity of admitting the constant agency of powers essentially different from the known qualities of matter . . . . The falseness of the analogy appears from this, that the moving force in every machine is some *natural power*, such as gravity or elasticity: and, consequently, the very idea of mechanism assumes the existence of those active powers, of which it is the professed object of a mechanical theory of the universe to give an explanation." — *Stewart's Prel. Diss. to the En. Brit.*, p. 125. Indeed, the mechanical theory cannot, in the nature of things, find any analogy in the universe. For man originates no motion whatever. In his most complicated machinery, he merely avails himself of pre-existing forces — properties which existed before he came into being. Now, the theory requires support from some analogy to these very properties which it assumes to be self-sustaining. But as the supposed parallelism of a piece of human mechanism fails, it can nowhere be found. To my own mind, the idea of a created universe existing in absolute independence of the Divine agency, is simply inconceivable.

and to turn his attention to other objects. He, a being of limited power, has constructed a machine which does not limit or detain that power, but which acts independently of it. Whereas, in this very particular, the analogy is totally inapplicable to the divine Creator. His presence with one object, or in one place, does not imply his absence from another; for his energy is omnipresent.

Besides which, is not our admiration, in the case supposed, excited rather by the wondrous mechanism than by the mechanist? At all events, would not our estimation of *his* powers be greatly enhanced, if, after examining the machine which was supposed to work alone, we discovered that he, though distant from it, held secret lines of communication with it; that these lines, on which its activity depended, were never out of his hand, by night or by day; and yet that, without any apparent limitation of his powers, he was occupied in the construction and movement of a similar machine elsewhere. Wonderful as we should deem the mechanism, we should regard the mechanist as more wonderful still. And the very feeling we are conscious of, of the impossibility of any human power being able to accomplish such a thing, is so much homage to the Divine power which can effect it. If the god of Epicurus had made the world, he would, doubtless, have retired from the cares and painstaking of sustaining and controlling it; that is to say, he would have acted the part of a great human creator. To be able, on the contrary, to originate the universe, and then to pervade it by an ever-present agency, unconscious of effort, is a perfection so far beyond our ordinary range of thought, so entirely unique and divine, that the mind does not easily reach the conception.

9. If, however, it be said, that the theory which leaves the universe to work entirely alone, enhances our views of the *skill* of the Creator, much more than that which supposes His ever-present and all-pervading agency, it seems sufficient to reply, first, that the display of His skill may not be (as the hypothesis supposes) the only, or even the highest, end aimed at in creation; and if it be not, the remark loses its force. But, secondly, while the skill of the Creator is sufficiently obvious, whichever view be taken of the present subject, it is clear also that the Divine skill has been actually employed, not for itself, but in subserviency to ulterior aims. Who can question, for example, the ability of the Creator to have complicated the proofs of His skill in the operations of nature much more than

He has actually done? or to have brought the world into existence at first in a more advanced state than He appears to have done? The reason why He did not, must then have related to an end or ends, distinct from the mere exhibition of His creative skill. And, thirdly, we can easily conceive of such ends, and shall have hereafter to enlarge on them; ends analogous to those, for example, attained by the family constitution, in which He has been pleased to arrange that the children shall not be born into a state of independence, (which *they* might deem the highest display of Divine skill) but that they shall owe their best advantages to the benevolent provision which keeps them dependent for years on their parents.

10. We entertain the belief, then, of the pervading agency of the Divine Being throughout the material universe, not in exclusion of, but in addition to, the doctrine of primary appointment; for He does that which He decrees. We believe this, because there are no valid objections to be urged against the view which do not lie equally against the theory of development by natural law; because the idea of an entirely self-sustaining universe is destitute of all true analogy; because we cannot conceive of a self-sustaining universe, any more than we can of a self-originated creation — dependence is its characteristic in relation to time, as much so as in its relation to space; and because (if the question is to be argued on the ground of what may be most honorable to the Divine perfections) we deem the view which represents the material universe as *directly dependent* on the Divine agency, more exalting to God than that which views the universe as released from such dependence; not to say that the reasoning which "compliments" Him out of the material universe not unfrequently ends in excluding Him from the throne of His moral government.

Other reasons in corroboration of this view will come to light as we proceed. For the present, it may suffice to suggest to the believer in Divine revelation, first, that the opposite view, if it does not necessarily deny the existence of the Divine attributes, denies, at least, their objective exercise — representing the Omniscient as if he saw nothing, the Omnipresent as if he were universally absent, and the Omnipotent as doing nothing. And, secondly, it seems impossible to harmonize such an abandonment of the universe to natural laws, with the testimony of Scripture, and with the evidence of geology to successive creations.

11. If to this it is replied that the Divine Being is not supposed to detach himself entirely from the universe, that he is yet regarded as being "virtually present in the natural world by a providential inspection and superintendence"[1] of it, we can only add, that this seems to fall very little, if anything, short of the ever-present and pervading agency which we advocate. At least, the arguments which would establish such a relation of the Deity to the material universe, as amounts to a *virtual presence* with it, a constant *inspection* and *actual superintendence* of it, and the *necessity* for such an agency, would go far to establish the sustaining and pervading nature of that agency. And this apparently near approach to the admission of such an agency, in the very act of denying it — a not unfrequent thing — only shows the difficulty of saying how much more or less relatively we affirm in a proposition of our own, unless we knew precisely how much is denied in the contrary position of another.

12. Before proceeding to the next law, let me recall attention to the important *distinction* which has now been disclosed to us, *between the relations of matter to space and to time.* One important distinction is disclosed to us under the law relating to necessary truth — the distinction between the subjective and the objective; the infinite mind and the created universe; the latter presupposing the former, having existed potentially in the mind of God before it existed objectively as a purpose realized. Here, we are called to regard the twofold relation which He sustains to it as it is viewed in connection with space and time. As it is regarded contemporaneously, or irrespective of time, and in relation only to space, He is its creator; but as it is viewed in relation, not only to space but to time, or as successively existent, He is its preserver. Creation introduces us to auniverse of objects; Providence to a universe of objects and events. By the first originating act, matter was made to take possession of space, as an objective reality; a moment after, and it had taken possession of time, as objective and successive.

13. But if this distinction be well founded, it follows that the properties and the distribution of matter, as constituted by

---

[1] Jones's Philosophy, quoted in a note in Tateham's "Chart and Scale of Truth;" one of the Bampton Lectures, vol. i. p. 169. So also Boyle, while comparing the universe to a vast machine, yet speaks of it as "*managed* by certain laws of motion, and *upheld by His ordinary and general concourse.*" — *Inquiry into the Vulgar Notion of Nature.*

creation, are distinguishable from the laws of matter as continued by Providence. The constitution of matter placed it in relation to space; the sequences of matter, in relation to time. True, we may know nothing of the properties but by the operation of the laws; nothing of the constitution of matter as created, except as disclosed by the sequences of matter as continued; just as the constitution of the mind may be known only as manifested in its operations. But as the laws or operations of the mind presuppose its constitution, so the sequences of matter presuppose the properties or constitution originally given to it.

XVII.

Necessary truth.— The existence and motion of the material masses imply *the existence of necessary truth.* Supposing that we had received and sustained the sublime and complicated impressions derivable from the contemplation of the new-made universe, what would have been the legitimate operations and consequent state of our minds?

1. We could not have beheld the unorganized masses, either as coming, or as come, into existence, without regarding the change as an effect. Nor could we have come into contact with a small portion of one of these masses, and have put it into motion by an act of muscular exertion, without regarding the cause of all the motion we saw around us as something more than a mere antecedent to it; as an efficient connection or power — an energy which has had a real operation.

We could not have contemplated these masses without perceiving that they were things distinct from ourselves, *without us*, external to us: but, our apprehending them as without us, takes for granted their existence in space. We could not, by sight, and touch, and muscular extension, have ascertained that they had figure, without perceiving their *relations* to space; for the line of one dimension, the plane of two, and the solid body of three dimensions, are all modifications of the conception of space. We could not have thought of space as the negation of all these things; as existing only that other things may exist in it; or as a condition without which the masses themselves could not exist; without regarding it as infinite in all its dimensions, and as indestructible. We could not have ascertained their figure, and externality, and solidity, without feeling that they existed independently of us, so that no act of our mind could make or destroy them. And as we should have perceived that these properties and special relations of the masses depended not on our perception of them, so we should have perceived that if these things themselves had never existed, the portions of space which they now occupy, would have borne the same relations to infinite space which the things themselves actually do — i. e., that the two sides of a triangle would have been greater than the third, even if there had never been a material triangle.

3. We could not have thought of the creation as new, or in connection with its former non-existence, or have marked its progressiveness, without being conscious of a sense of successiveness, or of time. Nor could we have reflected on time, as that in which both our perceptions and their objects exist, without feeling that time itself is independent of both. The first stage of creation, then, as far as it exhibited the existence of matter in motion, involved, at least, three necessary truths. For we *cannot* conceive of succession, without time; of body, without space; nor of effect, without the power which caused it — i. e., a Being or Substance potential to the effect produced. Time, space, power, are necessary ideas. All phenomena presuppose them; are not intelligible without them. They themselves cannot be resolved into anything antecedent; have no conceivable conditions; but exist independently, and as the conditions of everything else.

4. Here, an important distinction comes to light. While space is only the condition of body, and time of motion, *power*, as we have implied, *is not only the condition, but the cause of both.* As condition, it could not but be; as cause, its existence was contingent on the Divine will. As condition, it was from eternity; as cause, it commenced the succession of measurable time. As condition, it is a property of the infinite Substance — an attribute of the Divine Nature; as cause, it is the objective manifestation of that property, the creating exercise of that attribute. As condition, its activity from eternity was only subjective; as cause, its activity becomes objective also. Here, then, we have the *subjective* and the *objective;* for that which was possible has become real. What must that be, to which the real has always been possible? and what is that which, having been only possible, has now become real? What are the relations between the two? or, how do they co-exist? This is the domain of ontology — the doctrine which relates to the Substance of being.

XVIII.

Secular Change.—But *will this stage of the Divine operations be sooner or later succeeded by another?* For, according to one of our principles, the production of new effects, or the introduction of new laws, will be itself a law of the manifestation. For, were it to terminate at any given point, the proof of the Divine all-sufficiency for unlimited manifestation would terminate with it. Besides which, all-sufficiency, from its very nature, requires infinity and eternity in which to be developed; for it implies sufficiency for nothing less than these. If, then, the development of the Great Purpose be in its very nature progressive, this is only saying that the process must ever be kept open to receive the addition of new effects, or the superinduction of new laws.

1. Now, however, a new—an analogical ground for expecting an additional stage in the Divine operations has come to light. For, as we have seen, the activity of the primitive material universe has itself been the activity of *progression.* Nor can we imagine ourselves surveying this activity of progression, without more than suspecting that we are looking on the successive steps of a scene preparatory for a new stage of the Divine Plan. All that we behold—complicated and stupendous as it is—is only the play of inorganic matter, unconscious of its own existence and activity. The Divine Purpose and the Divine procedure alike combine to point us to the future.

2. The preceding section reminds us of the great principle that the law of ever-enlarging manifestation to which it relates *is itself regulated by a law determining the time and manner of each successive stage of the advancing process.* In the original statement of this law, I remarked, that the time for this change in any given department of the Divine Manifestation, will of course be determined *in a manner, and for a reason,* differing with the particular *nature and design* of the department:—first, by each existing stage passing through all the combinations and changes of which it admits, before another begins; or, secondly, by its existing long enough to show that it involves all the necessary possibilities for answering such and such ends, if its continuance were permitted; or, thirdly, until it has sufficiently taught the specific truth, and attained the proximate and particular end, for which it was originated.

But, whatever the *particular* reason for determining the period of change may be, it is evident that the law of the time and the occasion for every change must harmonize with the Great End of the whole — the manifestation of the Divine All-sufficiency. For, were a stage of the manifestation to be recalled or replaced a moment before it had, *in some way*, demonstrated the all-sufficiency of God for that particular stage, the Great Purpose would not be answered.

From which it follows that no such change or interposition takes place arbitrarily, but, as the laws of progression, and of the end, require it.

And that the *length* of the time which may be allowed to elapse, after the introduction of one law or change, before the introduction of another, so far from growing into an objection against any further addition or change, becomes, in a progressive system, an ever-increasing ground for expecting it.

3. Even those who advocate the natural-development hypothesis, cannot consistently entertain any valid objection against this law. For, even if the great changes which have marked the progress of the material universe have been, as they imagine, only the development of a law, or laws, originally impressed on matter, all these changes must have been foreseen — must have been actually included in the plan of the glorious Deity. But if their occurrence was designed, for the same reason that they were designed to occur at all, there must have been a right time for their occurrence. And this is the substance of the law now under consideration.

4. What was it, then, which made the time thus divinely selected, the appropriate time for a distinct advance in the great process? We have said that "no such change takes place arbitrarily; but, as the laws of progression and of the end require it." Here, then, is a two-fold law to be satisfied.

Now, the requirement of the law of progression, in the present instance, is obvious; — the event declared it. The inorganic world was designed by the Divine Creator to become the scene of organic forms — of life. When, therefore, the earth had passed through such foreseen changes, and had attained to such a condition, as adapted it to the existence of organic life, the law of progression might be expected, in harmony with the Divine Plan, to receive a new illustration. "The proximate end of the origination of this earth had been attained." It was in a state to become the means for the attainment of another particular end, if the Divine Creator chose so to employ it.

5. But is this the appropriate time for the change, accord-

ing to the law of the end? That is to say, admitting that the design of the creation and maintenance of the material universe is to manifest the Divine Omnipotence, is that ultimate end, in any sense, attained? Evidently, the first of the conditions of its attainment, which I have specified, is not fulfilled; — inorganic matter has not "passed through all the combinations and changes of which it admits." Vast and complicated as they have been, they are still in progress. And as long as the earth continues, these changes will go on multiplying. And who shall say whether, before the material system reaches a close, it will not have passed through all the great changes and combinations of which it admits? If, as the existence of a resisting medium implies, the period will come—immeasurably distant in the depths of futurity as it may be—when the planetary system, in its present form, will come to an end, who shall say that by that inconceivably remote period, the condition in question may not be literally fulfilled? Possibly, the limit of planetary existence, and the fulfilment of this condition are destined to coincide. The proof of the Divine All-sufficiency, for upholding the worlds which He had made, through all the great combinations and changes of which they severally admitted, would then be historically worked out and completed. Possibly, too, this awful crisis of the material system will arrive, only to be followed by its reconstruction in other forms, and for other ends, and for other immeasurable cycles. Solemn as these conceptions are, doubtless, something analogous, and as solemn, awaits our contemplation in relation to the material system, in the distant future.

6. But if the first of the conditions specified had not,—and, from the nature of the Divine Plan, could not have been complied with, at the time of the change, had the second condition been fulfilled? That is, were the creation of the inorganic universe, and the mighty changes which it had passed through, taken in connection too with the changes which it was yet to be conducted through prior to the arrival of man, sufficient to warrant the inference of the omnipotence of the Divine Creator? Let it be observed that the question is not whether Omnipotence had demonstrated its existence by doing all that it could do; by exhausting itself, so to speak, in its acts of physical creation. Yet this is the kind of evidence of the Divine Power which many persons inconsiderately suppose themselves entitled to look for. Whereas the existence of such evidence is not only inconceivable in itself, but, as we have be-

fore shown, would, if it were possible for it to be realized, defeat the very end of its existence. For, the attainment of that end — the display of omnipotence in the eyes of finite intelligence—requires that the display be progressive; that it include displays of power other than the creation of mere inorganic matter, and additional to it; — this is implied in the supposed existence of the finite intelligences themselves; and that it include power equal to every crisis that may occur in in the system created — otherwise it would be objected that proof of all-sufficiency was wanting in a most vital point. Accordingly, the manifestation of the Divine Power is still in progress; Power, not for the production of physical effects only, but for the attainment of other and higher ends. The manifestation of the Divine Wisdom, or Goodness, does not terminate that of Power; they co-exist and co-operate together. The question is, therefore, whether the creation of the material system, and the series of changes in it which we have referred to, furnish an adequate illustration, *of the kind*, of the Divine omnipotence.

7. That the power of God had demonstrated its sufficiency for the production of certain effects is evident; for these effects had taken place. But had all the effects taken place, which, under the circumstances, might have been expected? Novel as this question may be, and unanswerable, in a definite and categorical respect, as it must be, it appears to me that it involves that proof of all-sufficiency of which we speak, and that an approximation to a satisfactory reply is by no means impossible. In order, indeed, to a reply arithmetically accurate, it would be requisite — in reference to the earth, for example — to know (setting aside the power necessary for the origination of its material) how many changes that material could pass through, and the length of time necessary for the process. That is, we must know the number of the simple substances of which it is composed; the properties of each substance — its density, gravity, cohesion, elasticity, its relations to heat, electricity, and magnetism, together with all its chemical affinities; and the definite amount of each substance included in its constitution. With these *data* in our possession, we must determine the number of terrestrial changes possible; and then, having ascertained the lapse of time from the Great Originating Act to the period of which we speak, and the number of the terrestrial changes during the interval, we should be in a condition to furnish an answer to the question proposed.

8. Now, although such a reply, with our present limited means and powers, is not attainable, an approximation to the truth, sufficiently near, is not impossible. If it should appear, for example, that, of the number of terrestrial changes possible, a vast variety had taken place prior to the production of organic forms, and between that period again and the creation of man; that the *number* of inorganic changes which have since occurred, are as nothing in the comparison; and that the *degree* of all subsequent changes is as insignificant as the number; we may safely infer in favor of the affirmative of our question. If it should appear probable that the number and variety of our terrestrial changes are only a specimen of similar changes through which worlds and systems, beyond our powers of calculation, have been variously conducted from the beginning, the affirmative reply will be still further warranted. And if it should be made probable that cosmical changes, in every stage of revolution, and on a scale beyond our powers of conception, are still in process—what more could be desired to complete our conviction of the sufficiency of the Divine Power for the number of the physical changes in question?

9. That evidence of the truth of these suppositions exists in abundance will, doubtless, be freely admitted. Astronomy assures us of vast nebulous objects, exhibiting "no regularity of outline, no systematic gradation of brightness," and suggesting the idea that they are awaiting the slow process of aggregation into masses; as if on purpose to show the all-sufficiency of the Creator. The regions of space are inhabited by countless worlds and systems; exhibiting indications of an endless variety of color, density, magnitude, motion, relative position and mutual dependence, as if for the sake of showing the boundless resources of the Divine Power. Proofs of geological revolutions, in number not yet ascertained, if at all ascertainable, and in degree beyond all computation, are placed by the hand of God within the crust of the earth, as if in order to challenge our unquestioning faith in his all-sufficiency. Traces of a long and bewildering succession of changes, to the number, variety, and extent of which the imagination has never yet done justice, are there stored up, as if expressly that man might see and believe. The amount of evidence of the Divine sufficiency for all the terrestrial changes which might have been expected, is not merely adequate for conviction. For such a purpose, it exists in excess. It carries the mind into the future; awakening the idea that it is the design

of Omnipotence to conduct the earth, the material universe, through all the changes of which it admits; to occupy space without limit in unfolding the universe of matter, and duration without end in unfolding its properties by a succession of ever-varying change; and thus to display the sufficiency of His own power as the Originator and Sustainer of the whole.

10. The second condition of the law now under consideration, then, had been satisfied — the earth had existed long enough to justify the inference that the power which had shown itself sufficient for conducting it through all the changes of which it exhibits the evidence, is all-sufficient for every change of which the earth admits. Had the evidence of this truth been incomplete, when, according to the law of progression, the earth had become adapted to human life, I believe that the law of progression would have waited for the completion. Hazardous as this sentiment may appear, it is only affirming that the means would have been subordinated to the end; that one proximate end could not be sacrificed to another, without losing sight of the great and ultimate end. But, when it is remembered that we are speaking of the procedure of 'God only wise,' all appearance of hazard vanishes; for "seeing the end from the beginning," He makes all his operations harmoniously coincide, rendering the attainment of one part of his design 'the fulness of time' for commencing the attainment of another.

XIX.

Reason of the Method. — All the preceding laws relate, as I conceive, to the *method* of the Divine procedure. And, as far as we have gone, we have seen their application to the first department of that procedure — the inorganic universe.

The Reason for this method remains to be considered. It will be found, I submit, to be twofold. The first part is founded in the constitution of the beings by whom the method is to be studied, and involves the well-being of the creature; the second is founded in the destiny of the creature, and involves, in addition, the ultimate end of the whole — the glory of God. The reason relates, therefore, to the law, *that the beings to whom the manifestation is to be made, and by whom it is to be understood, appreciated, and voluntarily promoted, must be constituted in harmony with these laws; or, these laws of the objective universe will be found to have been established in prospective harmony with the designed constitution, and the destiny of the subjective mind which is to expound and to profit by them.* My remarks on the apparent reason for the Divine method must be, for the present, comparatively brief; on the obvious ground that we have not yet reached the human dispensation, or examined the constitution of man, and that, consequently, all we may now advance anticipates our consideration of that subject, or presupposes the knowledge of it.

1. Were it proper to enlarge on the law which I have just quoted, it would be easy and interesting to trace the harmony and coincidence of the constitution of the material universe with the constitution of the human mind. For the present, however, it will suffice to remark generally, *first*, that if the organic universe is to be understood by man, and to prove conducive to his well-being, it must be constructed according to a plan. Here we perceive, at a glance, a reason for that law of uniformity, without which man would possess his powers of observation in vain, and creation would be only and truly 'a fortuitous concourse of atoms:' — and for that law of all-connecting relationship, without which induction would be impossible, and inquiry would be constantly baffled and brought to a pause, but owing to which man is ever ascending to higher and wider generalizations, and an endless multitude of parts become a united whole: — and for that law of analogy, without which he could not take even a first inductive step, for nature would furnish him with no hint respecting the direction in which he should proceed; but by which he now possesses a clue for threading its most intricate labyrinths, and finds himself satisfactorily rising from physical science to natural theology, and thence to the domain of Revelation.

Without the laws in question, observation, experience, science, life itself, would be impossible. But, with them, matter becomes the educator of mind; aids in revealing it to itself, and in preparing it for higher revelations. While these laws are not so obscure as to defy his diligence, they are not so obvious as to force themselves on his involuntary notice. *If he will*, he can extract their secrets, and incorporate them as organic parts of his systematized knowledge. In the midst of an unknown multitude of worlds, man feels himself at home; since "the stars in their courses" are obedient to law. And when geology has led him back through an unknown succession of ages, he feels that he is only travelling through the ancient monuments of the same law, in the direction of the Divine Legislator himself.

2. And, secondly, if the inorganic universe is to be understood by man so as to answer the ultimate end, it must be constructed in a manner calculated to refer him to an Almighty origin. Here, again, if we were not presupposing the knowledge of man's mental and moral constitution, we might enlarge on the laws of ultimate facts, and of necessary truth, as pointing directly to such an origin. For the present, however, we shall limit ourselves to a remark on the single law, that the constitution of the material universe may be expected to be found contingent, or resolvable into the sovereign will of the Divine Creator.

If the inorganic universe did not exhibit marks of contingent arrangement, and if man had not the power of interpreting them aright, it would not be the means of the Divine manifestation, but would only manifest itself — disclose its own properties — proclaim its own nature. Instead of referring the human mind to God, it would literally stand between man and its Creator, and would tend to enclose man in its own material mechanism.[1] But we have seen that it does exhibit the expected signs of contingency. Its properties appear to be selected, and its relations to be instituted. Properties of some kind it must have, nor can we conceive it to be destitute of every kind of relation; but it cannot be shown that the actual properties were absolutely necessary, nor that the actual relations might not have been modified without end. On the contrary, choice, adaptation, and adjustment, are everywhere visible; and the mere facts that matter, though not capable of its own creation, should yet be found in existence; and though unconscious, should yet exhibit a scientifically arranged constitution, sufficiently point to the Divinity of its origin.

3. Here, then, we see the twofold *reason* for the chosen method of the Divine manifestation. Let the evidence that the power displayed in the material universe is *His* power sink below a certain degree, and man will be excusable for "worshipping the creature rather than the Creator." Let the evidence rise beyond a certain degree, and conviction will not be optional, nor voluntary adoration possible. The Divine method provides against each danger. If man will, he may

[1] Design implies freedom of choice; natural law means, as employed by materialists, a necessity. The fact of design may be inferred from any degree of regularity, however imperfect, which cannot *reasonably* be ascribed to chance. The establishment of a single exception is fatal to the hypothesis of a natural or necessary law.

make that uniformity of nature, without which there would be no evidence of the Divine power, the very occasion of forgetting and denying such power; or, if he will, he may make it the occasion of ascending to the proofs of that contingency and appointment on which the uniformity itself depends. The constitution of the material system told of an Almighty maker, in a way which foretold a race of intelligent and accountable creatures.

XX.

The ultimate End.—We are led to expect that both *the laws of the method, and the reason of it,* will find *their ultimate end,* in relation to this stage of the Divine Procedure, *in contributing to prove the all-sufficiency of the power of God.*

1. In our remarks on this subject, under the first law, we have stated distinctly that we do not claim for this opening stage a display of power exclusively, but preëminently. God himself is often found, in His word, appealing to the creation of the material system, as his own chosen proof of power. We remarked also that we were not then about to infer the extent of the power displayed in the material creation, whether it be limited or unlimited. Nor do we now say that this opening stage mathematically demonstrates the absolute infinity of the Divine power. If it did so, all the illustrations of power derivable from the subsequent stages of the Divine Procedure, would, as further evidence, be superfluous; for the proofs have been accumulating ever since, whereas we are only as yet dealing, by supposition, with the opening proof. And, we conceive, that as the metaphysically adequate proof of infinite power must itself be infinite, the only possible manner in which it can be furnished to finite beings, is by a progressive accumulation through infinite duration; and therefore can only be always in process. But we can conceive, also, of such a display of power within a space and a time not absolutely unlimited, as should furnish beings capable of reasoning from analogy, with ample, superabundant evidence of power unlimited. Such exercise of power we believe to have been displayed in the primary stage of creation.

2. Now, in order to fill our imagination for awhile with this illustration of the Divine Power, let us glance at the nature and magnitude of the vast system to which the earth belongs. And the point from which we might most advantageously start

would be an elementary atom. But where shall it be found? Animalcules — organized beings possessing life and all its essential functions — are in some cases so minute that a million of them would occupy less than a grain of sand. A grain of musk will continue to yield odour, to throw off an incalculable number of particles of matter, for twenty years, without any sensible diminution of its weight. Yet, on apparently conclusive grounds, it may be inferred that matter is not infinitely divisible. For the present, however, science must be content with an inference.

But it matters little that we cannot begin with a strictly indivisible atom; since, even if we could, the combination of as many of these as go to form a microscopic insect might baffle all our powers of arithmetic. Let us begin with one of these living atoms; and, remembering that every particle of which it is composed is a production of Almighty power, and that a million of these will only equal the size of a grain of sand,— according to Ehrenberg, a cubic inch of the tripoli of Bilin contains 40,000 millions of the siliceous coverings of the Galionellæ, — let us try to conjecture how many of these grains would equal a cubical mile of rock; and then recollect, that to equal the size of the earth we must accumulate 263,858,149,120 such masses.

3. Immense as this aggregate of matter is, when compared with the entire solar system it dwindles to a point. The mass of the sun itself is 354,936 times that of the earth, so that were its centre brought to the centre of the earth, it would not only fill up the orbit of the moon, but would extend nearly as far again. But this is nothing compared with the mass of some of the stars. Who can conjecture the magnitude of a body which would fill the vast orbit of the earth! But, though our mean distance from the sun is ninety-five millions of miles, and that of Uranus about nineteen times greater, or 1,800,000,000 miles, the bright star in Lyra has a diameter which, it has been said, would nearly fill even that orbit.

Among the planetary nebulæ there are masses so enormous, that, according to the computation of Sir John Herschel, if they are as far from us as the stars, their real magnitude, on the lowest estimation, must be such as would fill the orbit of Uranus; while among the nebulous stars there are some of dimensions so vast — not improbably systems of stars — that were one of them in the place of the sun, its atmosphere would not merely include the orbit of Uranus, but would extend eight times beyond it.

4. In the presence of such masses, indeed, the moon, the earth itself, may be omitted as an inappreciable quantity, and the space occupied by our system be passed by as an unassignable point. But the estimate is hardly yet begun The milky way derives its brightness from the diffused light of bodies each of which may be equal to that of Lyra, and of which 50,000 passed through the field of Sir W. Herschel's telescope in an hour: 2500 nebulæ, and clusters of stars, have been observed by Sir John Herschel; and an unknown number more remain to be observed. In some of those which he has examined, "ten or twenty thousand stars appear compacted or wedged together in a space not larger than a tenth part of that covered by the moon, and presenting in its centre one blaze of light." The number of the distinguishable telescopic stars of the milky way has been estimated at eighteen millions. But beyond the milky way of stars, and almost at right angles with it, there is a milky way of nebulæ. A nearer approach might resolve these into clustered myriads of stars, and reveal another milky way beyond.

5. Let us try to imagine the distance of one of the star-clusters in the nearer milky way. The earth, we have said, is ninety-five millions of miles from the sun. Uranus is nineteen times further. The great comet of 1680 recedes about forty times farther than Uranus, or about twenty times beyond the orbit of Neptune; and requires, according to Encke, 8,800 years for its revolution. The nearest fixed star is supposed to be 250 times farther from the sun than this comet at its greatest distance, while the star α Centauri is 11,000 times, the star 61 Cygni is 31,000 times, and the star α Lyræ is 41,600 times more distant than Uranus; so that light travelling at the rate of about 170,000 miles a second, would be three years, nine months and a quarter, and twelve years, in reaching us from these bodies, respectively. But if each of the stars in a nebulous cluster be a sun, and if they be separated by intervals equal to that which separates our sun from the nearest fixed star, light would require thousands of years in order to reach us from such a distance. "The rays of light of the remotest nebulæ must have been about two millions of years on their way."[1] They are therefore, as Humboldt remarks, "the voices

[1] Sir W. Herschel, in the Transact. for 1802, p. 498. Sir J. Herschel's Astr. § 590.

of the past which reach us. It has been well said, that with our mighty telescopes we penetrate at once into space and into time. Much has long disappeared from those distant regions before it vanishes from our view, and much has been newly arranged before it becomes visible to us." But were the means of vision which enable us to behold that remote point to be doubled, who can imagine that we should not see other clusters burning at a great distance beyond it, as it is beyond us; and that were we to be transported to that remoter system, we should not behold similar unterminated collections of suns and systems as far beyond?

6. But if such are the distances which intervene, the quantity of matter of which the sidereal heavens is composed, lost though we are in the greatness of the estimate, bears a very small proportion to the immensity of space. There are vast "openings in heaven," desolate and starless regions. "Large as the bodies are, the distances which separate them are immeasurably greater." But even this space is not a void. It appears to be traversed in all directions by light, and heat, and gravitation.

7. If we are lost in adoration of the Power which had only to say to this space, "Be filled," and it was occupied, what can we think of the Being who maintains every atom of the whole in constant yet harmonious activity! We might remind ourselves of the muscular force necessary to hurl a stone of a pound weight to the distance of a hundred yards, or to draw it to us; of the force requisite to project a cannon ball of 50 pounds weight with a velocity of a thousand miles an hour; but, in the same time, the earth woves 68,000 miles. Jupiter, equal in weight to 1,400 earths, moves with a velocity of 29,000 miles an hour. The rate of Mercury is 107,000 miles an hour. The velocity of the comet of 1680, is estimated at 880,000 miles in an hour. The *annual* motion of 61 Cygni is a hundred and twenty millions of millions of miles, and yet, as M. Arago remarks, we call it a fixed star! Such is its distance! But this is only a single motion of a single body. Besides the rotation of the earth on its own axis, and its annual motion, in common with the other planets, around the sun, there is ground to believe that the whole of the solar system itself is moving together in one direction; and beyond this, that the entire universe of stars is revolving around a common centre, in an orbit so vast, that no measurable arc, in no calculable period of duration, would ever appear otherwise to us than a straight line.

And what if that common centre be, as some think, a mass of matter bearing the same relation and proportion to the whole circulating universe as our sun does to its attendant planets — then is the view which we have hitherto taken of the quantity of matter in the universe reduced to utter insignificance. But whatever the merit of this supposition may be, the new and more enlarged impression which it gives us of the quantity of matter falls immeasurably below the sublime reality.

8. Here, in quick succession, our sight abandons the ground to our powers of calculation; our numbers fail, and resign the subject to imagination; and even imagination sinks, and seeks relief in exclamations of wonder, or in the silence of profound adoration. And yet the whole of this universal system of masses, vast beyond all that the eye can take in; speeding in every direction, with a velocity beyond all that arithmetic can calculate; through realms of space beyond all that the mind can conceive, is stable as the throne of God. If in the material universe there be one point of absolute repose, it is in that common centre of creation to which we have adverted.

9. Now, suppose we had been able to look on the great process on a much larger scale than we can at present; to place ourselves so as to obtain a view of these worlds, systems of worlds, collections of systems, in all the variety, velocity, and extent of their motions, what must have been our reasonable conclusions respecting the energy of the Divine Creator. Up to that period we should have lived, by the very nature of the hypothesis, in an empty, objectless universe; and we could not have beheld the numberless unorganized masses of matter rolling around us, where all had once been vacuity, without regarding the change as an effect, and the Cause, or the Being, who had produced it, as possessed of a power, to us, unlimited.

10. If, now, the question, to which we have already adverted, should be asked, whether or not the proper infinity of the Divine Power could be justly inferred from even this display of it — a display which, though indefinitely vast, must be necessarily limited? — it may be proper for the present, to submit the following considerations.

It is freely admitted, as before, that in the eye of strict *à posteriori* reasoning, a given mechanical effect implies only the operation of a mechanical cause adequate to the production. Beyond this, we admit, that the *à posteriori* argument, from effect to cause, cannot, by itself, demonstrate, respecting any cause, that it is the First Cause. "Though every true step made in this philosophy (*physical science*) brings us," says Newton, "not immediately to the knowledge of the First Cause, yet it brings us *nearer to it*, and on that account it is to be highly valued."[1] It is always conducting us in that direction, but can never certify us respecting any cause with which it has properly to do, that there is not another cause beyond.

11. But here, without stopping to examine whether or not an exclusively *à posteriori* argument be possible; whether, even in the present instance, it does not start with an *à priori* postulate, or belief — we have to remind the inquirer, *first*, that we are not speaking of a mechanical cause, but of an intelligent personal agent. "We must include a distinct personal consciousness of causation in the enumeration of that sequence of events by which the volition of the mind is made to terminate in the motion of material objects."[2] The cause and the effect are not homogeneous. The most, therefore, which he can affirm, is, that if the created effect be limited, the personal Creating Cause *may* be limited also; language which implies that He *may not* be limited; and, that if the effect be only of a physical nature, the Personal Cause *may not* be equally adequate to produce effects of any other kinds; language, again, which implies that He *may* be adequate; and we know that He has since proved it. A material cause is *measured* by the effect, an intelligent cause is only *proclaimed*.

12. *Secondly*, it is to be remarked, that this necessary limitation of the *à posteriori* argument is a tacit confession of its own incompetence and insufficiency, except within the circle of mere mechanical causes and effects. It professes to trace only the operation of laws, not to account for their origination. By this very confession, that its materials are not self-contained and self-sufficient, but derived, it refers the inquirer to a source of derivation beyond themselves. By acknowledging its own inefficacy, it emphatically directs him to carry his appeal from the laws of matter to the laws of mind. By exhibiting laws, it silently points to a lawgiver. The very tendency of the *à posteriori* process, in its ascent from effects to their apparent causes, is to awaken the idea of a First Cause. And, once the idea is awakened, the existence of such a Cause is felt to be an intellectual necessity; the mind cannot be satisfied without it. Aristotle himself has said, "All that is in

[1] Optics, Query 28, p. 345.
[2] Sir J. Herschel's Astronomy, p. 232.

motion refers us to a mover, and it were but an endless adjournment of causes were there not a primary immoveable Mover." That First Cause, indeed, must be immensely different, both in rank and *in nature*, from the subordinate physical causes to which it has imparted motion; but still the mind feels the necessity for such a cause with all the force of an intellectual instinct. The mind was constituted to feel this necessity, and thus to supply the last link in the chain of reasoning from itself, as much as it was made and meant to find the preceding links in the phenomena of nature.

13. The inquirer is to be reminded, *thirdly*, that in affirming the limitation of the created universe, he is quitting his *à posteriori* ground, and is inconsistently availing himself of an *à priori* assumption. True, he may start, on this point, from *à posteriori* ground — having observed that some parts of the material universe are divisible from each other; but he cannot make this the basis for the inference that all parts are in the same predicament, without either most unphilosophically jumping to a conclusion, or having recourse to *à priori* deductions. Certainly, observation has nothing to do with his supposition. Push his inquiries as far as he may, he nowhere finds vacuity or a limit. All the regions of space, as far as he can explore them, are occupied. Could he actually look on the frontiers of creation, he would not know that he was doing so; — there might, for aught he could say, be something beyond. But he has abandoned all thought of finding any confines to nature. Reasoning *à priori*, there must be limits; for a substance divisible into parts cannot be infinite. But observation, and the legitimate inductions of observation, can exhibit no proof of limitation.

14. We have to remind the inquirer, *fourthly*, that he is in danger of overlooking the power presupposed in the *creating* act — the act of the absolute *origination* of matter. He is thinking only of the quantity of matter in existence, and of its motions. The *nature* of the agency necessary to call it into existence is lost sight of. Now it seems impossible to conceive of that power as limited. Not only was there nothing, *ex hypothesi*, absolutely nothing, existing objectively to limit it; but that, in this state of absolute nonentity, the Deity should have "called the things which were not as though they were," can be conceived of only as the prerogative of Omnipotence alone.

Probably, the absolute origination of even a single atom would be proof demonstrative of infinite power in the eyes of exalted intelligences.

15. *Fifthly*, the inquirer is to be reminded of the very important fact that, on his own admission, the limitations of matter in space originate, not in the Cause, but in the very nature of the thing caused — of the material medium which exhibits the effect. He himself predicates of matter that it is conditioned by limits; that its nature forbids it to be properly infinite in extension. The question arises, therefore, what series of effects, exhibited in a substance necessarily subject to special limits, he — as a being constituted to infer, from what he sees, more than he sees — would deem an adequate illustration of uncircumscribed power? We just now intimated that the absolute origination of a single atom might be, in the estimation of superior beings, but the sole prerogative and the adequate proof of Omnipotence. But here is a universe of matter! He has no line with which to measure it. Words, numbers, imagination, fail, in succession, to do justice to the interminable reality. We say, interminable; for the inquirer must bear in mind that *our view of the Divine power relies especially on the phenomena of the material universe, regarded as successive and progressive.* Now, could its unimaginable masses be caused to roll or rush before him, in succession; surely he would not require many ages of such a survey to elapse, before he would feel constrained to exclaim, "It is enough!" Here, too, is a universe of matter *in motion.* Let him be given to understand the numerical amount of the forces implied in all this activity; surely, after the calculation had lasted for ages without any prospect of termination, he could not forbear confessing, "Nothing is too hard for God!" Here is a universe *perpetually changing in all its parts.* The changes which our own planet has passed through imply periods of time beyond our computation. Let him conceive himself to have beheld the first change, and the next, and so on, in succession; surely he would have exclaimed, ages, and cycles of ages ago, "Power belongeth unto God!" — all-sufficient power. He cannot but feel that, in such an imaginary position, the mere reasoning which measures the cause by the effect would soon be out of place; that, having prepared the way for a loftier rule, it would confess its own inadequacy, and be silent. Other and higher faculties than it implies would be awakened, and would assert their claims. And when he remembered that the mighty system was, both in the constitution of every particle and the collocation of its unnumbered worlds, entirely dependent on the will of God, he would feel that even here

" was the hiding of His power"—that He could reduce or enlarge the universe at pleasure. When he saw the innumerable changes which the great system had already passed through; and that no trace was visible of a failure of power, but, on the contrary, that everything was apparently constructed and conducted to evince its presence and its plenitude, he could not but feel himself challenged to say whether anything more was wanting to convince him of the all-sufficiency of God, in this department, for all the future. And when he recollected, that " the arm of God was still bare," still evolving and working out the immeasurable scheme; that every new moment brought with it an incalculable amount of new evidence of the Divine Power to be added to all the accumulations of the past; and that of such increase there was no prospect of an end; he would feel himself in the presence of a God all-sufficient, and spontaneously adore.

16. For, in the consideration of this subject, it should never be forgotten, that, as we have before remarked, man is not merely an intellectual, but also a moral being; a being meant for virtue as well as for reasoning, and partly, as the result of his reasoning. In relation to every moral truth, therefore, which he may be required to believe, evidence, depending for its due effect on his own diligence, attention, and state of mind, is to be expected, to a certain amount, but not beyond that amount. If wanting in that amount, belief would be impossible; if it be in excess of that amount, it would, by compelling belief, make virtue impossible. Constituted as man is, if his belief is to be at once rational and virtuous, the evidence on which it is to be based must be supplied in " weight and measure." Such evidence, it is conceived, is supplied in this opening stage of the Divine procedure—evidence calculated to call forth the intelligent and adoring exclamation, " Lo! these are parts of His ways; but the thunder of His power who can understand!" And thus the method and the reason of the Divine Plan, as evinced in this primary display, find their ultimate end, in contributing to prove the all-sufficiency of the power of God.

FOURTH PART.

ORGANIC NATURE.

The Second Stage of Divine Manifestation.

POWER AND WISDOM.

THE first stage of the Divine manifestation disclosed to us "enormous masses of matter rolling around the horizon of illimitable space," impelling us to the conclusion that the Creator of these must be a Being of all-sufficient power.

Let it be supposed that, haunted and bewildered with the sublime spectacle, and with the laws to which we saw matter successively subjected, we had retired to muse on the omnipotence of the Being who had produced the whole, and on the probable *design* of its production; and suppose, that now again, after the lapse of an incalculable period, it were permitted us to revisit some part of the material universe, to behold the manifestation of another perfection of Deity; what may we conceive that perfection would be?

1. But here, again, let it be premised that we do not contemplate anything like sudden transition in the Divine Manifestation, any distinct line which appropriates all within it to one attribute to the exclusion of every other. The very progressiveness of the manifestation implies the contrary; implies that which we actually find, that even the earliest attribute supposes the coëxistence of all that appear after it, and is itself to be carried on through all the intermediate stages of the great process, to the last.

2. But if, for reasons already assigned, we are warranted in concluding that the manifestation will be gradual; and if, in harmony with this expectation, we have found that the first display was an exercise of power, and that even this display

advanced from step to step, as if to point attention to something yet beyond; we are surely warranted in expecting that the period will come in the history of creation, when another attribute will characterize the manifestation as distinctly as power does already. What, we repeat, is that attribute likely to be?

We have already answered the question, in effect, by supposing that the manifestation of that power has filled us with wonder as to what is the *design* of the universe of matter. *Wisdom*, then, is the next perfection for whose manifestation we look; for with God, design and wisdom mean the same thing. Wisdom is evinced in *the adaptation and adjustment of means to ends*. Having seen the means, (we might be supposed to say,) let us proceed to examine the ends. Power has produced the material; in what way, and to what purposes, will Wisdom employ it? Immeasurable ages have elapsed since the first fiat went forth, and the universe seemed filled, or filling, with a new substance; what changes may not have passed on it, besides those which we witnessed, during the immense interval! What if, since our last survey, another fiat should have gone forth; and, in consequence, another effect have been produced as wonderful as the first, and by means of it!

Now what should we be willing to accept as such an effect? And here, if the mind would do anything like justice to those primary displays to which, in the order of the subject. we are now approaching, it should labor to divest itself, as much as possible, of all the impressions of the Divine Wisdom which it has received from the later and loftier stages of the manifestation. Placing ourselves, then, in the situation of beings to whom nothing of the kind has yet been disclosed, what, we repeat, should we be willing to consider as a display of wisdom — of wisdom so marked, as to constitute an era in the manifestation, so wonderful, that it should seem to unveil to us a new view of the Divine character, to bring us nearer than ever to the Divine presence, and to remove all bounds from our expectation as to the future?

3. We will suppose that the particular section of the universe visited is the solar system; and that, having marked the scientifically calculated intervals between the sun and the planets, and between the planets themselves, and especially the rigorous equality subsisting between the angular motions of rotation and revolution of each satellite, we have been brought to conclude, with Laplace, that the arrangement

is a protest against chance. We will suppose that the particular part of the solar sy tem to which we direct our attention is the earth; that we mark the progressive changes which it exhibits as compared with that primitive fluidity in which we beheld it untold ages ago; trace over again its laws of motion, and chemistry, and crystallization; and fancy ourselves one while standing in the midst of a vast chemical laboratory, where the great agent heat was crystallizing all things; and another while, amidst the conflicting operations of its well-matched antagonist, water, assailing, wearing, and reducing continents of crystal to atoms, and carrying them away to its own depths, but bearing them away only to lose them again by a subterranean force, which lifts them up from their submerged state to the light of day — a lofty table-land. Still, we should feel that all this was only the play or conflict of inorganic matter; that each form we beheld was lifeless, and each motion compelled, or impressed by a force from without, "ceasing when that ceased, and never proceeding beyond its compulsory impulse, either in direction or degree."

4. What, then, if some form of organic vegetable life had now for the first time met our view! It matters not whether that form came into existence slowly or suddenly, alone,[1] or in company with kindred tribes, and with millions of each tribe; the fact that the earth, after the existence of a "limited eternity," has become the owner of a new principle — a principle, be it remarked, hitherto unknown to the whole course of nature — a principle hitherto peculiar to the Creator himself, the sacred and mysterious principle of LIFE; and that innumerable pre-existing phenomena were now for the first time employed as *means*, for the development of this new principle as *an end;* this would surely be hailed by us as an epoch in the progress of the Divine Manifestation.

I.

Wisdom.— Here was *a result of which the supreme and ultimate reason is in the Divine Nature.*

5. We have not yet to speak of the *extent* of the wisdom to be inferred from this new form of existence. At present, we have only to regard it as evincing the *existence* of design in the Divine Creator. Hereafter, we shall have to treat of it as being also a new illustration of creative power, and of every attribute and relation of the Deity already dis-

[1] See Note D.

played in the preceding stage. And whatever illustrations of taste in arrangement, elegance in form, beauty in color, and majesty in magnitude and waving motion, are now for the first time brought before us in the botanical kingdom, are to be regarded as indications of the Divine complacency in the graceful, the beautiful, and the sublime. As effects, they point to correspondencies infinitely greater in their cause. But even the manner in which each of these effects is produced is a proclamation of the amazing wisdom of the Maker.

Every green leaf is a magazine of contrivances; every part of it capable of action, a theatre of different organic wonders. And these diversities are multiplied to such a degree, that, if we would not be bewildered, an attempt at classification is necessary at the very outset of our observations. Here, in the primeval earth, are the three classes which are still extant; the acotyledons, or those which, having no flowers, produce no true seeds; the monocotyledons, or those producing one-lobed seeds; the dicotyledons, or those producing two-lobed seeds. Of these classes, each exhibits an internal structure or organization peculiar to itself; the first being either vascular and cellular in its tissues, or else entirely cellular; the second, endogenous, its growth taking place by addition from without to the centre; the third, exogenous, the growth taking place by the addition of concentric layers without, immediately under the bark. But each of these classes includes numerous orders of plants, each order a number of genera, each genus many species, and every species a number of individuals defying calculation. Here, too, is "a new thing in the *earth*;" the great elements and phenomena of the inorganic world are seen subserving the purposes of organic life. The hand of the Creator has mysteriously bound them to the new principle. Every root in creation is, by a chemistry of its own, selecting elements from the earth; every leaf is silently feeding on the great air-field around it; every fibre is vibrating to the quickening influence of the light. Quiet as is the aspect of the new scene, repose is, in reality, a thing unknown to it. Movement, activity, multifarious excitement, pervade the silent life of this new creation.

Now could we have looked intelligently on this new, this organized, this living, kingdom of nature when first it came into existence, without saying respecting the Creator, "His understanding is infinite!" Here was the first utterance of His wisdom, in the adaption of means to ends.

II.

The Past brought forwards. — We have now to see whether or not *pre-existing laws and elements are brought forwards and employed in organic life.*

1. Preparatory to this, however, an important question claims our attention. Did the creation of vegetable life precede that of animal life? or were they contemporaneously produced? "The earliest forms of life known to geology [at present] are not, as might have been expected, *plants, but animals.*" A few species of coralloids and conchifers, in the slates of the Cambrian system, are, "the oldest monuments yet discovered of the creation of living things."[1] But this fact, geologists admit, leaves the question we have proposed unanswered. Lindley's experiments show that some species of plants entirely disappear in water. Had such plants, then, existed for ages prior to the introduction of animal life, their want of power to resist decomposition would sufficiently account for the loss of all trace of their existence. And geologists are well aware that no certain inferences can be drawn from the numerical proportion of fossil plants in different strata, respecting the numbers which actually flourished during the formation of those strata; since their preservation would depend on their more or less perishable nature, and on many other circumstances.

2. For the decision of the question, then, we are referred to other considerations. Some suppose they have adequate ground for ascribing priority of existence to vegetable life, in the evidences which they think they can adduce that the atmosphere of the primitive world was surcharged with carbonic acid; that this very excess, which would have been fatal to animal life, would have been conducive to the luxuriance of land vegetation; and that it was the office of such vegetation to purify the atmosphere of the ingredient in question, preparatory to the

[1] Phillips's Treat. Geol., vol. i. p. 129. Further investigation, however, enables us to qualify this statement in a manner which favors the geological precedence of the plant to the animal. In Sweden, in Norway, in Russia, and in the United States, there are certain rocks which occupy relatively the same place as the Lower Silurian or Cambrian system — the lowest in which fossils have been detected. The fossils which characterize them are fucoids — algæ or sea-weed. The Skiddaw slates bear their impressions, blent with graptolites — fossil zoophytes. They constitute that "fucoidal band" of Sir R. I. Murchison, which forms the base of the vast Palæozoic basin of the Baltic.

coming of land animals. As this supposition, however, is at present open to doubts, we will not rely on it; and we need not. A moment's reflection will show that in the system of things which God has been pleased to constitute, animal life necessarily pre-supposes vegetation, and is, indeed, very much regulated in its extent by the quantity supplied. Vegetable is the ultimate support of animal life; for, though some animals are carnivorous, those preyed on, if traced downwards, are found herbivorous; just as the herb itself derives its nourishment from the pre-existing inorganic elements. This is true of fishes and cetaceous animals which feed on the smaller plant-eating crustacea; and thus, in the ocean, the phosphoric acid of inorganic nature is, by means of plants, carried over to animals.[1] Both analogy and fact, then, authorize the inference that plants preceded and prepared the way for animal existence. And the reader of the scriptures need not to be reminded that, in the Mosaic history of the last creation, vegetable life *was* called into being first.

3. And as slowness characterises the processes of nature, except where the God of nature has an end to be answered by quickening them, analogy would lead us to infer that between the commencement of the Flora and the Fauna of the earth, a considerable period would elapse. This, at least, is certain, that the carboniferous group contains more than half the known species of fossil plants, and yet no trace of the existence of the great herbivorous land quadrupeds appears before the tertiary period. Besides which, it should be remembered that some of the vegetable tribes found in the earliest strata, appear to have had an end to answer prior, in the order of nature, to that of sustaining animal life—namely, the office of producing soil, and thus preparing the way for the superior tribes of their own order of life. But, whether the Flora preceded the Fauna by an interval longer or shorter, is of little present importance. It is enough for us that we have ground to believe that life began on the earth by the vegetable kingdom.

4. We are now prepared to see whether or not the pre-existing laws and elements of the inorganic world are brought forwards and employed in organic life. What more there may be in this new department, is not now the question; we have at present only to look for the continuity described. And first,

---

[1] See a paper by Professor Forchhammer, read by Sir R. I. Murchison to the British Association. [illegible].

we recognise it in the *external* relations of the plant. Botany has its geography. The plant is not only a native of the earth, but each different species has its peculiar territory, or, in technical language, its "habitat." Did light exist before the plant was created? The humblest herb requires it, turns towards it, seeks after it, and, without it, perishes. For water and air, it has the power of absorption. For the temperature, each species possesses a constitutional adaptation which can never be violated with impunity. The first seed that germinated claimed kindred with all the material elements which were in existence when it came. And the bud at this moment bursting, is holding communion with the distant sun, and comes to lay all nature under tribute.

5. But let us proceed from this general reference to the relation subsisting between the external conditions of the plant and its organization, to mark the presence and continuity of the laws and results of inorganic nature in the *internal* relations of the plant. Now, as to the organic constituents of plants, they are derived entirely, in the first instance, from the inorganic world; and consist chiefly of four of the fifty or sixty simple elements — carbon, hydrogen, oxygen, and nitrogen. Whatever there may have been originally included in the constitution of inorganic nature, with a view to the future Flora of the earth, no new materials were called into existence on the occasion of its creation. And, entirely distinct as was the new principle of life which was now to be introduced, the preexisting elements were sufficient in the hands of the Creator, for the means of its manifestation. Modern organic chemistry, we repeat, consists of little more than the study of four of these selected elements and their multiform combinations. Here is the law of gravity, carrying the root of the plant downwards, and making it one with the mass of the earth. Here is the attraction of cohesion uniting the parts of the plant, and giving it individuality. Here is motion, or mechanical force, carrying the fluids absorbed for nutrition from the root upwards. Here is chemical affinity, attracting the surrounding particles with elective forces, and completely changing their nature. Here is developed symmetry, answering, in form, to crystallization, giving determinate figure to the organized body.

6. In the preceding Part, we remarked that in the production of the crystal we saw what might be regarded as the most finished production of the inorganic world; and that, in its

symmetrical arrangement we beheld an image suggestive of the coming flower. But if the crystal is to be looked on, in respect to form, as a mineral flower, the flower, though much more, is a vegetable crystal. Cuvier affirmed even that the *form* of the living body is more essential to it than its matter. Be this as it may, morphology, or the subject of form, belongs to the science of botany.

III.

Progression.—The same theory which led us to look for the continuance of pre-existing laws and elements in organized matter, leads us farther to expect in this organization *the manifestation of new effects, or the introduction of a new principle.* Nor are we disappointed. Here are life and its manifestations.

1. But what is organic life? As we can acquire a knowledge of matter only by the changes of which it is susceptible, so life becomes known to us only by its effects or manifestations. And these may be summed up under the heads of Assimilation and Propagation; the nourishment of the individual and the continuance of the race.

2. An organic body is distinguished from an inorganic by the mysterious power of *assimilation.* The inorganic increases by *external* additions; thus particles allowed to coalesce from a state of solution, arrange themselves into crystalline forms, which can increase only by the further juxta-position of particles added to them externally. The organic is nourished by a power of appropriation within. The former only *finds,* the latter prepares, *makes,* what is added to its structure; re-casting the inert substance, and exhibiting it in new unions, not of binary merely, but of ternary and quaternary combinations. The inorganic changes that on which it acts *chemically;* the organic *vitalizes,* and imparts to the matter which it vitalizes the power of acting in the same way on other substances. This is the end and object of that series of functions which, beginning with absorption, conveys the absorbed matter through the stem into the leaves, then subjects it to a process of exhalation, submits the rest to the action of the atmosphere, conveys it back into the system, elaborates it by secretion, and ends in assimilation.

3. And the plant is also generative. The inorganic mass, as we have seen, can only increase by cohesion and agglomeration from without. But the plant "hath its seed in itself."

It exists in generations. Besides vitalizing that which is necessary to the conservation of each of its own parts, it is endowed with the power of giving existence to a new whole, and of providing the germ with the nourishment necessary for it in order to commence its independent being.

4. If now to the question, "What is life?" it be replied in the language of Schmid, "Life is the activity of matter, according to the laws of organization;" the question naturally arises, What is organization? Perhaps the best answer which has been furnished is by Kant, "An organized product of nature is that in which all the parts are mutually ends and means."[1] Let it be remarked, it is not said that the product is made up of mutually dependent parts; nor that the parts are mutually causes and effects; both of these descriptions might, in a sense, be true of a piece of machinery. But in a piece of mechanism, "the parts have no properties which they derive from the whole." In an organized body they have; the leaf, separated from the plant, begins immediately to lose the properties of a leaf, and soon ceases to retain even its form. Here, the causes and effects are so related as not merely to excite the idea of contrivance and intention; the light in which we feel impelled to regard them is that of means and ends returning into each other with a view to the constitution of a whole. The physiologist finds that each intelligible part of the system has a definite office; each organ, an appropriate function; that no portion of it exists in vain; and that each part not only answers an end, but is so formed as to lead to the conclusion that it was constructed for that end; and that that end, which is again to become a means, is the reason why it is where, and what, it is. Here, then, we find ourselves in a new department of Divine operation.

The notion of design in organized bodies — of contrivance, and of an end to be obtained by such contrivance — is natural and inevitable to the human mind. The mind is made to ask, *why* this function, or this member, just because the object is made to *reply*. And it is by wisely questioning nature, under the conviction that each organ and part was *intended* to answer a certain end, that physiology has been able to make any progress. Under this persuasion it is that Cuvier speaks of the combination of organs adapted to "the part which the animal *has to play* in nature." But there is another school of

[1] See Professor Whewell's Phil. of the Induc. Sciences, vol. ii. c. iii.

physiologists which attempts to decry the doctrine of final causes, though they will be found to be frequently using language in harmony with it; thus unconsciously rendering homage to the idea which they profess to repudiate. "I know nothing of animals which have to *play a part* in nature,"[1] says Geoffrey St. Hilaire. "I take care not to ascribe any *intention* to God."[2] But this, it appears to me, is mere logomachy and self-delusion. Some guiding idea to direct his inquiries the physiologist must have. The idea which Geoffrey St. Hilaire and his school profess to have taken, in opposition to the idea of design or final cause, is that of "unity of composition," or "analogues," or "morphology," which seeks to reduce all animated nature to one plan or principle of composition. Now let their writings be referred to, and it will he found that, in effect, they have only substituted one form of the doctrine of final causes for another; that "unity of composition" is their *final cause;* that they mentally assume it in every physiological inquiry, and find or fancy illustrations of it in every organized body.

5. That organization involves this idea of *means and ends*, as distinguished from *causes and effects*, contemplated in our last Part, will appear, if we remember, that it is here for the first time that we speak of failure or disease. "Physiology," observes Bichat, "is to the movements of living bodies what astronomy, dynamics, hydraulics, &c., are to those of inert matter; but these latter sciences have no branches which correspond to them as pathology corresponds to physiology. For the same reason, all notion of a medicament is repugnant to the physical sciences. A medicament has for its object to bring the properties of the system back to their natural type; but the physical properties never depart from this type, and have no need to be brought back to it. And thus there is nothing in the physical sciences which holds the place of therapeutic in physiology." On which Professor Whewell remarks, "Of inert force, we have no conception of what they *ought* to do, except what they *do.* The forces of gravity, elasticity, affinity, never act in a diseased manner; we never conceive them as failing in their purpose; for we do not conceive them as having any purpose, which is answered by one mode of their action rather than another. But with organical forces the case is

[1] Principles de Philosophie Zoologique, p. 65.
[2] Ibid., p. 10.

different; they are necessarily conceived as acting for the preservation and development of the system in which they reside. If they do not do this, they fail, they are deranged, diseased." And he founds on the distinction this aphorism: "The idea of living beings as subject to *disease* includes a recognition of a final cause in organization; for disease is a state in which the vital forces do not attain their *proper ends.*" Now physiological botany includes nosology, or the science which treats of the diseases of the vegetable kingdom.

6. Here, then, (and we only call attention to the fact in passing, with a view to its future application,) here, in the botanical kingdom, we find ourselves in a department of the Divine procedure essentially different from that which we have left behind us in the mineral kingdom. There we saw *events*, and thought only of their *efficient cause;* here we find *means*, and look for their *final cause* or *end.* There we found ourselves so near to the First cause, — for we cannot conceive of a *material* cause of the adjustment and motions of the planetary system, — that we naturally look back to recognise and adore it; here, we find ourselves so near to ends answered by proximate causes which we can recognise, that we as naturally look on to these ends in admiration of the Divine Contriver. There, we saw fixed laws in operation, so that nothing happened by *chance;* here we see the wise adjustment of means to ends, so that nothing is *in vain.* There we saw physical cause and effect taking place in a certain invariable order and symmetry, and we felt ourselves in the presence of Intelligent Power; here, we see fixed ends or purposes, the direction of means towards them, and changes taking place to attain them, and we feel ourselves in the presence of a Wise as well as an Intelligent Power.

7. And does not this important distinction account for the sagacious remark of Bacon,[1] that final causes are not to be admitted into physical or *mechanical* inquiries? For we see that, while there, we are only among causes and *effects.* It is not until we get into our present region of organization that we find ourselves among means and *ends.* As soon as we reach the first link of the living chain, "whose seed is in itself," we feel that the only adequate definition is, that "the parts are mutually means and ends."

8. And will not the distinction throw light also on the "dif-

[1] De Augment. Sc. ii. 105.

ficulty sometimes felt in the estimate of the proofs of creative wisdom and power supplied by the contemplation of organized life as compared with those derived from the study of the heavenly bodies?" The former — the organic phenomena — it has been noticed, do not furnish (to some minds at least) the same ready and conclusive evidence of a Deity as the latter — the mechanical phenomena.[1] And the view which we are now taking would have enabled us to show, *à priori*, that such would probably be the fact, and to assign the reason why. Organic phenomena disclose a number of visible proximate causes combined to accomplish a purpose, and we think only or principally of the *wisdom* of the Being who has designed it; the celestial phenomena simplify the theological argument by confining our attention to the *Being* himself, the First Cause of the whole.

Or thus; if we begin at an advanced stage of the Creative process — say, in the animal kingdom, where there is conscious enjoyment, we should find illustrations of the existence of a *good*, a *wise* and an *intelligent Power*. Descending to the botanical kingdom, we find that we have lost the proofs of goodness, and have narrowed our argument to the fact of a *wise* and *intelligent Power*. Descending again to the mineral and mechanical kingdom, we find that the proof of Wisdom is gone, and that our illustrations are restricted to the fact of the existence of an *intelligent Power*.[2] The argument tapers to a single term. But then it is all the more powerfully felt, owing to its very simplicity.

9. Kant's definition of an organized body, as "that in which all the parts are mutually ends and means," implies a *circularity* in the operation of the organized system. Hence Cuvier represents *life* under the image of a *whirlpool*, having a constant direction, and always carrying along its stream particles of the same kinds; individual particles of which are constantly entering in and departing out; so that the *form* of the living body is more essential to it than its matter.

Now without attempting to estimate the importance of the *form* — understanding by the term, the *structure* as compared with the *matter* of organic life, we would for the present, simply point attention to the fact that an organized body involves the idea of a determinate structural form. In addition, an organ-

[1] Professor Powell's Connection of Nat. and Div. Truth, p. 146. Dr. Turton's Nat. Theology, p. 54.

[2] In the same way, the mere *act* of creation, could we have witnessed it, would have furnished a proof of *power* only, without the intelligence.

ized body has the power of attracting into itself parts of surrounding substances, of detaining and changing a portion for its own use, and of giving up some of its own substance in return. This is in constant process. The structure not only retains its form, like the whirl of the vortex, though the matter constantly passes away and is renewed; but each particle is acted on at every point of the vortex, and is transformed in the whirl. On these grounds, the best idea we can obtain of organic life is, in the language of Professor Whewell, that *it is a constant form of circulating matter, in which the matter and the form determine each other by particular laws (that is, by vital forces).* Of the mysterious nature of these vital forces we shall speak hereafter.

IV.

Continuity. — By another of our laws, we are led to expect that the manifestation, *besides being progressive, will be continuous — leaving no intervals of space or time, but such as the modifying influence of other laws may require or account for.*

Now if, as we believe, such conditional breaches of continuity occur, and if, according to another of our laws, every inferior part of creation is destined to serve a higher moral purpose, we may be able to show that the exceptions to the rule of continuity contribute ultimately to the same end as the rule itself, only in a different manner. The exceptions may be as cogent against the doctrine of a necessity in nature, as the continuity may be in favor of design. At present, however, our concern is with the evidences of continuous progress in the *Floras* of the ancient earth.

1. For reasons already named, especially that of the absorption of plants, owing to their soft and destructible nature, during the consolidation of strata, no certain inferences can be drawn from the numerical proportion of fossil plants in the different formations. In the new list, by M. Göppert, the species of fossil plants discovered up to the present time all over the globe, amount to 1,792.[1] Their numerical distribution in the different rocks is stated to be as follows: —

Palæozoic	52
Carboniferous	819
Permian	58

[1] From a paper read by Sir R. I. Murchison to the British Association, 1845.

Triassic	86
Oolitic	234
Wealden	16
Cretaceous	62
Tertiary	454
Unknown	11
	1,792

From this table it appears that the carboniferous group alone contains nearly half the known species of fossil plants. This sudden outburst of vegetable life in the ancient earth, as compared with the Floras immediately preceding and following, intimates, at least, that the continuous progress to be looked for is not that of successive numerical increase. The living Flora, of about 80,000 species, is probably an increase on all the past; but then the increase has been numerically irregular.

2. If traces of a great botanical plan or system are sought for, they are not wanting; though they appear to be subject to interruptions similar to those which affect the numerical proportions of plants. Certain chasms now existing in the scheme of botanical organization, have been partially filled up by discoveries in the ancient Floras. Thus, by means of Lepidodendra, in the transition series, a kind of link is supplied between the flowering and the flowerless plants.[1] So also the Cycadeæ, of the secondary series, appear to fill up a blank which would otherwise have separated the three great natural divisions of plants — the seedless class, the one-lobed seed class, and the two-lobed seed class. Here, however, without stopping to remark on the existence of intermediate spaces which probably have never been filled up in the manner suggested, it is enough for us to know "that although many extinct genera and certain families have no living representatives, and even ceased to exist after the deposition of the coal formation, yet are they connected with modern vegetables by common principles of structure, and by details of organization, which show them all to be parts of one grand, and consistent, and harmonious design."[2]

3. But, chiefly, is continuous progress observable in the gradual increase, and final ascendancy, of the more complicated dicotyledons, or two-lobed seed class of plants, over the

---

[1] Lindley and Hutton's Fossil Flora, vol. ii. p. 53.
[2] Buckland's B. Treatise, p. 480.

more simple forms of the earlier periods. If we look at the ancient Floras, as distributed through the three great periods of geological history — the transition, the secondary, and the tertiary eras — we find that sea-weeds, or algæ, existed during even the early formations of the first period. Such structures are found in Scandinavia among the very oldest fossil groups.[1] But it is in the carboniferous series of this era, especially, that we are called to admire the fulness of vegetable life. Here are, already, the three great divisions of plants — the seedless, the one-lobed, and the two-lobed seed classes. But while plants of the second and third classes are here comparatively rare, those of the Cryptogamic, or first class, such as Ferns and gigantic Equisetaceæ, abound.

In the next era, a decided change is visible. The Ferns and Equisetaceæ are reduced both in size and number; being perhaps one-third of the whole. The greater part of the remainder are Cycadeæ and Coniferæ, with a few Liliaceous plants; the Coniferæ belonging to the two-lobed seed class, the Liliaceæ to the one-lobed seed class, and the Cycadeæ, which are so prevalent as to give a character to the upper formations of this era, resembling the palms of the monocotyledonous class in external appearance, and the Coniferæ in the structure of the flower and fruit. Here, then, is an approach to proportion between the first and third classes of plants.

In the third era the scale is decidedly turned. Most of the families of the first period, and many of those of the second, have disappeared. Plants resembling our own Flora have taken their place. We recognise our planes and firs, willows and elms, poplars, chestnuts and sycamores. The dicotyledonous, or two-lobed seed class, predominates. In our living Flora they form about two-thirds of the whole.

Taken as a whole, then, the geological periods exhibit botanical progression. It is easy to conceive of more striking illustrations of the rule. We can conceive, for example, of every family resembling the Coniferæ, which, beginning with the first stage of vegetation, has gone on " increasing in the number and variety of its genera and species," down to the last stage. But the plan of the Creator did not require such an illustration of the law; and, therefore, probably the conditions of the earth did not consist with it. It is sufficient to find that the Divine outline of botanical organization has been pro-

[1] Professor Forchhammer's paper to the British Association, 1844.

gressively filling up; and also that the order observed has been, on the whole, from the primary prevalence of the more rudimentary and simple, to the ultimate predominance of the more complex and perfect forms. Here is nothing, be it remarked, to countenance the idea of any want of permanence of species. The great three-fold distinction of acotyledonous, monocotyledonous, and dicotyledonous, existed in the first period as they do still.

V.

Activity. — This new principle of organic assimilation, may be farther illustrated if we proceed to inquire after the application of that law of creation which affirms that *every being will be found to manifest all that it is calculated to exhibit of the Divine nature, by developing or working out its own nature — by activity.* The activity of the mechanical and chemical forces we saw in the preceding Part. But these are constantly tending " to produce a final condition. Mechanical forces tend to produce equilibrium; chemical forces tend to produce composition or decomposition; and this point once reached, the matter in which these forces reside is altogether inert. But an organic body tends to a constant motion, and the highest activity of organic forces shows itself in continuous change." " So long as this motion subsists," observes Cuvier, " the body in which it takes place is *alive; it lives.*"[1] Even in popular language, *life* is a term employed to express the highest degree of activity. And in accordance with this view of the activity of the vital forces we find that they form an ever-whirling vortex. But even this is far from conveying an adequate idea of their activity. They leave nothing as they found it. They not merely move that on which they act, but subdue it; not merely change, but assimilate, organize, and share with it their own vitality. And though this activity is not always maintained at the same rate, so essential is it to the full development of organic life that it never pauses. Even during winter, when vegetable life is thought to repose, new fibres are forming at the roots, a slight progression of the sap is going on, and a trifling enlargement of the buds taking place;[2] while, wherever an organ is wanting to complete the symmetry of the plant, or any depart-

[1] Professor Whewell's Inductive Sciences, vol. ii. c. iv.
[2] Professor Henslow's Physiol. Botany, p. 234.

ure from the normal structure of the flower exists, it is to be ascribed to the restraint, or the diversion, of its natural activity.

Cavanilles, the Spanish botanist, conceived the thought of literally "seeing grass grow," by ingeniously adjusting his instruments, at one time to the tip of the shoot of a Bambusa, at another, to that of the fast-growing flowering stem of an American aloe. And who can doubt that, with our sight preternaturally sharpened, and the integuments of plants made transparent, we should see ceaseless motion in every tissue and every cell of the "germinating, leaf-pushing, flower-unfolding, organisms" of the great vegetable covering of the earth.

VI.

Development. — According to another law, *the same properties or characteristics which existed in the preceding stage are here found to be not only brought on to the present, but to be in a more advanced condition.*

1. Here every law seems double, or to have a counterpart. The vital power, as we have seen, is subject to the law of gravity; but while the plant tends downwards, it rises upwards too. The same power includes the mechanical forces producing motion; but it has the twofold force of attracting and repelling at the same point. It is also chemical, changing the nature of the substance on which it acts; but it also supports itself by the change. It exhibits affinity; but to affinity it adds assimilation. Not only has it forms of symmetry, and forms, some of which do not appear possible to crystals, (as the pentagonal); but while there is reason to believe that in the crystal the form depends on the matter, in organic symmetry the matter appears to be subordinated to form. It has activity, but, beyond this, it supports its activity by its action, increases its strength by exercise. Owing to its superiority over all the pre-existing powers of nature it is, that during its presence in the organized structure it holds them all in subjection. And hence, the vital principle no sooner secedes, than these ordinary laws return, dissolve the structure, and cause the separated parts to enter into new combinations, distinct from those under which they had existed as a living body.

2. And what is still more remarkable, different plant-cells possess different powers in this respect. With little more than the four elementary bodies — carbon, hydrogen, oxygen, and

nitrogen, they are found to elaborate an almost endless series of what are called "proximate organic principles" of the most diverse properties; one cell secreting one principle, and another, another principle, by simply combining these elements in slightly different proportions. Here, again, is the binary principle of inorganic union; but here is also a form of union entirely unknown in that division of science. Instead of combinations by pairs, here are three or four substances bound up together into a single group — a set of ternary and quaternary compounds — constituting one indivisible whole, and exhibiting properties before unknown. Nor, in many cases, can the stamp imparted to these properties, of their vital origin, be easily effaced by any means employed to destroy it.[1]

3. But this superiority of organic nature involves other points of distinction with which there is nothing in inorganic nature to compare. The vital principle includes *excitability*. We are aware that certain phenomena exhibited by plants have by some been regarded as proofs of the presence of *irritability* also, and even of *sensibility*. But as they appear to have nothing analogous to a nervous system, these phenomena seem to be only instances of the extreme action of excitability; by which we mean, generally, that property of the cellular tissue — the chief organ of nutrition — which "takes cognizance of the action of external influences upon it, and by which it resists those mechanical and chemical efforts which would otherwise soon succeed in decomposing its substance."[2] And even when the mystery of life closes in the mystery of death, it is only the death of the individual structure we are called to witness. The living plant includes the mystery of propagation — the power of self-multiplication during life, and of continued reproduction after death. Were it our object, then, to distinguish between the inorganic and organic parts of nature briefly and broadly, we might say, that while the former originate fortuitously, enlarge externally, and are terminated by mechanical or chemical force, the latter originate by propagation, grow by an internal power of assimilation, and terminate by death.

---

[1] See Fownes' Chemistry, &c., p. 41.
[2] Henslow's Botany, p. 161.

VII.

Relations.— The harmony of the plant with the conditions of its existence is necessary, because, according to another of our laws, *everything is related.* Were the continuance of the vegetable species independent of the reproductive process, or reproduction independent of nutrition, or were one organ independent of another, that compliance with law and order of which we have spoken would of course be unnecessary. Were botany unconnected with light, and air, and moisture, and heat, all these elements might depart, and yet leave a flourishing vegetable creation behind. It is because each plant is related to the whole by an appointment of the Creator never to be repealed, that every change in its external condition, and in its organization, involves a corresponding change in its well-being.

1. Relations are traceable between the various species of the subterraneous Flora and the co-existing conditions of inorganic nature. Not, indeed, — and, as we have already remarked, the difference is of the greatest importance, — not that there is any evidence that a change of inorganic conditions necessitates the production of new forms of organic life, (as if these conditions were independent causes,) but that the production of such new forms of life presupposes a corresponding change of inorganic conditions.

2. Internal relations are also traceable; or correspondencies between the various parts of the vegetable creation. *Type* is the very term which Naturalists have chosen to express this resemblance. It will be remembered that, when speaking of crystals, we remarked that their forms suggested the idea of likeness or resemblance. We may expect, then, that in organic bodies also we shall find this analogy, and something else in addition. And we do so; we find resemblance of *nature and habits.* Now this is the difference in natural history between analogy and affinity: analogy is superficial resemblance, affinity is resemblance of internal structure, properties, and habits. But in order to ascertain the affinity of organic bodies, the relative *importance* of the different parts compared must be determined; as, for example, whether resemblance between the organs of nutrition in two species is to reckon for more than resemblance between the organs of reproduction, or for less. The *number* of affinities present, which may be regarded as an equivalent for the absence of other affinities, must be

settled. Now when these laws of classification are ascertained, a *type* or *specimen* is to be taken, and the question asked, "which approaches the nearest to it in all the affinities which characterize the class; and which the nearest to this, and so on." The result will be, the formation of a natural group around the characteristic type. This will not be found to form a direct or linear series, answering to the figure of a chain, or of a cone of being, to a circular, quinary, or dichotomous system, or to any precise artificial arrangement. It may form a figure very irregular at its circumference, for it seeks no boundary line without; it enlarges from the central type. And as it ramifies in various directions, its continuity may be that of a branching tree. But so evident is its continuity, that the attempt at natural classification can hardly be begun before the mind becomes impressed with the firm persuasion that analogy and affinity reign throughout — that the whole botanical kingdom is constructed on a plan.

3. From the all-related nature of organic forms, it follows, also, that a modification of any one part of a plant supposes the modification of every other part. And, accordingly, it is found that a change of one organic function involves a corresponding change of the whole body.

VIII.

Order. — But, according to another of our principles, every law will be found to have its order, *and may be expected to come into operation on each individual subject of it, according to its priority of date in the great system of creation.* Thus, at the moment of separation from the parent plant, the seed tends to the earth *by gravitation.* The *chemical* conditions requisite for germination — moisture, oxygen, and a certain elevation of temperature — must next be satisfied. Having imbibed "moisture through its integuments, the embryo swells, the radicle protrudes and tends downwards;" the plumule, or terminal bud, expands and rises upwards; in other words, the law of developed *symmetry* obtains. Taking firm hold of the earth, it commences its own independent existence; its *conservative* functions come into play in orderly succession; all of which combine to prepare the way for the higher and orderly processes of *reproduction,* by which its species will be continued after its own individual existence shall have ceased. Here are "first the blade, then the ear, after that the full corn in the ear." The order of the progression is fixed, and no power but His who appointed it can reverse it.

IX.

Influence.—It is to be expected *that everything will bring in it, and with it, in its own capability of subserving the end, a reason why all other things should be influenced by it; a reason for the degree in which they should be influenced by it; and for the degree, in which it, in its turn, should be influenced by everything else.* If the powers of inorganic nature are to be ranged according to their activity and energy, or their capability of producing changes, it will yet be found that the most powerful are themselves susceptible of change. Action and reaction pervade the physical system, and are essential to its stability. For organic nature, all this action and reaction is "taken into account," calculated, and employed. The introduction of a single plant would have changed the relations of the whole. Its most wonderful property is the power which it possesses of influencing chemical action, and of thus secreting and preparing its own food, and securing its own growth. But while thus affecting everything external to itself, it is also modified by the very properties which it changes. While the leaf is decomposing the carbonic acid of the atmosphere, appropriating the carbon to the formation of its own proper juices, and returning the disengaged oxygen into the atmosphere, its own vital powers are affected by the quantity of carbonic acid which may happen to be present in the atmosphere—a fact, belonging to a class, suggestive of the difficult, but momentous truth, that human character is at once a constitution and a formation; a subjective power, at once modifying, and modified by, objective influences.

X.

Subordination.—Again, we find that every law subordinate in rank, though it may have been prior in its origin, is subject to each higher law of the Manifestation.

1. Accordingly, the productions of power are found to be subservient to the exercise of wisdom—the inorganic sustains the organic world. And not only so; it is prepared for its office by a process. It is subordinated by decomposition. No single earth, nor even a composition of two earths, is fertile.

The union of at least three — lime, silica, and alumina, is indispensable to fertility. For this the granite is decomposed, and the matter deposited by rivers in the bottom of valleys. And to this, every revolution and commingling of the strata of the ancient earth has been made subservient.

2. But this subordination is continuous, extending into the vegetable kingdom itself. Chemical and mechanical action almost fails to convert some rocks (as quartz) into soil. Yet not the less are these rocks made subservient to vegetable life. Here, where no other plants would exist, the Creator has placed the multitudinous and inexplicable tribe of lichens — "the pioneers of vegetation." These prepare the way for the mosses; and these, again, for other plants superior still; each retiring in succession, when it has contributed by its own life and death to place a better race on the spot; till at length the stately tree waves where once nothing but the apparently rootless, leafless, flowerless lichen could exist.

3. And this law of subordination is found to descend to the physiology of the *individual* plant. The organs of conversation are subservient to the organs of reproduction, the individual to the species. Though unconscious of a purpose, no plant lives to itself. In some tribes, the constitution and cares of the parent plant appear to be concentrated on this point, as on the end of its existence. The tribes of annuals die as soon as this end is answered. Others, in a sense, refuse to die, till they have answered it.

4. The same subordination obtains among the individual organs. "God hath set the members every one of them in the body as it hath pleased Him." And though no organ is useless, their value is graduated; and hence, a leaf, having answered its end, may fall off without any injury to the plant.

5. But then this subordination of one organ to another, of plant to plant, and of inorganic matter to the whole, lasts only as long as the plant continues to live. By death, it loses its *status* in the ascending rank of creation, and becomes subject to the ordinary inorganic laws.

XI.

Uniformity.—Profound as the subject of life is, all *its operations will be found to be impressed with the regularity of general laws.* On this condition alone can we hope to ascertain its operations, and mark the wisdom which they evince. Now the actual existence of such regularity is implied in the remarks we have already advanced. The vital principle, once superinduced by the Living God, acts, according to His appointment, and under His superintendence, with constancy and certainty. True it is, that in studying organic life we find ourselves for the first time in the regions of mutual adaptations; and that the writer on systematic botany is obliged to indite a chapter of anomalies.

Unlike the law of chemical affinity, which requires that the compound be in definite proportions, we find that Life asserts its freedom and its power by dispensing with this chemical exactness. But even this freedom is only within certain limits, or is bounded by law. This power of adaptation is according to particular rules, which are all ranged under a general rule. It is a law unto itself. For example: — Oxygen is indispensable to the germination of seeds; where it is entirely wanting, as in distilled water, they will not germinate; while, if acted on by more than a certain proportion, they will be over-stimulated. But let them have *about* the right proportion — one part of oxygen with three of azote, and they will germinate accordingly. The general law cannot be violated; while the power of adaptation by which the seed is adjusted to the circumstances is itself regulated by the universal law which measures the cause by the effect, and which determines that its action shall be always the same in the same circumstances. And as no compliance with the other conditions of germination will compensate for the want of the necessary oxygen, so no supply of this alone will atone for the absence of the other conditions of germination. Its constitution is defined by laws which must be complied with.

These laws, indeed, must not be confounded with causes. The life of the plant presupposes the organization which the Creator has been pleased to make a necessary condition; this condition, however, is not the cause of its vitality, but only the means of its manifestation. And organization presupposes certain inorganic conditions; but these conditions are not the cause of it; they are only employed and subordinated to organic ends. All that we recognise, in either case, is the law or rule according to which the organic and the inorganic are made to act; the cause of that action is entirely distinct.

XII.

Obligation.— Organic life exists under *an obligation to promote the end of creation, commensurate with its means and relations.* Of course, the only sense in which obligation can be predicated of the organic scheme is similar to that in which, like the inorganic, it is said to be governed by laws. The laws themselves suppose an agent; for they only express the mode in which he acts, the order according to which he proceeds. And as that agent is no other, can be no other, than the Lawgiver himself, the obligation of which we speak can be only the necessity which he has been pleased to incur, to operate in a certain manner in order to the attainment of a certain end. Having voluntarily determined on a given end, the adoption of the necessary means becomes obligatory; and as the means of which we are now speaking are merely organic existences, whatever obligation there is can rest only on a power external to themselves, the Power that employs them.

XIII.

Well-being.— In accordance with another of our laws, we find that *the well-being of the plant depends on its conformity to the laws of its constitution.*

1. Thus, in relation to the *internal* economy of vegetable life, let the process of reproduction fail, and the species ceases to exist. Let the organs of nutrition be obstructed, and the individual fails. Let the development of the plant be arrested, and deformity ensues; remove the impediment, and, if done in time, the dormant power of expansion awakes, and the development of the body is completed. And as to the *external* relations of vegetable life, the range of most plants — as to climate, for example — is very limited. If the average temperature adapted to the various families of plants were to vary as much as five degrees, they would, with their present constitutions, speedily suffer, languish and die. From first to last, the life of the plant depends on the maintenance of a definite adjustment between its constitution and external influences. Compliance with the conditions of its existence is indispensable to its well-being.

2. In this stage of creation, still more than in the preceding, the idea of perfection is forcibly suggested. In this domain of resemblances, we seek a *type* with which to compare analogous objects; and that type we select from among the most perfect

objects of its kind. Partly from finding that one specimen is better than another, the mind erects an ideal standard of excellence with which to compare everything comparable. But by this standard no specimen is absolutely perfect. No two roses, for example, have ever been entirely, in every property and particular, alike; so that no two have ever stood in precisely the same relations to the ideal standard. Even the individual flower which has approached the nearest to ideal perfection has fallen short of it. Some slight difference in itself, or in its circumstances — a difference inappreciable by man, would have been followed by a real, though equally inappreciable difference in its claim to perfection. Its approach to that standard is the measure of its harmony with the prescribed laws of its being.

XIV.

Analogy.— We have already found, to a considerable extent, that this second, or botanic, stage of creation, *is constructed according to a plan.*

1. We have seen that it is, in all its mineral and chemical elements, in complicated harmony with the first, and dependent on it. Either the inorganic stage was preconfigured to the organic, or the latter was entirely configured to the former. This correspondence extends even to that symmetry, or definite relation of form and number, which obtains first in crystallography. For while there are some kinds of symmetry common among flowers, which are unknown to crystals — such as the pentagonal, there are other kinds, such as the trigonal, which prevail in both, and which externally unite them together.

2. The various parts of the vegetable kingdom are also in harmony with each other. Indeed, no one family of plants could be naturally arranged, except as part of a natural classification of all plants. Now the symmetry to which reference is here made, involves numerical properties which afford a basis for such botanical classification. For it is found that the number *three* is the ground of the symmetry of monocotyledonous plants, and the number *five* of dicotyledonous plants, the numerical distinction harmonizing with, or expressing itself by, a leading difference of physiological structure.

3. The various parts of the vegetable kingdom, regarded as *successively* existent, not only do not derange the plan which classifies existing species, but seem necessary in order to com-

plete it. The large calamities of the coal formation take their place in the existing family of equisetaceæ. The fossil lepidodendra of gigantic stature, are intermediate between living lycopodiaceæ and coniferæ. And even the extinct sigillariæ, of which no living representatives exist, find, as far as the details of their organization are known, a definite place among existing families. In the Flora of the secondary series, the leading feature consists in the prevailing presence of cycadeæ. Now, of this family, the cycas revoluta exhibits an important physiological peculiarity, by which it forms a characteristic link between the living and fossil cycadeæ, while the existing cycadeæ can be shown to connect together the great cone-bearing family with the families of palms and ferns, and thus to occupy an intermediate station between the three great natural divisions of plants. And, speaking generally, the plants of the secondary series exhibit characters of an intermediate kind, between the insular Flora of the transition series, and the continental vegetation of the tertiary strata.

3. In addition to the evidence of a plan which arises from this constant adherence to a determined class of primitive types, and to the consequent reduction of every species to its appropriate place in the great system, there is the remarkable fact of the existence of *apparently abortive*, yet always symmetrical, parts in plants. Botanical physiologists "find parts existing in a rudimentary or abortive state in one species, which in others serve some manifestly important design." In this rudimentary state, they seem to exist only for the purpose of suggesting the idea of symmetrical arrangement, and of inviting and facilitating classification. And "it must be considered an additional proof of arrangement, when, as in many instances, we are able to show that they become subservient to a new purpose, by being unfitted to their primary one."[1]

4. Classification. — Now, according to our theory, the true system of botanical classification is that which arranges the relationship of plants according to the *order* of progressive nature, taken in connection with the relative *importance* of the progressive steps. Thus, beginning with mechanical properties, as those of the lowest value, we ascend to those of chemical affinity; to symmetry, or relations of form and number; then to the organs of nutrition, each organ rising in value as the process advances; and, finally, to the organs of reproduction, as of the highest value; — the relationship being nearest where

[1] Dr. Daubeny's Inaugural Lecture on Botany, p. 24.

the affinity lies between those characteristics which are of the highest value.

5. This method, 1, so far from arbitrarily selecting any one part of the plant as the basis of arrangement, — as the corolla, by Tournefort; or the stamen and pistils, by Linnæus, — requires a minute investigation of every part and property. Its peculiarities of chemical composition, the "proximate principles" which distinguish it, as well as its geographical and climatic relations, are all to be taken into the account. 2. Although it assigns the highest value to a particular function, it by no means follows that such principle is to be universally the basis of arrangement; inasmuch as resemblance, in this particular, may be outweighed in some families of plants, by a combination of characteristic differences in other particulars. The law of the *subordination of characters* is itself subject to a more comprehensive law, which takes cognizance of the entire scale of their values, and divides and combines them according to the relation of those characters. 3. As an organic body is all-related, so that a change in one part of its constitution involves a corresponding change in every other part, our method supposes that an arrangement correctly formed on one function will harmonize with an arrangement correctly formed on another function. 4. Our method provides, not only for the formation of groups, but also of series of groups, ranging according to organic perfection. The distinction between the cellular class, lichens, algæ, &c., without sexes, flowers, or spiral vessels, and the vascular class, is obvious. And a more intimate acquaintance with the physiology of the latter class would, doubtless, enable us to range all its species in the order of their ascending organization.

6. The multiplication of the points of agreement which the organic kingdom presents as compared with the inorganic, prepares us to expect an increase of such points with every advancing stage of creation; and, consequently, an increasing power of testing the truth of our classifications.

XV.

Contingent. — According to another of our laws, we may expect to find *that this new department of organic life exhibits marks of its contingency, or dependence on the sovereign will of the Divine Creator.* In the section corresponding to this, in the preceding part, we saw the cosmical and terrestrial arrangements taking law directly from the will of God. Here the illustrations of the Creative Will are still further multiplied in the constitutions and properties of organic forms.

1. For example: there is in plants a cycle of functions requiring about 365 days. There is a lesser cycle, or alternation, requiring about twenty-four hours. There is a measured force in the motion of the sap of every flower; and there is an appointed degree of stiffness in the stalk. Now there is no inherent necessity whatever, in the plant itself, why it should have these particular cycles, alternations, and forces, and no others. We can conceive them increased or diminished to any degree. But these exact phenomena and no others, it may be said, are made necessary by the previous conditions of the earth, of which they have come to form a part. Unquestionably, the first peculiarity is adapted to the annual motion of the earth, the second to its diurnal revolution, and the third and fourth to the mass of the earth. But, we have shown that this motion, revolution, and mass, were themselves originally dependent on the Divine appointment. Whether, therefore, we regard inorganic nature as preconfigured to the preordained constitution of organic life, or the organic constitution as adapted to the pre-existing plan of inorganic nature, we have alike a twofold proof of the exercise of a Designing Will.

2. True, the farther we remove from the first stage of the Creative process, the less manifest becomes the direct intervention of the Creating Will in the subsequent stages, and the less marked the direct dependence of the things created. This second stage, for example, from being adjusted and made to fit into the first, appears to some as if it were directly and entirely derived from it. He who is admitted to have originated the first, is supposed to have less to do with the second, just because, in His all-comprehending plans, the organic is made to presuppose the inorganic. The first, from being made a mere condition of the second, is in danger of being promoted into the place of the great originating Cause.

3. Even if vegetable life could be shown to be a necessary development of material elements merely, still, as no one who admits that the laws of matter were derived from God, would deny that He foresaw all the developments and results of which these laws were capable, and therefore foresaw their development in organic life as one of those results, such development must be held to furnish a new illustration of His manifold design in the creation of matter. The illustration only takes

a different date. And this, let me restate, is a sufficient reply to those who, admitting the Divine origination of nature, would have every subsequent stage to be a mere natural development; partly, on the ground of saving the Divine dignity from the supposed trouble or unworthiness of a more direct interposition. For this view, besides involving an anthropomorphic misapprehension of the nature of the Divine Greatness, implies that it may be worthy of the Deity to devise a law in eternity, which yet it would be unworthy of Him to carry into effect in time; and thus overlooks the fact, that in relieving the Deity from an act of immediate creation, it does so by supposing that He has yet from eternity designed and contemplated the results of such a creation.

4. But the idea of a natural and necessary development of matter, is a mere assumption. While the fact of the Divine origination of matter, at first, is itself a strong presumption in favor of the Divine origination of every new use subsequently made of it. In accordance with which, we find that fossil vegetation exhibits no indication of a regular development of species from the most simple onwards to the most perfect. The dycotyledon of the present day is not derived from the rudimentary acotyledon of the palæzoic series; even then they grew together side by side. Nor has the rudimentary vegetable of that day been absorbed in higher forms, and gone out of existence; it exists, unchanged, by the side of the ancient dicotyledon. The vegetable kingdom of the early carboniferous group, requires to be distributed into three classes; nor does the botany of the present day require a fourth class. Even from that early period, the plan, or outline, of vegetable life had been laid down by the Designing Will.

5. Such direct creative interposition is to be inferred also from the ground there is to believe that plants have a character of their own, more or less independent of mere external influences. That they are related to all the great pre-existing laws and elements of inorganic nature, we have shown; but, according to the views of the best botanical writers, they have characteristics which no external forces can account for, and which can be ascribed only to independent laws.[1] "Deciduous plants, when carried across the equator, will put forth leaves at the approach of winter; evidently because it is their habit so to do after settled intervals of time. In the experi-

[1] Decandolle's Physiologie, vol. ii. 478.

ments made by Decandolle on this subject, it was found that some plants kept their habits, without regarding either the artificial light or heat to which they were subjected. And it is admitted to be among " the unsatisfied problems of geology" to account for " the uniformity of the types of organic life over great areas, accompanied as it was by considerable diversity of local association."[1] Great as is the power of plants to adapt themselves to external changes, they have laws and a constitution of their own. Stimulated they may be, but not forced. In their creation, a principle was superadded to all that had gone before, subjecting matter to itself, but not to be subjected by it.

6. And is not the same direct interposition to be inferred from the apparent want of correspondence observable between the inorganic conditions of existence, and the organic existences themselves? That the appearance of organic life has been made by the Creator to depend on certain inorganic conditions, we hold to be a point settled. But we submit that it is not consequent on this, that the presence of the mere physical conditions shall always be followed by the presence of the life. According to creation by natural development, indeed, life *must* follow the physical conditions, directly, necessarily, universally, and to the utmost amount; for these conditions are supposed to be the only causes of life. If the new creation did not invariably follow the new condition, the law of natural development would be at an end; for it is supposed to act inevitably. And yet such apparent irregularities do exist. For example, some families of land plants, as the coniferæ and the palms, have pervaded all the series of formations. Why did the physical conditions of the secondary series fail to reproduce the sigillariæ, as they did the coniferæ, both of which had existed together in the first series? Or what was there in many of the plants of the second series less suited to the temperature, and other conditions of the first series, than in those of the first to the conditions of the second, throughout which they both afterwards concurrently flourished without any apparent deterioration? While we believe it to be fully established that organic life does not exist, except in connection with certain physical conditions, we believe also that the conditions are not the causes of life, and may exist without it; and that the Will which originated the first, is the cause of the second.

---

[2] Mr. Phillips, at British Association. 1845.

7. In the organic, then, as well as in the inorganic world, all that we can recognise are conditions and laws; and only *some* of these. The originating cause in each alike was the Divine volition. The same free scope which existed when matter was yet to be created, as to everything which related to its properties and arrangements, existed in relation to the introduction of vegetable life. The precise period of its commencement; the plan of the great system; the varieties which it should include; and the laws of its historical and geographical distribution; all are referrible to "the good pleasure of His will," in whose purpose it is allowed to have originated.

XVI.

Ultimata. — If organic life be thus dependent on the will of the Creator, we may expect to find that it reveals the *existence of ultimate truths.* Accordingly, after all the inquiries into the phenomena of organization, if the question recurs, what is life? or, what is the cause which produces these effects in living bodies? or, what is the principle which unites all these organic functions in the single result called life? we are as far as ever from being able to furnish an explanation. We have only described some of the phenomena. The thing itself is indefinable.

1. The organs by which life acts, may be anatomically examined, and correctly classed; but life is something independent of them all: for not one of them is universal in organized nature, and therefore is not essential to the vital force. The functions of these organs may be known, and the chemistry of their operations be silently and perseveringly watched; but the principle of that chemistry, the cause of these functions, are meanwhile presupposed and unapproached. The "proximate organic principles" which the chemistry of life produces, and submits to our examination, may be minutely analysed and correctly named; but they have been produced "in circumstances which we cannot imitate, and, in fact, do not understand." They are, at best, only *proximate* principles; effects, which refer us to the existence of a cause, the nature of which they do not reveal; their very number and diversity not explaining, but multiplying the mysteries in which it is involved. The little "nucleated cells" evolved from these proximate principles, and by the development of which the organic mass is supposed to be enlarged, may be known and truly describ-

ed; but this is something already existing; the cause which has led to it is still presupposed. The analogy between certain crystalline, and certain vegetable forms, may be interesting and familiar; but if those crystalline forms be referred to electric action, here is something which deals with electricity, and employs it; or, if they be referred to the form or quality of the ultimate atoms, here is something which subordinates both. Organization is, as we have seen, not an affair of outward form merely, but of inward structure. Admitting even the possibility of the artificial imitation of some of the proximate principles, and of the cells or globules of organic life, still they are inorganic principles and globules; the very absence of the vital power shows that it is something distinct from form and elementary composition, though it may employ both, and that these artificial imitations are not organization.

2. Vegetation involves an orderly series of processes. And all that the physiologist can do is to describe the results of each, and the order in which they occur. Having done this, he is said to have explained the subject; but all that he has done is to state *what* takes place; *how* it has taken place, is as mysterious as before. He shows you the circulation of the sap, but the force which circulates it is presupposed. He takes a flower, and discloses all that has taken place in order to its production, since he deposited the seed in the earth; but with that seed he deposited an already existing principle which he cannot disclose. He has told you only of laws; but with each law he has left a cause unexplained. Like the astronomer looking at his supposed nebula, let the physiologist trace back the process of organization as far as he can, he cannot detect it in its primary state; he has to refer it "back to some previous state, out of which it appears to have emerged imperceptibly and explicably." He sees the phenomena of life only after it has begun to work. Life itself is presupposed and ultimate.

3. Now organic life, like inorganic matter, is to be viewed, first, as an object, or in its relation to space: and the question arises, how came it really and objectively to be? What relation did the Divine power and wisdom bear to its creation? We may be able to describe the organization in which life is developed. But, having done this, and having traced the organization back to the seed, and searched the very elements of the seed itself, we find that we have reached an impassable barrier. It contains nothing in itself to account for its own

origination, as a living organific power. And could we have looked on the first seed that germinated, or the first vegetable creation that lived, we should have felt, instinctively, that the only ground of its existence must be the will of God.

4. But if the first moment of its existence revealed a wise Creator; the second moment revealed a Providence, for vegetable life was seen in relation, not only to space, but also to time — it continued. Organic processes were constant and universal. What was the Divine relation to the vital forces implied in all this new kind of activity? Here we come to ultimate laws. For in tracing the sequences of organic phenomena, we find a series of laws, each of which is related to all the rest; and all of which refer us to a cause of which they are only the results, or the means of manifestation. And the only conclusion warranted is, that the continuance of vegetable life, no less than its origination, has its ground in the will of God. We are as unable to conceive of a self-sustained, as of a self-originated organization. Dependence is not less its characteristic, in relation to time, than it is in relation to space. The regularity of the organic processes, so far from denoting the absence of the Great Agent, is the very circumstance which indicates His presence. It is the only way in which we can conceive of His agency. The laws proclaim the presence of the Lawgiver.

5. Life, then, as imparted in creation, and revealed in the phenomena of organization, is something distinguishable from the phenomena or laws which reveal it. We may, indeed, know nothing of the vital principle, but by the operation of these laws; just as the properties of matter as created, are disclosed to us only by the sequences of matter as continued. But, as the laws of matter presuppose its properties, so the phenomena of life presuppose the life which they reveal.

XVII.

Necessary Truth.— The existence of ultimate truth, reminds us of the law which prepares us to recognise *the existence of necessary truth.*

1. In the former inorganic stage, we saw matter take possession of space; and we saw that, besides implying the preexistence of space as a necessary condition, it implied the necessary existence of the Divine Power both as condition and cause. Here, we see life take possession of matter; and we cannot but feel that the idea of a Living Cause is indispen-

sable. The contrary is impossible. Such a cause might have been inferred, indeed, from the creation of inorganic matter; but the existence of organic life proclaims and represents it.

2. In the laws of organic phenomena, too, we recognise proofs of the wisdom of God. We see a vast and complicated system of means employed for the attainment of certain ends. And thus, if the creation of organic life, in its relation to space, implies the necessary existence of a Living Cause, the laws of its existence as related to time, imply the necessary wisdom, as well as the life-giving power of the Creator. We cannot but conceive of that Living Wisdom as existing prior to all objective manifestation, and independently of it. As condition, its activity from eternity was only subjective; as cause, it has now become objective also. Here then we have the subjective living wisdom, and the objective; for that which was possible, has become real. The nature of Him who is "the Life," begins to be manifested. Things not only are, they live; and live by means which give us a deeper insight than we possessed before, into the necessary perfections of the Divine Creator.

XVIII.

Change.—This stage of the Divine procedure not only prepares us to look for another, but, according to our theory, the law of ever-enlarging manifestation is itself regulated by *a law determining the time and manner of each successive stage of the advancing process.*

1. That the process itself cannot consistently terminate, is evident; for then the proof of the Divine sufficiency for unlimited manifestation would terminate with it. That it was not yet to terminate, might now have been inferred from a new analogical ground; for not only was the activity of the inorganic universe from the first the activity of progression, but addition of vegetable life furnished an entirely distinct ground of expectation for the addition of yet another stage. Nor can we conceive ourselves as surveying this second display of the Divine resources, without becoming conscious of the persuasion that we shall "see greater things than these," and that these are intended, in some way, to prepare for them.

2. But what was it which made the time of the actual change, the right time? For here again I may remark, that even those who adopt the hypothesis of development by natu-

ral law, must admit that every stage of development was prospectively included in the plan of the Lawgiver; and that for the same reason that any stage was designed to occur at all, there must have been a right time for its occurrence, or a reason which made the period of its actual occurrence the right period. And the law with which we have now to do, respects the nature of that reason.

3. Believing that no such change takes place capriciously; but as either the law of progression, or of the end, or the coincidence of the two, requires, we have to remark, first, on the claims of the law of progression. What these were, was declared by the event. The introduction of vegetable life was designed by the Creator to become subservient to animal enjoyment. As soon, therefore, as the vegetable and other foreseen conditions were present, the law of progression might be expected to receive a new illustration in the addition of animal existence, provided no other law intervened. I am aware, indeed, that by those who advocate natural development, the presence of certain conditions would alone constitute, not merely the fitness of the occasion for the addition of animal life, but even necessitate such addition. But this is a position which, from the nature of the case, can never be susceptible of proof. And is it philosophical to conclude that, because a thing does not exist without certain conditions, therefore it must exist with them? That certain events *may* invariably follow the presence of certain conditions, I do not deny; for it may be the law of the Divine procedure that they shall do so; and, further, the Creator may have arranged that this coincidence in the law of progression shall fall in with the law of the end, and, indeed, with other laws also of which we know nothing. I object only to the manner in which what may be, is confounded with what must be — the possible with the necessary, and in which conditions are gratuitously promoted into the place of causes.

4. Admitting, then, that the organic creation was not originated without a design, or, that it forms part of the Divine plan; and that, as a great system of adaptations of means to ends, it proclaims a Divine designer, the question arises, whether or not that ultimate end was, in any sense, adequately attained. That it had not been attained, when animal life commenced on the earth, if such attainment depended on the diversity and multiplication of vegetable structures to the utmost extent possible, is evident; for this multiplication was most

probably much greater after that period than it was before. Then, was the original creation of organic life, taken in connection with its subsequent reproductions, and successive enlargements prior to the creation of man, adequate to warrant the inference of the all-sufficiency of Creative wisdom? Does the long series of vegetable worlds, including the present, exhibit all the changes, and consequent displays of Design, which, under the circumstances, (such as the geological revolutions and the size of the planet), might have been expected?

5. In order to answer this question otherwise than inferentially and approximately, we should require to be put in possession of data which can never come within our reach — to know possibilities, for the comprehension of which our minds would need a different constitution. It is enough for us to yield ourselves up to the inferences and impressions flowing from the data which we do possess. If, for example, it should appear that the inorganic creation, in all that closely woven web-work of mechanical, and chemical operations, of which man, as yet, has unravelled so little, was only a world of prospective contrivances for the coming of organic life: if, further, it should appear that vegetable life has been adapted to every inorganic change and variety — to the bare granite and the recent cinders of the volcano, to the emerging coral-reef and the dark recesses of the mine, to the sand of the torrid zone and the perpetual snow of the poles — as if Wisdom rejoiced in the occasion which such apparent difficulties and extremes afforded for displaying the fertility of its resources; showing that the conditions, destructive of one form of life, can be made essential to the existence of another, and that, in its hand, the same general plan admits of diversity of adaptation without end: and, further, that of all this variety, there has existed a fulness to which Wisdom alone has assigned the limits, what more can be necessary to assure us of the all-sufficiency of the Creative Wisdom?

6. Now, the truth of these suppositions is undeniable. Vegetable physiology brings to light the fact that, even if the material universe had been constructed solely for the reception of organic life, it could not have been more studiously adapted, in all its great elements and operations, to the attainment of the end, than it actually is. The most scientifically constructed plant-house, and the most elaborate apparatus that may be introduced into it, can only pretend, not to originate, but simply to take advantage of, two or three of these natural adaptations.

But the wonders of the great Nursery are only as yet in process of discovery. "The half has not been told." Scientific botany has arranged between eighty and a hundred thousand species of plants; and still it continues to add to the number. Literally, its "field is the world." Every clod of earth belongs to it, and the floor of the ocean. While fossil geology brings to light the remains of departed floras, and suggests the idea of species not only extinct but effaced; — as if, amidst the prodigality of evidence of design still extant, some of the earlier illustrations might well be spared. The abundance of vegetable life is equal to its variety. "In order to form an idea of the luxuriance of vegetation in the former world, and of the masses of vegetable matter accumulated by running water, and which have certainly been converted into coal in the humid way, I remind the reader that in the Saarbrück coal field there are 120 seams of coal lying one over another, exclusive of a host of smaller seams; and that some of these single seams of coal are of thirty, and others of more than fifty feet thick, as at Johnstoun in Scotland, and Creuzot in Burgundy. . . . . It is also well to remember, that these coal measures are indebted for no inconsiderable portion of their materials, not to the trunks of mighty trees, but to small grasses, and to frondiferous and low cryptogamic vegetables."[1] At the mouth of the Mississippi, and in the "wood hills" of the icy Siberian Sea, the same process of vegetable accumulation is, probably, still going on. But to estimate the existing fulness of vegetable life, it is necessary to remember the mighty forests of the tropical zone of South America. And yet, could the whole be surveyed, it would be as nothing, probably, compared with the seeds of organic life enclosed in the crust of the earth. Kneaded up with the inorganic material, to an unknown depth, are the germs of vegetation; and only awaiting exposure to air and light, in order to "bring forth and bud" as if the hand of God had but just sown them. And, not only so, but almost every variety of material is found to contain a corresponding variety of vegetable existence. So that not only may it be said of organic life that its "field is the world," but world upon world.

7. Here, then, is evidence enough to justify the conclusion that the Wisdom which has shown itself sufficient for all this unexplored range of organic life, is sufficient for every change

---

[1] Humboldt's Cosmos.

of the same kind of which the earth, or even the material universe, admits. The question, be it observed, is not whether this range, extended as it is, might not have been more extended; this demand is of a kind which no range short of infinity could satisfy. For even if instead of a hundred thousand species, every individual plant had been different from all the rest, and every inch of the earth's surface had been crowded with vegetable life, the question might have been still raised whether the earth itself might not have been larger, and so on, *ad infinitum.* In other words, it is to ask for that, which, if possible, would yet be useless. But the question is, whether the Creative wisdom displayed in the organic stage of the Divine plan, does not warrant the conviction of its sufficiency for the *same kind* of display to any possible extent. And every one who considers the question must feel that it admits of only one reply. And hence it is that we can hear of the discovery of new vegetable species, not only without surprise, but as if the fact merely gratified a feeling of antecedent probability. Nor can we doubt that if the earth were to be once more stripped of its verdant robe, and if the conditions of organic life were to be afterwards restored, sooner or later, it would again look like "the garden of the Lord." And, with the same confidence, we feel assured that, if similar conditions exist in other worlds, the same wisdom which has so often "renewed the face of the earth," is sufficient to clothe them with similar beauty, in diversities without end.

But, if the design of the organic creation be to illustrate, in the sense explained, the sufficiency of the Creative wisdom, we shall be ready to admit that not until the evidence of such sufficiency was complete, could "the fulness of time" for man's creation have arrived. Not until it had existed long enough to accumulate all the proofs of the truth which it was designed to teach, would the "set time" arrive for the coming of the creature destined to interpret that truth. And whatever may be the apparent hardihood of this view, it entirely vanishes when we remember that He who forelaid the plan of the whole creative series, makes every part to harmonize with every other part, and the whole to subserve the ultimate end.

XIX.

Reason of the Method. — In passing from the method of the Divine procedure to the *reason* of the method, we find it to be two-fold; — being founded *partly in the constitution of the creature by whom the method is to be studied, and involving His well-being, and partly in his destiny,* and so involving, in addition, the glory of the Divine Creator.

1. As to the first part of the reason; it would be easy to show that, if the organic world is to be made subservient to human interests, the laws of the method are indispensable. Without the uniform sequences and dependencies, for example, which vegetable life exhibits, its cultivation would be impossible; indeed, without amenableness to law, it would not be even useable.[1] And how impossible would it be for man to turn his observations to any scientific account, were it not for those relations of analogy and affinity which arrange the members of the botanic kingdom in an orderly plan!

And that which especially marks the wisdom of the Creator is the manner in which the medium is observed between bewildering irregularity on the one hand, and an uninstructive and depressing sameness on the other. Only imagine these laws to be so obvious as to cost man no effort; and they would yield him no interest. On the contrary, suppose them to be but slightly illustrated by fact, or to be inextricably entangled by circumstance; and they would defy his utmost diligence and application. In the first instance, he could not be said to learn; and in the second, nature could not be said to teach. But as it is, his position somewhat resembles that of a child into whose lap its parent has thrown a handful of flowers selected for a nosegay, but intentionally mingled together, that the taste of the child might be cultivated in their re-arrangement; the parent taking care that the exercise shall not be so difficult as to be hopeless, nor so easy as to be useless. The organic world is so constituted that, without either forcing its lessons, or dis-

---

[1] See on this subject Professor Liebig's "Organic Chemistry in its application to Agriculture and Physiology;" a work devoted especially to an explanation of the proper food of plants, and to the modes in which, and the sources from which, they receive this nourishment. In harmony with the subject of this chapter he remarks: —"Innumerable are the aids afforded to the means of life, to manufactures and to commerce, by the truths which assiduous and active inquirers have discovered and rendered capable of practical application. But it is not the mere practical utility of these truths which is of importance. Their influence upon mental culture is most beneficial; and the new views acquired by the knowledge of them enable the mind to recognise in the phenomena of nature proofs of an infinite wisdom, for the unfathomable profundity of which human language has no expression." — p. 6.

pensing with attention, it invites observation, and rewards well-directed diligence of every kind and degree. Its "doctrine drops as the rain; its speech distils as the dew. But its instructions are all optional; man receives them only if he will.

2. And as to the second part of the reason, if organized nature is to be construed by man so as to subserve the ultimate end, all the laws which we have considered as belonging to the method of the Divine procedure are, in one respect or another, indispensable. In the absence of law, it would be impossible for the mind to infer a Law-giver. In the absence of all signs of dependence, organic nature would be regarded as proclaiming its independence. But, here, every vegetable family has its place; every species, its type; every function, its order; every fibre, its prescribed rule. Here life is found in union with organization; a union, however, which can only be shown to be uniform, not necessary. And here, everything relating to the commencement of organic life, to its progress, and to the filling up of the great plan on which it is formed, must be resolved into the will of the Divine Creator; for even those who believe only that laws were originally impressed on matter of which all this is the developed result, must admit that the entire result was in the original contemplation and choice of the Deity.

3. But here again the evidence needs to be balanced between two extremes. If the proof of a Divine agency were to be so obvious and cogent as to leave man no option whatever as to the nature of his conclusions respecting it, this would be as unsuited to his moral freedom, as the absence of all or of adequate proof would be to his rational conviction — a consideration which applies to every department of the Divine procedure; and which, if seasonably remembered and applied, would answer many objections, and solve many difficulties, respecting it. Accordingly, the evidence is supplied in "weight and measure." It is as reserved to one, as it is open and communicative to another. To some, the laws of organic life answer the purpose only of self-manifestation; and seem to publish both their own sufficiency and the sagacity of the party discovering or apprehending them;[1] while to others, they con-

---

[1] Dr. Macculloch has well remarked of certain philosophers, who never "think of a designing and wise Creator — they search, and when they have found, they produce the discovery as a proof of their own wisdom.

vincingly declare that their "sufficiency is of God." To each class the same evidence is supplied. For the former, it is not so scanty as to excuse their impiety; nor for the latter, so overpowering as to constrain belief, and make virtue impossible. It is so graduated and adjusted, that it may be regarded as having formed, from the first, a mute prophecy, both of the voluntary constitution of the being destined to interpret it, and of the end it was designed to answer.

XX.

The ultimate end. — According to our theory, *both the laws of the method, and the proximate reason of it, will find their ultimate end,* in relation to this stage of the Divine procedure, *in contributing to prove the all-sufficiency of the wisdom of God.*

1. But first, having distinctly stated that each preceding display of the Divine perfection may be expected to be brought forwards and enlarged through each successive stage of creation, and having assigned the grounds of this expectation, we have to begin by remarking on its fulfilment in the continued exercise of the Divine Power. During the entire period, from the introduction of organic life to the creation of man, all the pre-existing forces of inorganic matter continued in activity. The argument for the power of God, therefore, remained unabated; rather it was augmented during every moment of the period.

2. But here were new displays of power. It originated and introduced the new principle of life. It was present in the motion of every plant that waved; as well as in the mechanical and chemical action constantly going on for the production of soil. It was present in the mountain cedar braving the tempest by resistance; and in the slender flower evading the storm by elasticity: in the plenitude of vegetable life which crowded the wilderness; and in the lichen of the almost inde-

They seek for ends and uses; and they boast of having seen the means and the end, as much as if they had intended the end and invented the means. Yet they who boast, should not forget that there was a Wisdom which anticipated their own; that had there not been a Sagacity which planned, their own sagacity in tracing the execution would never have appeared; that they are but students, and that in their pride of assigning the wisdom and the design, they ought not to overlook Him, the Designer and the Wise, their own designer, and the great Being who gave them the power of knowing Himself, their God." — Vol. i. p. 607.

structible rock which appears to live on through ages, the only form of life in a region of desolation. It proclaimed its presence in the molecular movements and ceaselessly diversified currents of every minute cellular structure; and in the organic force which pumps up the sap and diffuses it throughout the most gigantic and branching tree. If, for example, as it can be shown, a tree of thirty-three feet high, requires a pressure of "fifteen pounds upon every square inch in the section of the vessels of the bottom, in order merely to support the sap," how great must be the power which propels the sap upwards so as to supply the constant evaporation of the leaves. And if this be true of an individual tree, who shall calculate the amount of the forces which came into play with every outburst of vernal life during the era of the great coal formations!

3. But power is here seen waiting on Wisdom; laying out her resources to be employed as adaptations and means. Wherever we look we are impressed with the idea of difficulties overcome, difficulties originated as if for the purpose of overcoming them, — and overcome, not in one way merely, but in ways so gratuitously varied and multiplied as if to impress us with the conviction of the inexhaustible resources of the Being who has overcome them; and, further, that He actually intended to produce this impression.

4. We have just been showing that the displays of power co-exist with those of wisdom, and are even multiplied in her service. We have now to recognise the prospective contrivances of wisdom even in the inorganic world, where before we saw nothing but power. Take, for example, the fact that granite should have been selected from many other substances to constitute the great framework of the earth, in connection with its peculiar chemical fitness for the support of vegetable life. Animals do not ultimately depend on vegetable food, more certainly than vegetables depend on mineral sustenance. Primarily, indeed, they depend on the surrounding water, and on the moisture which bathes their roots: but experiment demonstrates that there are certain other bodies — such as potash and phosphoric acid, which are universally present in vegetable structures, and essential to their existence. Now there is satisfactory evidence to show that these substances formed specific ingredients in the granites of the ancient earth; and that, consequently, they were provided ages before the commencement of organic life. But in vain would this provision

have existed, if, in addition, these granite masses had not been elevated to form the great mountain chains of the earth; for in this way only could that slow disintegration take place by which their liberated materials contribute to produce the fruit-bearing soil of the earth. Now who can fail to recognise here the bearing of one part upon another, the presence of conspiring means, of preparation and completion?

5. We may notice, also, instances of the remarkable manner in which organic life has been adapted to pre-existing laws. Had the earth, for example, its astronomical year and its diurnal rotation? The entire life of annual plants agrees exactly with the former, and the circle of action in the perennial tribes with the latter. Is the force of the earth's gravity specific? Then must the forces of organic life be precisely adjusted to it; for, were they below a certain amount, the rate of vegetable circulation would stop; or were they in excess, it would be accelerated in a manner equally destructive of life. Creative wisdom, however, has nicely adapted the minutest parts of vegetable structures to the mass of the earth on which they exist. Is matter endowed with the properties of tenacity, hardness, density, flexibility, and elasticity? So exquisitely is the vegetable constitution adapted to all these, — not in a single way, but in a different manner for each species, — that a slight alteration in any one of these laws would require the reconstruction of the whole. The magnitude of the ocean and its extensive currents are related to the magnitude of the moveable atmosphere, the repository and the moving force of the clouds; and both combine to the production of such a distribution of the temperature as is essential to vegetable life, and determines many of its forces. The laws of radiation, evaporation, electricity, all sustain vital relation to the organic economy; while light, besides administering the necessary stimulus to its functions, paints and beautifies every flower that blows.

6. But the same system of adaptations has reappeared, and been applied, through a prolonged succession of geological changes; so that its accommodative power has been always receiving additional confirmations. Had we seen the earliest organic products of the primitive earth, we should most likely have concluded that the then existing condition of the globe was essential to their existence. But other conditions of the planet succeeded, and the mighty forests now entombed as coal formations came with them. And as other changes fol-

lowed, plants, of forms and characters now unknown on the surface of the earth, succeeded; specimens of which were stored away in the grand natural Herbaria of the earth, as if reserved for the purpose of shaming us from setting limits to the Creator's power and wisdom.

7. In speaking of the boundless variety of vegetable life, we may take the existing flora of the earth as a specimen of all those which have preceded it. The Divine Being might have clothed the earth with verdure, and yet have limited the whole vegetable variety to two or three species; but between eighty and a hundred thousand species are already classed. Had we seen land-plants only, we should have considered the existence of aquatic plants an impossibility; and yet forests wave at the bottom of the ocean. Had we seen them only in a fertile soil, we should have deemed such a soil essential to their existence; but God has appointed the apparently insignificant lichen to live on the rock, and it eats for ages into a substance which defies the chemical and mechanical forces. From the sea-shores, from the bed of the sea, from the deep caverns of the earth, upwards, as the land rises, in stages, to the line of eternal snow, organic life is to be found diffused over the entire range. Is land to be rescued from the sea? A succession of plants effects the process, each giving place as soon as it has prepared the way for a superior species; others, again, being ready to defend and retain the rescued territory. Did the Creator determine that the plant should be distinguished by definite form? All the species are obviously constructed on a general plan; but, while that plan is never lost sight of, the characteristic of figure, color, fragrance, and duration, is diversified without end; and, in many instances, as if for the sake of showing that, in the hands of Infinite Wisdom, any single idea admits of endless illustration. Are plants to grow by nutrition? The food which they elaborate and store up is not of a single kind merely; in one tribe it is oil, in another fecula, in another lignine, in another sugar, in another gum, &c.; while "an interminable catalogue of other substances may be extracted from the juices of different plants, all of which have been formed by secretion in some part or other of their structure." Are they to be continued by reproduction? The modes of sustaining the feeble parent plants are so variously diversified, as if for the sole object of showing that such variety was practicable; some of these are supported by different kinds of hooks, others by voluble stems, by claws, by

voluble leaves, by radicles, by tendrils, &c. The modes of protecting seeds comprise unnumbered inventions; many of them so far from simple, that they would seem to be adopted only for the sake of demonstrating a power of invention. From some plants the seeds simply fall; from others a mechanical force projects them to a distance; others yield them to the power of the winds; and the seeds of others are winged for distant flight.

8. Now, we do not say that this diversity and exuberance of organic life, together with the complicated inorganic arrangements which it involves, scientifically demonstrates the absolute infinity of the Divine wisdom. If it did so, all the illustrations of wisdom exhibited in the subsequent stages of the Divine procedure would, as further evidence, be superfluous. A similar remark to this we made in the preceding Part, when inferring the extent of the Divine power from the evidence then before us. And from the advanced point we have now reached, we can see how great would have been our error if we had limited our views of that Power by the evidence afforded by that first stage. For, here we behold it putting forth fresh displays, and demonstrating that "the Creator of the ends of the earth fainteth not, neither is weary." And, in a similar manner, the illustrations of the Divine wisdom have been accumulating ever since, and in new departments of creation. In harmony with which fact, we repeat our conviction, that an infinite proof of infinite wisdom can be furnished to finite creatures, or be received by them, only by a progressive accumulation through infinite duration, and therefore can only be always in process. But we can conceive also of such a display of wisdom, within a space and a time not unlimited, as should furnish beings capable of reasoning from analogy, with abundant evidence of wisdom unlimited. Such an exercise of wisdom we believe to have been displayed in the organic creation.

9. In bringing this conviction home to the mind, it is to be remembered, as a fact of universal admission, that the *special* limitations of matter, and therefore the limitations of the uses made of it, are necessitated by the nature of matter itself. The material medium for exhibiting design is itself inherently conditioned by limits. So that we have to determine the question, what amount of evidence of design, exhibited under circumstances in which the medium of design itself forbids absolute infinity, we, as beings, constituted to infer more than we see,

should deem an adequate illustration of wisdom unlimited. Now we think we are uttering a very sober supposition in saying, that the production of the first form of organic life that appeared, would be, in the estimation of superior intelligences, both the sole prerogative and the adequate illustration of infinite wisdom. We can conceive of beings to whom that simple form would furnish a key to the material universe. For them, the full exposition of that single constitution would involve the exposition of the whole physical creation. But, that single specimen was accompanied or followed by a world of diversified organizations. It would have been in vain for man, had he then lived, to attempt the individual enumeration. Now, surely he could not have listened to such an exposition of organic life as that to which we have adverted, — a tale of ages,—for it must have included the mechanical and chemical history of our planet from the beginning; could not have marked how all physical science was presupposed by each organic form, and met in it; how it stood the centre, not of a system merely, but of plan within plan, and system within system, with all the inorganic laws and elements, like angels, ministering to it; and that the same was true of every species, but with an endless diversity of details in each; he could not have required ages of such occupation, in order to feel constrained to admit, of the Divine Creator, that " His ways are past finding out!"

Long as that early geological period may have lasted, it would doubtless have come to an end before the supposed exposition was completed, for every returning season would add to its subjects. While yet the investigation was in process, a new epoch would dawn, and a new world of organic wonders come to view. And thus the illustrations of Creative wisdom would be accumulating on him in an ever augmenting ratio. Surely, as these worlds came before him in a succession which promised no end, and yet every one of them exhibiting myriads of differences from all the rest, he would have confessed, unnumbered ages ago, " There is no searching of His understanding!" Further, when he found that each of these varying organic worlds as it came before him was not only perfect in itself; and perfect from the first; but that each formed part of a plan which comprehended the whole; a plan presupposed by the whole series, and which had been invariably adhered to amidst all the endless modifications which its principles were always receiving; and a plan which, while retaining in the original and appropriate places the fossil remains of every extinct family, provided a definite place for every new creation, and every additional species, he could not forbear exclaiming, " O Lord, how manifold are thy works; in wisdom hast thou made them all!" In the imaginary position we have described, he could not but feel, as every onward step in the organic series brought with it an incalculable amount of evidence of the Divine wisdom, to be added to all the accumulations of the past, that the Being who had designed all this could have covered the earth, had it been ten times larger than it is, with a proportionate enlargement of the organic plan; that, if He has not clothed every distant star with vegetable life, it is not owing to any limit or exhaustion of His designing power; and that the organic worlds of past time are only a specimen of the manner in which He could go on varying the details of organic adaptations for ever. And when he saw that there was no prospect of an end to His designs; and remembered that, as the Divine power of the inorganic stage had been brought on into the organic, so the Divine wisdom of the organic stage would probably receive fresh illustrations in some new economy, he would feel that he was in the presence of wisdom all-sufficient, and acknowledge, " Great is the Lord, and of great power; His understanding is infinite!"

FIFTH PART.

SENTIENT EXISTENCE.

The Third Stage of the Divine Manifestation:

POWER, WISDOM, AND GOODNESS.

LET it be imagined that another extended period has elapsed since we took our last survey of creation, and beheld the wisdom of God as displayed in the wonders of vegetable life. It seems but natural that the view, so far from leading us to conclude that we had reached the ultimatum of Divine Manifestation, would have awakened rather an expectation of beholding ulterior displays. The Being, we might have said, whose Power called this visible universe into existence, and whose Wisdom has ever been conducting it from one stage to another, till it is literally organizing its elements and exhibiting them in the possession of life, can surely know no limits to His operations but such as the same Wisdom may see fit to prescribe. The use which He had made of matter when last we looked on the scene of creation, seems to warrant the conjecture that, if life can be added to matter, something equally wonderful may be added to life. What if that addition should consist of enjoyment! Who can say but that in the revolution of ages, the period may come when forms of organized being may not only live, but move and be happy!

1. Another visit to the object of our meditations is at length permitted us; and a scene opens to our view which compels us to exclaim, "How great is his goodness!" For the sake of illustration, let the season of our supposed visit be fixed, long after the new era of animal existence had commenced, yet before the time of the Adamic creation; and let it be imagined that the various changes which, at long intervals, had

occurred since our last visit, were all laid open to us. We should find that not only had the great change itself, which had been the subject of our conjectures, taken place — that vegetable life had been actually succeeded by animal enjoyment — but that even that enjoyment had reached a point which awoke the expectation of something greater still at hand.

2. In the last Part, we saw vegetable life in the solitary and entire occupation — we say not for any length of time — of the advancing earth; we saw it in busy and diversified activity, preparing the way, in some places, both for the coming of higher orders of its own kind of life, by producing the necessary kind of soil, and for the Divine origination of that animal life which it was destined to support. We beheld in its presence, and varieties, and rapid increase, an indication that the Great and Provident Householder was contemplating the arrival of unnumbered guests. Now we find, not only that they have come, but that, since their first appearance, the crust of the globe has undergone many a revolution, and has exhibited many a rich and varied surface of vegetable life, crowded with corresponding forms of animated existence. While, on each occasion, there is reason to believe the same order has been observed as to the subsequence of animal to vegetable life: an inorganic change being followed by a corresponding change in vegetation; and a change in vegetation followed by appropriate species of animated beings.

I.

3. *Goodness.* — We have not yet to speak of the *extent* of the Divine benevolence to be inferred from this new form of existence. We have only, at present, to regard it as evincing the *existence* of goodness in the Creator. Hereafter we shall have to view it as furnishing new illustrations also of the Creative power and wisdom already displayed in the preceding stages. But, for the present, we have only to do with the law, *that every Divinely originated effect is a result, of which the supreme and ultimate reason is in the Divine nature.* Now, here, in the animal kingdom, is a being constructed for enjoyment; each of its movements yielding it gratification; each of its senses an inlet to pleasure: and the whole is ever preparing the way for greater enjoyment still, and finding happiness in the occupation. If the reason for the existence of this creature is to be sought in the Divine Creator, so also must be the rea-

son of its enjoyment. Even if there were no purpose of manifesting the Divine All-sufficiency — if the creation were to be limited to a single creature — still, as every effect must be, in some sense, like its cause, that single creature would be, not indeed, formally, but virtually, a manifestation, *pro tanto*, of some property of the Divine Nature. But here is not merely an individual animal designed for enjoyment, nor a single species, but a world, a succession of worlds, filled with animal enjoyment. What property of the Divine Creator can this fact be supposed to manifest, but that He, "the Happy God," is good, or delights to impart happiness!

4. But is animal pain and death, especially the system of prey, compatible with the goodness of the Creator? We admit, first, that death, and even the system of prey, were originally intended by God. That the former was, will be, in general, readily admitted. In proof of the latter, we have merely to call attention to the fact that whole tribes of animals are expressly constructed for it. Their instincts and organization prepare them to be engines of destruction.

5. But, then, secondly, the pain attending animal death by violence is apparently reduced to its minimum. For, 1, the animal knows not that death is the extinction of life. Yet this is the very consideration which, in the case of man, gives to death all its bitterness. 2. As the animal knows not that it is ceasing to be, even when it is in the article of death, the difficulty is, in reality, reduced to one of physical *pain* merely. For as to its unconscious removal by death, no objection can be consistently raised against such an arrangement in the animal world, apart from the attendant pain, any more than against the corresponding arrangement in the vegetable world. And yet we there admired the wisdom which made a lower order of vegetable organization subservient by death to a higher order. Now, it should be remembered that the dying animal is as unconscious of its *fate* as the dying plant; the only question to be resolved then, we repeat, is one of animal pain. 3. There appears to be a law of graduating sensibility pervading the animal kingdom; according to which, the degree of feeling diminishes as the organization descends in the scale; till, as we approach the point at which it touches the vegetable kingdom, it verges on total insensibility to pain. We are aware that in proportion to this reduction must be the reduction also of animal enjoyment during life. But while death is the event of a moment, the enjoyment of life is to be multi-

plied by all the moments though which it is prolonged. Now, as the myriad tribes of these inferior orders constitute the staple of animal food, the arrangement provides, in so far, for the least possible amount of suffering; if, indeed, in their case, there be any suffering at all. 4. And then, as to one large animal preying upon another, though the sensibility is greater, it is subject to great deductions on some of the grounds already adverted to; and, by a simple, if not a special, contrivance, death is rendered as sudden, and therefore as easy, as possible. That the predatory animal should kill before it begins to devour, is a beneficent provision. Some animals, it is well known, seize on the carotid arteries; in consequence of which, death speedily ensues. But the fact to which we allude is, that at one particular point of the neck, near the skull, a wound of the spinal nerve produces instant death, and apparently without suffering. Now, while man has discovered this fact only by experiment, the predatory animals have always made this part of the spine the object of attack.

6. This animal death is an unavoidable part of the present constitution of creation. That constitution, we have shown, is progressive. In order to prepare the earth for man, it has been subjected to successive revolutions. The coal which forms our fuel is the produce of the destruction of plants, preserved from former worlds. But that provision involved the death of all the myriad forms of life and enjoyment with which the woods of the ancient earth were crowded. And were unknown ages of animal enjoyment to be then withheld, because a physical revolution was eventually, and for a time, to interrupt it?

7. "But might not these revolutions have been spared, and the earth have been created at the first as we *now* find it?" In many respects, it is progressive still. The lichen and the moss produce a soil on which they can no longer live; new races of plants follow in succession, improving with every change, and occupying the once arid waste. Insects and reptiles at first possessed it, for it could maintain nothing better; but as it has improved, superior races have successively come into possession. Were ages of reptile and insect life to be withheld, because the progressive change involved their ultimate extinction, for a higher order of life?

8. "But might not such progression have been rendered unnecessary by making the entire amount of animal and vegetable life, as well as the state of the globe, unchangeable from

the beginning?" The inquirer may not foresee that this is to ask, in effect, whether the Divine Being might not have adopted a mode of government entirely and essentially different from that which He has chosen; for if one part be changed, every part must undergo a corresponding change. A world of immortal animals and plants; a world that knew no climatic change, no seasons, no organic nor inorganic variety — a stagnant and unprogressive creation — would be as unsuited to the created as to the Creating mind.

9. It might be suggested, also, that the continuance of the first created animals, and of everything else to correspond, would force on the attention of man evidence of their miraculous origin, too obvious and overbearing for a system of free agency. Besides which, (and this is the adequate answer to the implied objection,) such an unchangeable state of the animate creation would inconceivably diminish the amount of animal enjoyment. So that if the greatest degree and diffusion of such enjoyment be the object in view, the supposed change would defeat itself. That object can be obtained only by death, and specially by the system of prey. And shall the comparatively small amount of pain which that system involves prevent the incalculable amount of animal fecundity and enjoyment which it necessarily presupposes? For the right view of this part of the question seems to be that, if animals are to be sustained by food, it is more consistent with the greatest amount of enjoyment that a certain proportion of that food should be animated, and be filled with pleasure until it is wanted, than that it should be inanimate and incapable of enjoyment.[1]

10. "Then might not animal life have been sustained on vegetable food alone?" Not only would such an arrangement—as we have seen — inconceivably diminish the amount of animal life and enjoyment which exists under the present arrangement, it would still leave death in the animal world, from the ten thousand sources of what are called accident. The foot of the ox would crush the insects in the grass; the breeze waft them by myriads into the stream; and the evaporation and exhaustion of the lake leave the fish dead on the shore. Nothing less than perpetual miracle could have saved them from destruction. And thus it is, in the all-related system of creation, that a single essential alteration would throw

---

[1] See Note E.

the whole into disorder, or be a virtual repeal of the entire scheme; and that every objection made against it involves an *incalculable reduction of animal life and enjoyment*, and is therefore incompatible with the Divine benevolence.

11. "Then might not animal death have been unaccompanied even with the smallest degree of suffering?" To this objection it seems to be a sufficient reply, that sensibility to pain is but the necessary alternative to sensibility to pleasure; — that in few things is the beneficence of God more strikingly apparent than in the arbitrary manner in which he has arranged the animal system so as to *economise* pain; rendering each nerve belonging to a sense, for instance, sensitive to pain only from the excess of that impression which constitutes its peculiar function, (as the optic nerve from excess of light, but not from excess of sound also, and that of the ear from excess of sound, but not of light;) — that this sensibility to pain operates as a necessary warning of danger, without which the animal would soon and inevitably perish; so that its benevolent language is emphatically, "Do thyself no harm; take timely warning, and be happy;" — and that this possibility of pain could not be separated from the powers of sense without miraculous interposition, since it is the natural consequence of their functions. In addition to which, it should be observed, that where death is the simple consequence of age, the power of feeling does gradually cease before that event arrives. It is benevolently arranged that the prior departure of physical sensibility shall leave the final struggle to be carried on by the vital powers alone. So that the animal passes through a state of stupor into the sleep of death.

12. According to the existing arrangements of creation, then, we behold, on the one hand, a system of provisions for securing the greatest amount of animal life; for only a small proportion of it could find the necessary sustenance in any other way than that of prey; so that if animals, we repeat, are to be sustained by food, it is more consistent with the Divine goodness that a certain proportion of that food should be animated and filled with enjoyment until it is wanted, than that it should be inanimate and incapable of pleasure. While, on the other hand, we find a number of remarkable provisions for reducing the pain involved in this system of animal enjoyment, to the smallest amount. Other and higher considerations we omit; such as the fact that animal sensibility forms a perpetual appeal to human sensibility, and is an important means of its improve-

ment; and the manner in which the progressiveness of creation is made subservient to the moral education and advancement of the beings to whom the Divine Manifestation is made, and worthy of Him who makes it. But we are content with having shown that a fact which might at first appear to diminish the claims of the Divine goodness, becomes, when viewed in its relations, an occasion for enlarging our conceptions of Creative benevolence, by showing that it secures animal existence and enjoyment to the greatest amount.

13. And thus we have found, as the great Reason led us to expect, that every stage and object of creation is an exponent of some characteristic of the Divine Nature.

II.

The past brought forwards. — By the principle which requires *that the laws of the past should be brought forwards to the present,* we are led to expect that the elements and results of the mineral and vegetable kingdom will be found brought on into the animal kingdom.

1. Accordingly, though the animal is more withdrawn from the inorganic world, in point of rank, than the vegetable, it is still amenable to all those laws of inanimate matter which make it a part of the great material system. Here is the law of gravitation, by which the animal stands. Here is mechanical force, illustrating its laws, and distributing its levers and fulcra, in a way which enables it to fulfil a thousand distinct purposes. The various secretions are complicated products of chemical action; though no *artificial* chemistry can imitate them. Here light and air find appropriate organs; and electricity finds functions and properties expressly adapted for its development and action. The same laws which operate in the formation of the silicious crystals, here compose the skeleton of many zoophytes, and the calcareous crystals of many radiated animals. The *simple* symmetry of vertebrate animals, and the *pentagonal* symmetry of radiate animals, show that we are still investigating the productions of a Being who is acting on general principles, and filling up a plan. While the presence of organic life in its leading functions, nutrition and reproduction, shows that the vegetable and animal kingdoms are connected parts of a great whole. Of these facts, numerous illustrations will occur as we proceed; none of them, however, tending to efface the great chacteristics which separate the

organic kingdom from the inorganic, and the animal kingdom from both.

2. Thus we have seen pre-existing laws brought on into each succeeding stage of creation; the inorganic into the organic, and both these into the animal kingdom.

III.

Progress. — Our theory leads us to inquire next for the indications of progress, or for *the introduction of new laws.* And we find animal life superadded to the vegetable or organic life.

Now it is obvious to remark that the comparison of the two must be drawn, not between the highest form of the one and the lowest form of the other, but between the more elaborate and perfect forms of each division. Were it our object to show the contiguity and continuity of the two organized kingdoms, we might then (as we shall hereafter have occasion to do) point out the principles which they have in common, and the points at which they appear to touch and even blend. But in illustrating their distinctive characteristics, it would be as irrelevant to compare the lowest state of animal life with the highest form of vegetable life, as it would be to compare the lowest form of vegetation with the highest form of animal existence. Taking both, however, in their more perfect states, it will be found that the animal world differs from the vegetable, as widely as both these differ from the mineral. So marked is this difference, that were the various endowments which are distributed separately throughout the whole vegetable world to be concentrated in a single plant, the superiority of an animal, taken promiscuously from the herd, would still be instantly and abundantly manifest.

2. When treating of vegetable physiology, we saw that organic life includes a series of functions by which the individual plant is preserved and the species continued. Now the physiology of animals discloses the fact, that they possess functions analogous to those of vegetables; and that, in addition to these, and distinct from them, they possess also the functions of a higher order of life, involving sensibility and locomotion. *Each kind of life has its own system of organs.* The centre of the organic life is the heart; of the animal life, the brain. The functions of organic life act continuously; those of animal life intermittingly. The former operate unconsciously and involuntarily; the latter not so. Such are some of the lead-

ing distinctions between the functions of organic and animal life.

3. Accordingly, Bichat has shown (and the distinction is now generally accepted,[1]) that the natural division of the complex animal system is twofold. Such parts as the heart, the intestines, and whatever acts independently of the will, and without the consciousness of the subject, belong to what he denominates *the vegetative or organic life*. While the senses, and the parts that bring the system into voluntary relation with the external world, he calls *the animal life*. In the plant, life is endowed only, at most, with the property of excitability; in the animal, it superadds to this property, those of sensation, perception, passion, mental association, and impelled volition, followed by the expression of that volition in muscular contraction. To the plant is assigned the power of drawing nourishment from inorganic matter — mere earths, salts, and airs; while the aliments by which animals are nourished are derived from animal or vegetable substances alone. Whence plants, says M. Richerand, may be considered as the laboratories in which nature prepares aliment for animals; and thus, we may add, emphatically seals their superiority.

4. But what is the nature of that instinctive mind by which the animal is especially distinguished from the vegetable creation? The difficulty of giving what may be deemed a satisfactory reply to this question, arises, perhaps, not so much from any inherent profundity in the subject, as from our necessary ignorance, or inability to obtain the requisite data; and from the prepossessions respecting it of those who are too much amused with the facts to examine the reasons, and who would rather "see in the shifting cloud what shapes they please."

5. With a view to a reply, however, let us first mark the distinctions which exist among the functions of the animal life itself. Analogous in office to the *excitability* of the plant, is the *sensibility* of the animal; though the latter is secured by a nobler arrangement than the corresponding property in the vegetable, and is made to answer additional ends. The animal is placed in new and wonderful relations to the external world by the organs of touch, hearing, sight, &c. United to these organs is a system of nerves which conveys "*sensations* from the organs of sense inwards, so as to make these sensations the

---

[1] See Dr. Playfair's Abstract of Liebig's Report on Organic Chemistry applied to Physiology and Pathology, read at the Meeting of the British Association, 1842.

objects of the animal's consciousness." And in "the higher animals these impressions upon the nerves are all conveyed to one organ, the brain." Here then is one step towards an explanation of the functions of animal life.

6. But what part of its physical structure is it by which the animal on receiving these impressions changes its posture, its place, or its action? It is now satisfactorily ascertained that the immediate agents in such motions are the muscles. The property by which, under natural stimulus, they produce motion, has been termed *irritability*, or, more properly, *contractility*, from the manner in which they contract in the movement of the limbs. Here, then, is another and a distinct step in the explanation. The sensations which the animal feels, and the muscular action which it consequently exerts, may be inseparably connected; yet are they obviously distinguishable. Animal sensibility has the nerves for its organs; animal contractility, the muscles. The former is the passive; the latter, the active element of animal life. The former seems preparatory to whatever of instinct, intelligence, or mind may be expressed by the latter. So that between these two extreme terms, lies the sphere of our present inquiry.

7. Now, if we mark the effect directly consequent on certain sensations, we shall find that the animal appears to have received a notice or knowledge of the external object which has occasioned them. And the knowledge thus acquired is called *perception*. Here, then, is a connection apparently mental. The knowledge resulting from the sensation, reveals the existence of animal mind; of something, at least, which is not material, and which is not merely vital; but is distinct from, and superior to, both.

8. If next, we mark the effect consequent on certain perceptions, we shall find that they are apparently followed by *volitions:* by which we mean that mental act which immediately determines muscular action. And thus there intervenes between the two states of sensation and muscular contraction, the two links of perception and volition. So that "the cycle of operations which appears to take place when animals act in reference to external objects is this, sensation, perception, volition, muscular contraction;"[1] the brain being the seat or centre to which sensation tends, and from which volition proceeds.

[1] Dr. Whewell's Philosophy of the Inductive Sciences, ii. p. 71.

It is not intended by these remarks that the supposed mental part of this process *clearly* and *consciously* attends every animal action. At least, man, while performing the ordinary acts of breathing, walking, &c., is but faintly conscious of the sensations and volitions which these acts imply. So that, in representing the sensation and muscular action of animals as connected by the intermediate process of perception and volition, we must be regarded as stating only an extreme case.

But, at this stage of the subject, the question arises, whether the cycle we have described includes the whole of the process belonging to the operation of animal mind or instinct; or, whether, in addition to the four steps named, there may not be at least a fifth. In entertaining this question, indeed, we shall be anticipating that side of the subject which compares the animal with the human mind; yet, an adequate view of the inquiry will not allow us to postpone it.

Now, it will be admitted, that, in the human mind, at least, one additional link intervenes between perception and volition. To this link we will give the general name, not of understanding, but of reason; by which we mean, the power which the mind has of deducing universal truths from particular appearances, or of contemplating the ideal relations of things; and of willing or determining, in harmony with such ideas, on the means necessary to the attainment of a proposed end. The question to be decided, then, may assume this simple form, is the volition of brutes determined without the intervention of reason?

The great end of instinct appears to be the preservation of life in the individual, and its perpetuation in the species. That man occasionally trains and turns it to a different account, does not affect the truth of the statement. During all the ages prior to human existence, and wherever the animal is left undisturbed by the influence of human reason, the direct and only reference of its instincts is to the continuance of its race. And as this is their only obvious end, so the various ways in which it is gained, by the different species, is evidently predetermined by the organization peculiar to each. From which it is inferred by some that wherever there is life there is instinct; or, *that instinct and life are co-extensive.*

9. Instinctive motions, viewed in this enlarged sense, are of different classes. First, there are those which belong to organic life, and which may be called *vital.* These are common to plants and animals; such as the involuntary processes of

secretion and assimilation. But whether these processes should be regarded as instinctive or not, is immaterial to the principal point at issue.

10. Second, there are those instincts which call into action the muscles considered to be under the control of volition, and which may be called *adaptive*. Such are the actions of the new-born young of animals; the beautiful and perfect nest-building of birds; and the mathematical cell-making of bees. These constitute the great class of actions, allowed, on almost all hands, to be strictly instinctive; and whose direct tendency is to the continuance of animal existence. And yet, as far as the animal is promoting this object, it is evidently acting towards an end which is unknown to itself; and, therefore, acting blindly. Agreeably to Paley's definition of instinct, it is acting "prior to experience, and independent of instruction," and, we might add, with a perfection which no instruction could teach, and no experience improve.

11. And, thirdly, there are those which appear to be the result of experience, and which discover a power of selecting means for proximate ends according to varying circumstances: these may be said to be mental. To this class of actions pertain those remarkable instances of animal sagacity, at the recital of which every one has been more or less interested and astonished, and which have even suggested to some the extravagant idea of a system of animal metaphysics.

The remainder of our remarks on instinct will be restricted to this class; and our object will be to show that, even allowing some mental act to intervene, in such instances, between perception and volition, that intermediate act or operation is *not* what we intend by *reasoning*.

1. That an action ascribable to reason in man, would, when performed by an animal, be hastily ascribed to the same principle, was antecedently probable. But to do this is to forget that just as rational, and quite analogous, would it be to infer, that because the bird constructs its nest by instinct, and the bee its cell, therefore, if a man attempts an imitation of that nest or that cell, he acts under the impulse of instinct also.

2. If what the animal does evidently from instinct, is done better, and is of greater importance to the end of its existence, than that which it does from what some would ascribe to a higher faculty, it seems unphilosophical to ascribe the superior efforts to the inferior principle, and the lower efforts to the higher principle. Now, probably, no one supposes that the

lamb when it first follows its mother, and adapts its muscular action to the form of the ground, knows anything of the geometrical relations which the action involves; or that the dog, in hunting only a certain kind of animal, and in crossing the field repeatedly, to scent it, knows anything of the doctrines of Resemblance and of Space; or that the bird, in its first flight, adjusting its effort to the distance and height of the flight with mechanical precision, really recognises the doctrine of force. All this is attributed to instinct. If then, under different circumstances, the animal should afterwards be found acting differently, consistency would seem to require that the difference should be ascribed to the provisional operation of the same instinct. If the bird on perceiving that the rising stream is approaching its half-finished nest, begins to build higher up the bank, it does but build on the spot where it would have placed its nest at first, had the waters then been as high as they have since become, and the end in both cases is the same—the continuance of its species.

3. If animals ever perform actions from instruction or experience, to which human sagacity would be unequal, it must result either from an *instinctive* intelligence, or (which would be proving too much,) from the exercise of a reason superior to man's. Now the great majority of the remarkable feats related of animals are of this description. The advocates of brute rationality, in their anxiety to do the best for their clients, adduce illustrations of so remarkable a nature as to show that no human reason would have been competent to such doings. Such, for example, are those instances in which an animal reads in the countenance of its master that he contemplates its destruction, and absents itself accordingly; or in which it knows, better perhaps than its master, that he is about to take a certain favorite walk, and runs on before to secure a share in the enjoyment; or, in which it finds its way straight home again when it had been taken by a circuitous route, and blindfolded, to a great distance. It was this want of discrimination, in ascribing to reason, actions which had not afforded scope for reasoning, and which were too quick and too certain for anything but instinct, which led Descartes [1] to say, "their doing many things better than ourselves does not prove them to be endowed with reason, for this would prove them to have more reason than we have, and that they are capable of excell-

[1] In his treatise De Methodo.

ing us in all other things also; but it rather proves them to be void of reason."

4. If the most wonderful feats of animal sagacity are the result of human instruction, such instances only show the adaptiveness, within certain fixed and narrow limits, of the mental instinct. It was antecedently probable, in a world whose regularity is made consistent with variety, and whose every principle admits of diversified application, that the higher order of animals would find scope for their instinctive mind within a certain range. Even the plant has a confined power of adapting itself to circumstances. It is only in analogy with nature, that the dog, for example, the most instinctively sagacious of animals, if he become the companion of man, and so be made to feel indirectly the influence of the human mind, should have all its better adaptations brought to light; though itself entirely unconscious of the fact. Compared with its condition in the preadamite earth, the domestic dog is now in another world, walking among gods. "Man is to him instead of a god, or *melior natura*."[1] And, while there is no ground to believe that, if the canine race existed a thousand ages before man appeared on the earth, a single trait of the instinctive sagacity we now so much admire, had ever been exhibited by them, so neither is there reason to conclude that such sagacity is now the result of anything higher than an instinctive adaptiveness, of which they themselves have no intelligent perception.

5. If, again, the power of performing extraordinary feats be *hereditary*, it cannot be the result of reason or of knowledge; for knowledge and reason are not, in this way transmissible. A paper of Mr. Knight's, read before the Royal Society,[2] shows that even the acquired faculties of dogs — the expertness they gain by teaching, descends in the race. "He found the young and untaught ones (springing spaniels) as skilful as the old ones, not only in finding and raising the woodcocks, but in knowing the exact degree of frost which will drive those birds to springs and rills of unfrozen water." It is evident that such a fact cannot be adduced in favor of animal rationality; for the knowledge exhibited was strangely possessed without instruction or experience; and the reasoning, if there had been any, being destitute of data, must have been nothing less than a train of *à priori* speculation.

---

[1] Bacon's Essay on Atheism.

[2] Quoted in Lord Brougham's Dissertations, &c., vol. i. p. 140

6. Among the presumptive proofs against the rationality of animals, it is, we think, justly alleged that, while man can transmit the knowledge which he has gained by experience, from generation to generation, conscious of its being experience, and that it is capable of receiving indefinite addition and application, the experience of animals, confined at most within narrow limits, is incapable of accumulation and transmission. So that the bee and the beaver of to-day, build no better than the bee and the beaver of a thousand years ago.

7. Another fact, of the same class, noticed by Adam Smith, is, that animals practice nothing approaching to barter. The most barbarous South Sea Islander will eagerly part with his rude ornaments and his food for a piece of iron. But even the animal which collects stores for the winter, shows that, in making this provision, he is impelled by instinct and not by foresight, for he is incapable of making an exchange which might exempt him from the trouble of collecting stores.

8. But, perhaps, the great fact which lies against the rationality of brutes, is, that they are destitute of the power of speech. To say that they have voices, or articulate language, adequate to the indication of certain appetites and passions, only increases the force of the remark. For how unlikely is it that they would be endowed with the means of expressing animal feelings, and be denied the power of imparting ideas, supposing them to have ideas to impart. And besides the inconsistency, perhaps few things would seem to impugn the goodness of the Creator more, than to withhold from a creature capable of even very limited reasoning, the faculty of expressing and imparting its reasonings.

9. But it may be asked, whether the power of inarticulate signs which animals possess, may not be adequate to the communication of thought? "The intention and the capacity, of expressing *thought*," says W. Humboldt,[1] "is the only thing which characterizes the articulate sound; and nothing else can be fixed on to designate its difference from the animal cry on the one hand, or the musical tone on the other." To which it may be sufficient to add, that, arguing from analogy, inarticulate cries serve only for the expression of sensations and passions. Hence man, during infancy, when he has only feelings to express, has only the limited signs and cries of the animal. With the dawning of thought comes its appropriate

[1] Quoted in Lieber's Political Ethics, p. 12.

vehicle, speech; and, although, afterwards, thought and feeling are generally combined in his vocal communications, it is worthy of remark that, in proportion as he essays to express unmingled feeling or passion, as in moments of great danger or pain, he invariably falls back on inarticulate sounds and interjections.

10. As little would it serve the purpose of an objector, and as much serve our own, to say that the animal is not entirely denied the organs of speech; for this would only increase the incongruity of giving an animal both reason, and organs for expressing it, and yet withholding from it the medial link, whatever it may be, necessary to connect and develop both. That some animals, especially birds, have at least imperfect organs of speech, is evident, for they can be taught to speak; and the only reason which can be assigned why they do not utter a single untaught sentence of their own, is that they have not a single thought to express. For "in a question respecting the possession of reason, the absence of all proof is tantamount to a proof of the contrary."[1]

11. But, while the train of our remarks impels us to the conclusion that, in the mental process of the animal, reason does not intervene between its perceptions and its volitions, it forcibly indicates what may or does intervene, namely, the operation of appetites, passions, habits, and, not recollection, but memory or associations of past impressions. To the expression of these alone, its sounds and signs are adequate; and of these alone we believe it to be conscious. As sensation issues in perception, perception awakens desire or attachment, aversion or anger, fear or the operation of habit, or some past impression or mental association; the influence of this again determines the volitions necessarily, and determines them differently according as they act feebly or powerfully, singly or in combination; while the volitions, so determined, issue in corresponding muscular action. The relation of the Divine agency to animal instinct, will be a subject for after consideration.

12. Having thus considered the subject independently, we may now be allowed to glance at it in its relation to the unfolding of that great system of Divine procedure of which it forms a part. We are not aware that the conclusions at which we have arrived have been in the least degree biassed by a

[1] Coleridge's Aids to Reflection, p. 291.

reference to that system. If, therefore, on comparing them with the expectations which that system would naturally suggest, we find them harmonize with each other, we shall be entitled to regard such harmony as additional evidence of the truth of our conclusions. And besides this, we shall feel the advantage of being able to bring our independent conclusions to the test of an independent system, and of there finding, so to speak, a place awaiting these conclusions. For to the want of such a test it is, we think, to be chiefly ascribed that so much diversity and uncertainty of opinion on the subject, prevails. We will only premise farther, that it is not our purpose to do more at present than barely to indicate some of those expectations to which we refer; leaving the more complete exposition of them to their proper places in the coming sections.

13. If, for instance, in our hypothetical visit to the scene of the advancing creation, we had been forewarned that the animal kingdom was only to form a part of the creation, but was not to be that part to which the Divine manifestation was to be made, what more reasonable than to expect that we should find a form of existence naturally incapable of recognising the great design? Now this is to expect that the animal kingdom will be found irrational; destitute alike of that faculty of concluding universal truths from particular appearances, which would have referred it back to its origin; and of that power of proposing an ultimate end, and of determining the will by ideas, which would have pointed it on to the chief and last end of all things. And accordingly, we do not find that it exhibits the least evidence of reason thus interpreted.

14. But if this stage of creation is to manifest the *goodness* of the Creator, the animal must not be endowed even with the power of recognising its humble position in the scale of creation, otherwise its enjoyment might be completely marred. Accordingly, it occupies its place as a link, unconscious of its office, in the yet ascending but unfinished series of being; and is incapable alike of mentally "looking before or after."

15. But, though unconscious of the ultimate design of creation, an end it must and does answer. The tendency of all its motions, voluntary and involuntary, is to preserve its own life, and to perpetuate its kind. Yet must it not be allowed to be conscious that it is answering even this end; otherwise the same mental power, which would enable it to recognise this fact, would enable it to recognise other truths, and might fill

its life with care and anxiety. Accordingly, the bird, while patiently sitting on its eggs, week after week, is ignorant of the end to be answered. An intermediate or present end may be answered of which it is conscious; for, during every moment of the time, some sense may be receiving present gratification. But the purpose to which this present enjoyment is subservient is that great favorite object of nature, the continuation of the kind; and this end the animal is accomplishing blindly and unintentionally.

16. But if the great object of its life is to answer this end, and if the circumstances in which, and the external means by which, this end is to be gained, vary, we may expect that it will not be destitute of adaptive power and instinctive intelligence. Even the plant, we have seen, possesses the former; it is only analogous, then, that to the nobler animal should be superadded the latter. Accordingly, the power which the animal possesses of unknowingly profiting by experience, is simply the slightly diversified application and perseverance of instinct in gaining its own great end.

17. Farther, if the animal be thus insensible to the ultimate end of creation, and even of the part which it is made to act for the attainment of that end, we may expect that its signs of communication will be of a very humble description. Having no thoughts to disclose, speech, the vehicle of thought, will be unnecessary. Having nothing to express but the feeling of the moment, nothing more can be necessary than inarticulate signs; and nothing more does it possess. "The minister and interpreter of nature" is yet to come.

18. In resumption of the law now under consideration, then, we remark that a superior order of life is here found added to the vegetable or organic life. By the wonderful addition of the senses, the points of relation between the animal and the external world are multiplied above those of the plant a thousand-fold. By the properties of animal mind which we have already considered — sensation, perception, passion, mental association, and constrained volition, comparatively inferior as these may be, those relations are further increased. The powers of muscular contraction and locomotion, by changing the position of the animal in relation to external objects, and by enabling it to put itself in proximity or even contact with them, augments these relations still more. And the faculty of communicating by sounds and signs with the creatures of its own kind, renders the number of these relations indefinite.

While each of these innumerable relations is a designed and calculated part of an elaborate system of *animal enjoyment.* And thus have we illustrated and substantiated the law of progress.

And, here, it is obvious to remark, how as each part of creation comes into existence, and becomes related to the preceding parts, certain terms progressively enlarge their meaning. There was a time, for example, when the word *creation*, supposing there were beings to employ it, meant only, in reference to the material system, *chaos;* and when *life* meant only *vegetable* existence. The doctrine of *Providence*, in relation to the same material system, originally indicated much less than it has come to mean, for there was but little comparatively to provide for. And so also of the *medial* relation, — expressing itself at first in effects representative of an originating cause; then adding to these the attainment of ends by the organization and employment of prepared means, representative of power guided by wisdom; and then endowing certain organic forms with susceptibilities of enjoyment, thus adding to power and wisdom, goodness, and awakening the idea that, as we are looking on a progressive scheme, the relation in question will yet express itself in other and higher forms.

IV.

Continuity. — Distinct as is the animal kingdom from the vegetable, and numerous and striking as are the additional characteristics which, in some of its departments, it exhibits, the progression will be found to be, in that general sense in which alone it can be expected, *continuous.*

1. It is continuous if regarded *organically*, or in relation to the vegetable kingdom. This is evident from the appellation given to a large division of organized bodies, *zoophytes*, or animal plants. So imperceptible are the gradations by which the two kingdoms are apparently connected at their origins, that naturalists are often divided as to the kingdom to which many well-known bodies belong. And a proposition has been entertained by more than one scientific society, that certain classes of organized beings should be placed in a new kingdom, occupying a place between plants and animals.

Still, it should be distinctly remembered, that this continuity is only apparent or general. It may be an insensible gradation to us. To superior powers, the passage from the vegetable to the animal would be visible, and could be measured. To suppose that, because it is difficult to assign the boundaries of the two kingdoms, therefore there are no boundaries, would be as irrational as to conclude that, because material atoms disappear, first from our unaided sight, and then vanish even beyond the reach of microscopic power, there is a point at which they graduate into nothingness. A moment's reflection will show us that, between that supposed point and the point beyond, there is all the difference between body and space, something and nothing — an infinite difference. In the same manner, however slight the *break*, where the vegetable appears to graduate into the animal, such an interruption there is; and it is nothing less than an interruption in *kind*, a transition from identity to essential difference. Accordingly, Cuvier affirms the universal application of the graduating principle to be philosophically untenable; and disclaims its rigorous application to the objects even of one and the same kingdom of nature.[1] And even Lamarck, than whom no one, perhaps, entertains more extravagant views of a structural gradation in animals, expresses his belief that plants and animals, when most resembling, are always distinguishable.[2]

2. Progression is also traceable, in the same *general* manner, in what may be called a *geological* or *historical* continuity. Physiologists regard the animal kingdom as susceptible of a fourfold division, in the following ascending order, — *Zoophytes* or *Radiata*, animals whose parts are distributed around a common centre, as the star-fish; *Mollusca*, pulpy animals, inclosed wholly or partially in a muscular envelope, as the cuttle-fish; *Annulosa* or *Articulata*, jointed animals, as the lobster; and *Vertebrata*, or animals with a spinal column.[3] This last division is composed of four classes, in the following order, — Fish, Reptiles, Birds, and Mammals, or animals which suckle their young. Now, as the fossil remains of all these divisions and classes are not found together in the lowest strata of the earth, are they found by geologists in any order; and, if so, what is that order?

The lowest or earliest system of rocks in which any traces of organic structure have been discovered are the Cambrian.

---

[1] Règne Animal, Pref., pp. xx. xxi.

[2] Philosoph. Zoolog., tom. i. pp. 377, 384, and 398, in note. See Professor Kidd's B. Treatise, pp. 310, 311.

[3] This is the order of arrangement adopted by Geoffrey and others. Cuvier's order reversed the position of the second and third divisions.

Here are found in abundance the remains, not of *radiata* alone, but of the second division of the animal kingdom also, predaceous cephalopods, the most advanced of all molluscs in organic structure; and, of the third division, highly organized crustaceans — trilobites, with reticular eyes. In the next system of the ascending series, the Silurian rocks, some of the preceding species are found, " but, as a group, the species are new and characteristic." Here, first, a vertebrate appears — a fish. But while the class to which it belongs is the lowest of the four vertebral divisions, the specimen itself belongs to the highest order of its class — the placoid. Indeed, all the fishes found in this system are of a high organic structure. The old red sandstone above the Silurian rocks, contains numerous genera of placoids, and of the order next below — ganoids. Above the old red sandstone comes the carboniferous system: here fossil footprints of a large reptilian first appear. Above this, comes the zechstein or magnesian limestone formation, charged with Palæosaurs, thecodonts, and monitors. But while reptiles compose the class of vertebrata next in order above fishes, the fossil bones of these three first-found species show them to have belonged to the order of lacertilians — the third from the top of Owen's nine orders of fossil reptiles. Ascending to the secondary class of rocks, we reach first the new red sandstone and saliferous marls. Here the gigantic frog or toad-like labyrinthodons occur; and here, for the first time, are the traces of birds. Still, as far as their structure can be ascertained, they do not appear to have been of the lowest order. Next comes the oolitic or jurassic system; and here occurs the didelphys — the first known example of mammalian remains, though not so low in organic structure as some living mammals. The green sand and cretaceous systems follow. The latter exhibits great changes of organic types; for while some of the preceding families have become degenerate, and others extinct, new families are called into being; and here we have the first traces of animal species still living. Leaving the cretaceous, we enter the tertiary system; and here we find ourselves in a comparatively new world of organic remains. " Among the millions of organic forms, from corals up to mammals, of the London and Paris basins," we find hardly one species belonging to the secondary rocks. Here, in the first subdivision of the system — the eocene — we find numerous extinct species of vertebral animals — fishes, reptiles, birds, and mammals; but the first and the last coexist. And, of the mammals, the carnivora are as old as the pachyderms; nor are monkeys wanting even in this opening page of the new chapter. And, then, as *eocene* implies that the subdivision exhibits the dawn of species still existing, the *miocene* subdivision above contains more of the species now living, though extinct species still predominate; while in the *pliocene*, or upper division, extinct species decline, and species now living predominate.[1]

From these remarks, it will be seen that geology affords no ground whatever for the hypothesis of a regular succession of creatures, beginning with the simplest forms in the older strata, and ascending to the more complicated in the later formations. The earliest forms of life known to geology are not of the lowest grade of organization; neither are the earliest forms of any of the classes which appear subsequently the simplest of their kind. The fanciful hypothesis which derives the higher animal from the lower — and of which we shall speak hereafter — is here contradicted at every step.

Neither have we any reason to believe that, of the species found in the older fossiliferous rocks, the *individuals* belonging to each existed in smaller *numbers* than they did afterwards. Animal forms, too, appear there in as full development, as to *size*, as they do in the analogous forms of existing creatures.

But the continuity which we do find is truly remarkable. As to *the uninterrupted maintenance of life;* from the time of its first creation, there does not appear to have been any break in the vast chain, till we reach the existing order of things: "no one, geological period, long or short, no one series of stratified rocks, is everywhere devoid of traces of life."[2] As to *the increase of species;* "although the older fossiliferous strata often contain *vast quantities* of organic remains, the *number of species* is much smaller than in more recent deposits."[3] Chiefly, as to *the succession of the vertebral classes;* notwithstanding the subordinate exceptions to regular progress we have noticed, the geological order in which we find them is that of an ascending series — fishes, reptiles, birds, and mammals. And, as to *the gradual conformity of the successive ani-*

---

[1] See Professor Sedgwick's Address to the Geol. Society, p. 2; and an admirable article in the Edin. Rev., July, 1845.

[2] Note by Mr. Phillips, in Professor Powell's Connection of Natural and Divine Truth, p. 309.

[3] Sir R. I. Murchison's Silurian System, p. 583.

mal creations to the existing types; "we find successive stages marked by varying forms of animal and vegetable life, and these generally differ more and more widely from existing species, as we go further downwards into the receptacles of the wreck of more ancient creations."[1]

3. The animal kingdom exhibits *physiological* continuity. Here, again, we employ the term continuity, only in a general sense, and as opposed to any essential departure from the original plans of animal function or structure. From the lowest *radiate*, up to the most complicated and perfect animal structure, endowed with digestive, intestinal, circulatory, respiratory, and nervous functions, a gradation may be traced of an easy, and, in some parts, almost imperceptible ascent. The types which represent the great divisions of the animal kingdom, exhibit points of resemblance; showing that they are all parts of one general plan. In the progress of discovery, species are often occurring which seem to fill places in the general classification which were previously vacant. Thus the numerous pachydermata found by Cuvier among the earliest fossil mammalia, enabled him to supply many intermediate forms which do not occur in the species of that order now living; the cetacea seem to occupy the interval between fishes and warm-blooded quadrupeds; and the ornithorhynchus between birds and mammalia.

It is not to be inferred from this representation, however, that the gradation of animal being is absolutely continuous and complete. Man, probably, will never succeed in recovering fossil specimens of all the forms of past creations. But even if he did, and if to these were added any given number of new species, the existing plan of animal life would find *room* for them all. They would form a *continuation* of the present system; not one of them would stand isolated. *Thus* interpreted, we have no objection to the doctrine of "the unity of organic composition." It was by a masterly application of it, in this sense, that Cuvier was able to supply from the fossil genera of former states of the earth, many of the links that appeared to be wanting, in order to connect the past and present forms of animal life as parts of one great system.

4. In our examination of nature, then, we have found, not only progression, but continuity — the only kind of continuity which we were led to expect—that which discloses the Divine

---

[1] Dr. Buckland's B. Treatise, vol. i. p. 113.

manifestation in the order of power, wisdom, and goodness; and we have found this graduated connection existing, not merely between the several stages of the advancing creation, but also, in various respects, between the multiplied parts of each stage separately considered.

V.

Activity. — Another of our laws is, that the animal structure and functions are *developed by regulated activity.*

1. "All parts of the animal body," says Liebig, "are produced from the fluid circulating in its organism. A destruction of the animal body is constantly proceeding. Every motion, every manifestation of force, is the result of the transformation of the structure or of its substance. . . . At every moment, with every expiration, parts of the body are removed, and are emitted into the atmosphere." Every part of the frame of a vertebral animal, for instance, circulates more or less rapidly. Its food circulates quickly in the fluids, more slowly in the flesh, more slowly still in the bones; but its life requires that every part should be in motion.

2. Besides which, as animals rise in the scale of existence, the systems of digestion, circulation, respiration, and sensation, bear a proportional increase; which is only saying that organic activity and animal perfection correspond with each other.

3. Again, an organ being given, its development or degree of perfection is regarded as depending on the extent and number of the uses to which it is applied. Thus the teeth, the special use of which is to triturate the food, to which alone by some classes of animals they are applied; are by the graminivorous class applied to the further office of prehension; and in the carnivorous they become, in addition, organs of attack.

4. Hence too, all those defective formations, formerly deemed mis-shapen or monstrous productions, or *lusus naturæ*, are now found to be occasioned, as in abnormal plants, by the irregular development — the activity in defect or excess — of some parts of the embryo, while the natural process was carried on regularly in the rest of the system.

5. And, in harmony with the locomotive power, and organization of the animal, the external world is adapted to call forth its activity. The senses, and the objects which excite them; the appetite, and the food which gratifies it; the passions, and the means of appeasing them, mutually operate to excite the

activity of the animal. And on the constant exercise of its functions, in conformity with their nature, its well-being and enjoyment depend.

6. Every stage and part then of the progressive and all-connected scheme of creation is found to manifest all that it is calculated to exhibit of the Divine nature, by developing or working out its own. Every being, every organ, element, and particle, is in constant activity. Much of this activity, indeed, is so subtle and rapid, as to defy our means of measurement and calculation; yet has every atom an appointed place, and obeys a definite law. And much of this activity may appear to be objectless; yet is everything acting its appropriate part, and answering a momentous end; for, here, everything is ever tending to realize the great end.

VI.

Development. — According to another law, *the same properties and characteristics which existed in the preceding stage are found to be, not only brought on to the present, but to be in a more advanced condition; in the sense of being expressed in higher forms, or applied to higher purposes.*

1. We saw that, while the plant, in obedience to the law of gravity, tends downwards, it rises upwards too. But the animal is able to resist this law so far as to maintain a variety of motions and attitudes at variance with its tendency; or even to rise, like the eagle, many thousand feet into the air, in opposition to its own natural weight. Many plants will bear a very limited variety of temperature; but many animals preserve an elevated and steady temperature, whether exposed to severe cold or to excessive heat; some will even bear exposure to the intensest cold of the Polar regions, without having their own temperature reduced even by a single degree. The plant receives its nourishment by a slow and nearly constant supply, and by being rooted in one spot: the animal is furnished with a receptacle into which it can receive at once a large supply of food; by which it is rendered independent of local situation; and enjoys the privilege of moving from place to place, and of selecting its food. The animal has all its organs of nutrition within itself; for, while the plant absorbs from the soil without, it is not until the food is deposited in the stomach of the animal, that the lacteals, or absorbing vessels, answering in their office to the *roots* of vegetables, imbibe nourishment. The

sexual distinction of diœcious plants is, at most, little more than an obscure intimation of the same distinction developed in the animal kingdom; where it is made the basis of the strongest sympathies, relations, and affections. The parent plant is constructed to provide the seed with that nutriment on which, when it falls to the earth, it may live during its germination, before the roots have sufficiently enlarged to absorb the moisture from the surrounding soil; but from the moment in which it is shed, its separation from the plant is complete. While, in the animal kingdom, the moment of birth is, in the case of some tribes, the commencement of a series of parental cares; some species continuing to *protect* their young; others, both male and female, uniting *to protect and to feed* them; while the mammal protects and feeds them *with food drawn from its own life*, and even continues to associate with them and to be mutually dependent, to the close of life.

The *excitability* of the plant is, as we have seen, succeeded in the animal by *sensibility* and *contractility*— that *passive* and that *active* element of animal life by which it is distinguished, not only from mechanical, chemical, and all other merely physical forces, but even from organic vital powers. For, in addition to the nerves of sensibility for conveying sensations to the sensorium, there are also nerves of motion for conveying the mandates of volition to the muscles.

2. These illustrations may remind the reader of the following admired passage in Coleridge's "Aids to Reflection:"[1] "Every rank of creatures, as it ascends in the scale of creation, leaves death behind it or under it. The Metal at its height of being seems a mute prophecy of the coming vegetation, into a mimic semblance of which it crystallizes. The Blossom and Flower, the acmè of vegetable life, divides into correspondent organs with reciprocal functions, and by instinctive motions and approximations seems impatient of that fixture by which it is differenced in kind from the flower-shaped Psyche, that flutters with free wing above it. And wonderfully in the insect realm doth the irritability, the proper seat of instinct, while yet the nascent sensibility is subordinated thereto — most wonderfully, I say, doth the muscular life in the insect, and the musculo-arterial in the bird, imitate, and typically rehearse the adaptive understanding, yea, and the moral affections and charities of man. Let us carry ourselves back, in spirit, to the

---

[1] Pp. 111, 112. 1st ed.

mysterious week, the teeming work-days of the Creator: as they rose in vision before the eye of the inspired historian of 'the generations of the heaven and the earth, in the days that the Lord God made the earth and the heavens.' And who that hath watched their ways with an understanding heart, could contemplate the filial and loyal bee; the home-building, wedded, and divorceless swallow; and above all, the manifoldly intelligent[1] ant tribes, with their commonwealths and confederacies, their warriors and miners, the husband-folk that fold in their tiny flocks on the honeyed leaf, and the virgin sisters with the holy instincts of maternal love, detached, and in selfless purity, and not say to himself, Behold the shadow of approaching humanity, the sun rising from behind, in the kindling morn of creation! Thus all lower natures find their highest good in semblances and seekings of that which is higher and better." This is the poetic but guarded language of a mind which more than "half creates that which it sees." No one could be more fully aware than its author that, in thus subjectiving nature, and allowing his active but trained imagination to speak, he was only *illustrating* a moral truth; or be less in danger of mistaking rhetoric for science.

The gradation of a plant into an animal, or of an inferior animal into one of a higher class, by any process of natural and necessary development, is a hypothesis requiring far other data. In preceding chapters it has been shown that development, in such a sense, is entirely unknown to fossil geology; and in the fourteenth and fifteenth chapters of this part it is made apparent that the hypothesis is at variance with the facts, both of geology and of animal physiology.

3. The facts which we have adduced, however, are sufficient to illustrate the law of development in the limited, but important sense in which alone we hold it to be true. We have seen that pre-existing laws are not merely brought on into each succeeding department of creation, but are there expressed in higher forms, or promoted to higher offices. The scheme of the Divine Creator advances and ascends. His last and greatest display virtually includes, and provisionally completes, the exhibition of all that had preceded it. His wisdom is the perfection of His power; His goodness, the provisional complement of both.

---

[1] See Huber on Bees and on Ants.

VII.

Relations.—Every part is mutually and medially related to the whole.

1. Numerous and complicated relations exist between the earth and every animal which inhabits it. The magnitude of the earth determines the strength of its bones, and the power of its muscles. The depth of the atmosphere determines the condition of its fluids, and the resistance of its blood-vessels. The common act of breathing, the transpiration from the surface, must bear relation to the weight, moisture, and temperature of the medium which surrounds it. The external form of every part of its body, and every organ of sense, relates to the properties of the objects around it. All its parts are created in accordance with the condition of the globe, and are systematic portions of a great whole.

2. From this it may be expected, not only that an adaptation will be found between the animal and the particular element of air, earth, or water, which it inhabits, but between it and the different states of the earth at different geological periods. Accordingly, the fossil remains of animals inform us, not only that certain races of animals, now extinct, existed at certain remote periods; they even reveal the prevailing condition of the earth during those periods, and the nature of the changes which it successively passed through.

3. May we not expect, then, if the relation be so close, that similar adaptations will be found existing between the animal and the region which it inhabits? They exist in abundance. It is this fact which explains to us, for example, the periodical changes in the plumage of birds, and the furs of quadrupeds, the migrations of animals, and the theory of their geographical distribution.

4. Nice adjustments are observable in order to preserve the balance between the different races of animals existing at any time on the earth. The produce of so minute a thing as a fly, if unchecked, would soon darken the air and render whole regions desolate. Had there been an error as to the grouping of the different races of any one period, there might have been a destruction of the whole. But, so nicely have all the varieties been balanced, that they have mutually conduced to the existence of the whole. Even the conflicting instincts of animals — as, of one to pursue and another to flee — are related parts of this whole.

5. A single living animal is the result of a system of relations. It is this fact which enables the comparative anatomist to infer from a single fossil bone, the division, class, order, and even species and habits of the being to which it belonged. *Ex ungue leonem.* To say that there is a perfect relation established between the bones and the muscles, or that everything remarkable in the outward configuration of an animal is always attended with some corresponding change in the anatomy, would give but an imperfect view of its organic relations. "With each new (animal) instrument, visible externally, there are a thousand internal relations established; the introduction of a new mechanical contrivance in the bones or joints, infers an alteration in every part of the skeleton; a corresponding arrangement of all the muscles; that the nervous filaments, laid intermediate between the instrument and the centre of life and motion, have an appropriate texture and distribution; and, finally .... that new sources of activity must be created, in relation to the new organ, otherwise the part will hang a useless appendage."[1] So perfect is this system of relations, that whatever part or function of the animal engages our attention, we feel inclined to conclude that the whole has been adjusted for that particular point. Though a thousand parts consent and conform to every single act, the nervous system, besides being the medium of sympathy among the organs, secures a consentaneousness of action among the parts, and establishes instrumentally a unity of consciousness in the individual being.

6. But more remarkable than all, perhaps, and the type of mysteries beyond itself, is that sexual relation, by which one entire being becomes the complement of another, and sustains a medial relation to all the generations of the same kind, from the first of the race to the last that shall exist.

7. Thus we have seen that the whole universe, organic and inorganic, presents a system of instrumental relations. The last effect of any particular kind, which the pre-adamite creation exhibited, was variously connected with the first of the entire series. The bare coming into existence of that first effect proclaimed a Cause; and the bare continuance of that effect, for a single moment, proclaimed a distant end; why else did it continue in existence even for that moment? Its continuance not only foretold an end, but announced that by means of all the intermediate effects which should instrumentally flow

[1] Sir C. Bell's B. Treatise, p. 180.

from it, it would be representatively present in that end, however distant—thus connecting the origin with the end of all things.

In a similar manner, each of the several kinds of effects in nature is found to be related to all the rest. The object of the Creator is ultimately one; and they all stand in the relation of means to that one end. Vast as is the space they may have occupied from the beginning, and ever widening as it may have been through each successive moment since, the Divine plan circumscribes the whole. Nothing wanders at large and unrelated in that immeasurable circumference. And nothing, once related, can ever break away, and reach a point beyond. Every atom is bound to the system as effectually as if it formed the centre of the whole. And the last and most finished specimen of sentient life that has come from the Creating hand, is variously related to that apparently insignificant atom. On no one point can we lay our finger and positively affirm, "Here ends one class of effects and begins another:"—this is the province of the Creator alone. The very partitions of nature are denoted by disjunctive conjunctions. Range where we will, we never find that we have passed into another sphere—a strange department of creation. There is, says Paley, "a certain character, or style, (if I may use the expression,) in the operations of Divine Wisdom; something which everywhere announces, amidst an infinite variety of detail, an inimitable unity and harmony of design." How obvious the inference, then, that no one science can be properly arranged, which does not provide for its relation to every other science. Philosophy, says Adam Smith, is the science of the connecting principles of nature.

VIII.

Order.—We may expect *that laws will come into operation on every subject of them, according to their order in the system of creation.* Were our knowledge of the physiology of the subject sufficiently accurate and minute, we doubt not that this principle would be found to hold good in every respect in which it could be legitimately applied; whether tested from the first moment of *embryonic life* to the birth of the animal, or from the first moment of *independent existence* at birth to complete maturity. At present, however, physiologists differ respecting many of the phenomena concerned, so that we could not rely on them either for argument or illustration. Thus, the view, that animals occupying the highest place in the scheme of organization present, at the commencement of their embryonic existence, a marked resemblance to that which is the permanent condition of the lowest animals of the same division; and that in the course of their progress to their own mature and distinctive form, they assume in succession the characters of each class of the division to which they belong, corresponding to their consecutive order in the ascending scale, would seem to promise a strong corroboration of our principle. Nor would the serviceableness of this view be much diminished, even if accompanied by the important admission, that at no period of embryonic development does an animal of a higher class resemble *in all its parts* an animal of a lower class; for, at the same moment that one of its organs resembles the corresponding organ in a lower animal, another will be found to resemble a corresponding organ in a much higher animal. But we cannot accept a view which rests, as we shall presently show this does, on very insufficient and doubtful data.

It is sufficient to find, however, that, generally, and as far as physiologists are agreed, our principle proves to be in harmony with fact. Does it imply, for example, that the development of the organic life would precede that of the animal life? The pulsations of the heart, the centre of the organic life, give the first indications of vitality in the embryo, while the sensorial functions are the last which attain perfection. Would it lead us to expect that the nutritive organs would be found to precede the reproductive? "The apparatus first perfected is that which is immediately necessary for the exercise of the vital functions, and which is therefore required for the completion of all the other structures."[1] Even the prior appearance of the spinal cord,[2] is no impeachment of our principle; for as it presents itself before the embryo has any life, or organs of life of its own, it can only be regarded as an extension of the parental life;[3] and to that life our principle does apply.

---

[1] Roget's B. Treatise, vol. ii. p. 540.

[2] According to Müller, the first trace of the nervous system is not merely that of the spinal cord or of the ganglionic string, but is the potential whole of that system, of the brain and all its appendages.—*Physiology*, vol. i. p. 20.

[3] Up to this point, the embryo cannot be spoken of as a separate existence. Even those organs which ultimately become single are said to be formed in halves; or to present, at first, a double appearance. They

And would it further lead us to expect that the nutritive process would correspond with the order of the same process in plants? From the *mechanical* operations to which the food is, in the first place, subjected, and the *chemical* changes which it next undergoes in the stomach, through all the intermediate stages, to that of absorption, the order of the process is the same in each economy.

IX.

Influence.—It may be expected *that everything will bring in it, and with it, in its own capability of subserving the end, a reason why all other things should be influenced by it; and for the degree in which it, in its turn, should be influenced by everything else.*

1. In our preceding illustration of this law, we saw the living plant decomposing the carbonic acid of the atmosphere, appropriating the carbon to the formation of its own juices, and returning the disengaged oxygen into the atmosphere; itself, meanwhile, influenced by the amount of the element present and subject to decomposition. We have now to remark that by this very process, the plant was not only rendering the atmospheric air more fitted than it was before for the support of animal life, and thus preparing for the support of a higher order of life while absorbing its own means of nourishment, but that it was preparing to become the food of that superior order of life.

2. Looking up the scale of creation, the highest order of being at any time existing is to be regarded as the relative end of all the orders below it.[1] This is its prerogative by right of its comparative importance, or of that greater power which it possesses of answering the great end of creation. But as all inferior beings possess a measure of the same power, and therefore, of the same right, their subordination to the higher is never absolute. It is regulated by the degree in

are individual; they do not yet form an individual. It is not until the halves approach, infold, and unite, that an intimation is given of a distinct system. At first, too, the formation is said to proceed from without inwards, showing the external dependence of the process; it is not until the order is reversed that an intimation is given of the approaching self-dependence of the animal.

[1] Liebig shows the closeness of the connection between vegetable and animal life, from the fact that "the *first* substance capable of affording nutriment to animals is the *last* product of the creative energy of vegetables."

which they can conduce to the well-being of that higher order of existence. This is at once the extent and the limit of their subordination. Hence, one of the nobler species no sooner dies, than he loses his *status* in creation. The lowest forms of animal life become his superiors, and prey on him. And even the physical laws regain their ascendency over him. So that in this sense, " a living dog is better than a dead lion."

3. The law now under consideration is recognised in all our natural classifications of objects. For it provides not only for the calculation of all the points of resemblance, for the subordination of characters, and for the arrangement of animals in natural groups, but also for the arrangement of these groups in an ascending series according to the degree of value or intensity in the leading phenomena of the animal economy. Indeed, the principle is recognised in that system of Providence which, while it " feeds the young lions," notes " the fallen sparrow," and " taketh care for oxen," is represented as apportioning its regard according as its objects are of lesser or of " greater value ;" according, that is, to the measure of the capacity which an object has to receive and exhibit the proofs of the Divine care, and so to answer the end of creation.

X.

Subordination.—Every law subordinate in rank, though it may have been prior in its origin, may be expected to be subject to each higher law of the manifestation.

1. Accordingly, we here find the productions of Wisdom subordinate to the exercise of goodness ; the vegetable sustaining the animal creation.

2. But this subordination is continuous ; extending into the animal kingdom itself. Each class of animated being is, generally speaking, food for those immediately above it in the scale of existence.

3. The same principle of subordination obtains among animals of the same species. For instance, if, as we have already seen, the perpetuation of the species be a later and a higher law than the preservation and enjoyment of the individual, we may anticipate that the earlier but inferior law will submit to it. Accordingly, numerous tribes, especially of insects, appear to live only to propagate their kind. And, among the mammalia, the parental instincts, while they last, subordinate every other. The " bear bereaved of her whelps" is reckless of her own life.

4. Nor is the law of subordination less traceable in the organization and functions of the individual animal. Indeed, here it asserts itself in a new and remarkable manner. For, as we have seen, while the primary object of vegetable germs appears to be the preparation of the functions of nutrition, the *primitive trace* of the animal structure in its embryonic state, is that of a part to which all the functions of vitality are to be placed in subordination; namely, the rudiments of the central organ of nervous power. The same early intimation of the ultimate supremacy of the organ of sight is given by the appearance of a rudimental eye, before any of the other organs of sense. — I say, the supremacy of the eye; for, if the value of the senses is to be estimated according to the degree in which they enlarge the circle of our objective perceptions, the order in which they would rank would, probably, be this — touch, taste, smell, hearing, sight.

5. But though intimation is thus early given of the nervous system, and of the higher senses, the order in which they come into active use is in strict accordance with our preceding law. For, the parts first perfected are those which are immediately necessary for the exercise of the vital functions. The heart, the *punctum saliens* of organic life, begins its pulsations while yet it resembles a mere tube; the sensorial system is perfected last. And, to the last and highest power of the animal — the power of volition — all the earlier functions of vitality are placed in subordination. To this, its organs of locomotion are subservient. And, when they are wearied, for this it reposes and sleeps, while the heart keeps vigil, and all the organic system continues at work; that, when it awakes, it may be able again to obey its volitions, gratify its desires, and resume its enjoyments.

XI.

Uniformity. — This stage of creation is found to be pervaded by the operation, and impressed with the regularity, of *general laws*. All these are doubtless contained in the Divine mind; for they are only the rules of that agency by which all animated nature is sustained in activity.

1. The uniformity of such activity, or the presence of such laws, is implied in most of the views already advanced. How else, for example, could we speak of the animal scheme? What would prevent one class of beings from assuming the form of

another, till the animal kingdom presented a scene of inexplicable confusion, if each of them were not kept within the limits assigned to it? Especially is this reign of law discernible in the arrangements of animal sensation. The function of each nerve of sense is determinate, and can be performed by no other part of the system. The optic nerve alone can give rise to the sensation of light; "no part of the nervous system but the auditory nerve can convey that of sound; and so of the rest." While it is evident that the relations subsisting between the nervous system and the external agents capable of affecting it, must be maintained by laws equally determinate.

2. Fossil geology shows that such relations have existed from the first appearance of animal life to the present day; binding the whole together as the successive parts of one great system. Paley has well remarked, respecting the variations observable in living species of plants and animals, in different regions and under various climates, that "we never get amongst such original or totally different modes of existence, as to indicate that we are come into the province of a different Creator, or under the direction of a different Will."[1] The philosophy of Dugald Stewart carries him a step further, when he acutely remarks, that the uniformity of animal instinct "presupposes a corresponding regularity in the physical laws of the universe, insomuch that, if the established order of the material world were to be essentially disturbed, (the instincts of the brutes remaining the same,) all their various tribes would inevitably perish."[2] Geology immeasurably enlarges the range of this truth. "Any naturalist," sagaciously observes Mr. Lyell, "will be convinced, on slight reflection, of the justice of this remark. He will also admit that the *same species* have always retained the same instincts, and therefore that all the strata wherein any of *their* remains occur, must have been formed when the phenomena of inanimate matter were the same as they are in the actual condition of the earth. The same conclusion must also be extended to the extinct animals with which the remains of these living species are associated; and by these means we are enabled to establish the permanence of the existing physical laws throughout the whole period when the tertiary deposits were formed.[3]

[1] Nat. Theol., p. 450. Chap. on the Unity of the Deity.
[2] Phil. of the Human Mind, vol. ii p. 230.
[3] Geology, p. 161. 1st Ed.

3. But while the uniformity contended for is essential, in order even that any reasoning respecting the past may be possible, it should be borne in mind that the same source which supplies the means of proving it, furnishes also abundant evidence of its interruption. Because no other physical laws than those which are now known to us have ever existed, it by no means follows that these have, in no sense, known interruption. Every destructive earthquake, though itself the result of general laws, is, in so far as it is destructive, a breach of that stability of nature for which the animal is made, and shows that such uniformity is not inviolable. While the successive appearance of races of animals, entirely unknown to pre-existing nature, shows that it is an uniformity as compatible with the addition of new creations as with the destruction of old ones.

XII.

Obligation. — Animal life exists under *an obligation to promote the end of creation, commensurate with its means and relations.* Here, again, obligation can be affirmed of the animal kingdom only in the same figurative sense in which all the kingdoms of nature are said to be governed by laws. The mind of the Lawgiver is the only conceivable seat of these laws; for they only and simply express His modes of operation. If, moreover, these created existences have been originated for a purpose, the mind of the Creator is the only conceivable seat of that purpose; for animal natures are only, at most, instinctive and impulsive. The mere proximate ends, indeed, for which they blindly live — their own conservation and the propagation of their kind — may be regarded by the imagination as a foreshadowing of a being capable of consciously aiming at a higher end. But of such an end the animal itself knows nothing. Whatever obligation may exist, therefore, to employ the means necessary for the attainment of the end, and to create and sustain the animal kingdom as a part of those means, can be binding only on Him with whom the purpose of their creation has originated.

The idea of this law is thus recognised and poetically expressed by Hooker: "The world's first creation, and the preservation since of things created, what is it but only so far forth a manifestation by execution, what the eternal law of God is concerning things natural? And as it cometh to pass in a kingdom rightly ordered, after a law is once published, it presently takes effect far and wide, all states framing themselves thereunto; even so let us think it fareth in the natural course of the world: since the time that God did first proclaim the edicts of His law upon it, heaven and earth have hearkened unto His voice, and their labor hath been to do His will. He 'made a law for the rain.' (Job xxvii. 26.) He gave His 'decree unto the sea that the waters should not pass his commandment.' (Jer. v. 22.) Now, if Nature should intermit her course, and leave altogether, though it were but for a while, the observation of her own laws; if those principal and mother-elements of the world whereof all things in this lower world are made, should lose the qualities which now they have; if the frame of that heavenly arch erected over our heads should loosen and dissolve itself; if celestial spheres should forget their wonted motions, and by irregular volubility turn themselves any way as it might happen; if the prince of the lights of heaven, which now, as a giant, doth run his unwearied course, should as it were, through a languishing faintness, begin to stand and to rest himself; if the moon should wander from her beaten way, the times and seasons of the year blend themselves by disordered and confused mixture, the winds breathe out their last gasp, the clouds yield no rain, the earth be defeated of heavenly influence, the fruits of the earth pine away as children at the withered breasts of their mother, no longer able to yield them relief; — what would become of man himself? whom these things now do all serve? See we not plainly that obedience of creatures unto the law of nature is the stay of the whole world!"[1]

XIII.

Well-being. — In accordance with another of our principles — *that everything will be entitled to an amount of good, or enjoy a degree of well-being proportionate to the discharge of its obligations*, or to the measure of its conformity to the laws of its being; we find that the well-being of the animal depends on its conformity to the laws of its own constitution.

1. The laws of its own being, physical, organic, and mental, are in conformity with each other, and with the laws of the external world; and, provided nothing occurs to disturb that

[1] Works of Hooker, by Keble, vol. i. p. 257.

harmony, its well-being is secure. If the germ form which it springs be perfect, and if its embryonic development be unimpeded, it will come into existence as a complete organization, sound in its whole constitution; but, if either of these conditions be wanting, it will be feeble and sickly, or else a malformation. If, from the first moment of its separate existence, it is supplied properly, as to quantity and quality, with food, air, light, and every physical element requisite for its support, the result will be a healthy development of its organs and powers, a pleasing consciousness of existence, and an aptitude for the performance of its natural functions; but the result of non-compliance with these conditions, will be a stunted growth, imperfection, or an early death. If it duly exercises its organs according to the laws of its constitution, enjoyment will be experienced in the very act of exercise, and appropriate gratifications be acquired; but the absence of such activity will result in the sluggishness and consequent derangement of the functions, together with the want of the appropriate gratifications, and with a sense of uneasiness or of positive pain. "The whole life of animals," says Liebig, "consists of a conflict between chemical forces and the vital powers. In the normal state of the body of an adult, both stand in equilibrium. Every mechanical or chemical agency which disturbs the restoration of this equilibrium is a cause of disease. Disease occurs when the resistance offered by the vital force is weaker than the acting cause of disturbance. Death is that condition in which chemical or mechanical powers gain the ascendency, and all resistance on the part of the vital force ceases."

2. But this animal well-being does not depend, in a mere general and indefinite manner, on conformity with the laws of its constitution, but is exactly regulated in its kind and degree by the nature and relative importance of the laws obeyed. Some laws were intended to be subservient to others. If they are so subordinated, they both yield their own peculiar kind and degree of pleasure, and instrumentally enable the higher laws to minister their superior enjoyment. If the law of appetite be limited to its appropriate gratification, the pleasure of eating is enjoyed; and, besides this, the animal is prepared for all the higher pleasures arising from muscular activity and the exercise of the senses. But if they are not so subordinated, though the higher enjoyment is lost, they do not, therefore, necessarily and at once, cease to be productive of their own peculiar kind of pleasure. By feeding inordinately, the ani-

mal may render itself incapable of higher gratifications, of even avoiding the attacks to which it is exposed; and may thus hasten the end of its life, and therefore, of this solitary pleasure of eating; still, while its appetite continues, it continues to enjoy the animal gratification which arises from eating.

3. Here, again, we are reminded of the ideal perfection to which we have referred in the corresponding sections of the preceding parts. The chances, so to speak, that no two animals of the same species have ever stood in precisely the same relations to the standard of absolute animal perfection, are here multiplied by all the additional laws, and all their possible combinations, which characterise the animal as compared with the vegetable economy. For the same reason, the chances are equally increased that no one animal has ever reached that standard. In the case of even that one which may have most nearly approached it, if certain incidents had been added to the myriads which had actually combined in its history, it would have approached still nearer to perfection. Its resemblance to the ideal standard is in exact proportion to its conformity to the laws of its being.

4. And thus we have found that everything in the vegetable and animal world has an end of its own; and that all such proximate ends are so placed in a line with the ultimate end, that everything answers it most effectually, by aiming at its own immediate end. The happiness of the creature and the glory of the Creator are thus seen to harmonize and become one.

XIV.

Analogy. — The relation of every part of the animal kingdom to every other part, as well as to all that had been created previously, suggests another of our laws, that *the whole is in analogy, or is arranged on a plan.*

1. Accordingly, it is found that, notwithstanding the almost interminable variety of animal forms with which the earth, the air, and the waters, teem, the whole are reducible to a very small number of types, or principal schemes of organization. Cuvier, as we have seen, limited these models to four — the radiata, the mollusca, the articulata, and the vertebrata. Take any of these divisions — say the vertebral — and it would almost seem as if, in its construction, a definite type or standard

had been kept in view; and to which, amidst endless modifications, all the species had been conformed. For, in many instances, where the greatest diversity might have been expected, this original type is departed from only just so much as is necessary for the purpose of adapting it to the destiny of the particular species; while, in other instances, where the greatest dissimilarity of size, and form, and habit, exists, the closest analogy to the type is still traceable. Thus, the longest necked mammalian at present known, and the shortest necked, have the same number of bones in the neck — the giraffe the same as the hog or the mole. And the bones which we recognise in the paddle of the turtle, are, by slight changes and gradations, adjusted so as to form the fin of the whale, the wing of the bird, and the paw, the foot, and the hoof of the land mammifers.

2. Instances of particular change are always accompanied by the corresponding readjustment of the entire structure. No limb, organ, or structure, is isolated. Every part conforms to every other part. "We are inclined to say, whatever part occupies our attention for the time, that to this particular object the system has been framed." Hence it is that the physiologist acquainted with comparative anatomy can infer from the fossil fragments of a skeleton — a mutilated bone — the entire structure and the habits of the animal to which it belonged.[1] And were all the bones of any geological period to be laid at his feet, he would be able to build up all their frames, "bone coming to his bone;" to reduce each species to its class, and each individual to its place, as harmonious parts of an all-related system.

3. This unity of design is further illustrated by the fact that the same parts which are fully developed in some classes, exist in others only in what is termed "a rudimental" state. Thus, a row of small teeth are said to exist in the lower jaw of the young of the whale, before its birth; but, as they do not rise above the gums, they are useless for mastication, and gradually disappear. "Rudimental" organs of this kind may have special applications, of which we know nothing. In the instance named, for example, both the coming and going of the teeth may minister to the pleasure of the unborn animal; in which case, there would be the same reason for the process, as we are accustomed to assign for the existence of the animal at

[1] Cuvier's Discourse, prefixed to his Ossemens Fossiles, p. 47.

all. Our knowledge must not be made to limit the creative designs. But even if such rudimental parts answer no other end, they indicate the relation of the species; they point to a type, and are suggestive of the general plan. And as man could know little or nothing of the Divine Wisdom, apart from the classification of created objects, here are some of the innumerable helps to the necessary arrangement.

4. This comprehensive plan of animal life, viewed co-existently, is still further illustrated by the recovery of the fossil remains of animals which have existed in successive states of the globe. They fill up the apparent blanks in the plan. Novel as many of these ancient forms are, they are never at variance with the order of the general system. Not one of them stands apart in isolation. The scheme is all-including; so that the strangest organization belongs to it, and finds an appropriate place in it.

5. Now it was only to have been expected that such indications of a great plan of animal existence would give rise to a number of hypotheses respecting both the mode of its production, and the principle of the classification of its members. Accordingly, by dint of overlooking some phenomena, of seeing others which existed only in the imagination, of occasionally exalting particular instances into general principles, and of torturing doubtful circumstances till they seemed to utter the language desired, various theories have been formed, and have flourished in succession; each being considered, for the time, a most remarkable discovery of science.

6. As to the mode of production, Lamarck took occasion, from the obvious traces of a scheme of animal life, to advocate, in his *Philosophie Zoologique*, the extravagant hypothesis of the transmutation of species; according to which, there was no distinction of species originally; but each class has in the course of ages been derived from some other and different class, less perfect than itself, by a spontaneous effort at improvement. Now the only reply which is really due to this fancy, falsely called philosophy, is the origination of some counter fancy, equally baseless, but equally aspiring to the honors of philosophy. If, however, the reply must needs partake of a grave character, it is obvious to remark, first, that while fossil geology exhibits abundant remains of distinct species, it presents no remains of any species in a state of transition into other species. Striking as the resemblance may be between any two species, still, what more can be said than that the difference is specific?

Short as the step may appear to be from the one to the other, it is an impassable chasm. And hence the same species is found, in many instances, to retain its essential characteristics through a long succession of strata, while, in some one of these very strata, new species come into view, not by a gradual change, but suddenly and completely; leaving it to be inferred that all other species have had the same independent origin.

On this subject, let us listen to the weighty testimony of Agassiz in his Report on the Fossil Fishes of the Devonian System, or Old Red Sandstone. "One of the first observations to be made on the ichthyological fauna of the old red sandstone is, that it is wholly peculiar to this formation; its numerous species differ alike from those of the Silurian system, and from those of the carboniferous strata; the greater portion of the genera, even of the Devonian system, are restricted to the duration of this geological system. . . . It is a truth which I consider now as proved, that the '*ensemble*' of organized beings was renewed not only in the interval of each of the great geological divisions which we have agreed to term *formations;* but also at the time of the deposition of each particular *member* of all the formations. For example, I think I can prove that in the oolitic formation, at least, within the limits of the Swiss Jura; the organic contents of the lias, those of the oolitic group properly so called, those of the Oxfordian group, and those of the Portlandian group, as they occur in Switzerland, are as different from each other as the fossils of the lias from those of the Keuper, or those of the Portlandian beds from those of the Neocomian formation. I also believe very little in the genetic descent of living species, from those of the various tertiary layers which have been regarded as identical, but which, in my opinion, are specifically distinct. I cannot admit the idea of the transformation of species from one formation to another. In advancing these general notions, I do not wish to offer them as inductions drawn from the study of any particular class of animals, (of fishes for instance,) and applied to other classes; but as the results of direct observation of very considerable collections of fossils of different formations, and belonging to different classes of animals, in the investigation of which I have been specially engaged for many years, in order to assure myself whether the conclusions which I had drawn from the tribe of fishes were applicable to this class only, or whether the same relation existed in the other remains of the animal kingdom."[1]

7. The advocate for the progressive transmutation of a species may be fairly pressed with the inquiry, why the essential *parts* which characterize every individual member of that species, have not exhibited any corresponding development. The eye of the extinct Trilobite, for instance, one of the most ancient forms of animal life, but which has not been found in any strata more recent than the carboniferous series, exhibits an optical instrument as perfect as that of any crustacean now existing. Now surely if the condition of any crustaceous animal of the present day is the result of a long series of improving transmutations from an inferior condition of preceding crustaceans, we may analogically look for a corresponding improvement in all its parts; and, of all its parts, especially in its characteristic parts; and, of these, especially in so complex an organization as the eye. But the eye of the earliest crustacean is found to be as perfect as the eye of the last living Serolis that was caught; leaving us to infer that the eye of this class has not depended for its structure on any preceding and progressive improvements, but that "it was created at the very first, in the fulness of perfect adaptation to the uses"[2] for which it was designed; and, further, that if such changes had not been necessary in order to account for the condition of the crustacean eye, neither have they been necessary to the present condition of that animal as a whole, nor productive of that condition.

8. The observations of mankind for thousands of years, have furnished no instance of a transmutation of species.[3] Exploded statements to the contrary are sometimes revived, and vague phenomena are, for a time, confidently reported. But on investigation it will be found, that all the imaginary instances of such changes may rank under one or other of the following heads, — supposed spontaneous generation, which is a thing distinct from the translation of species, and which will be presently noticed; or else a variation of the *individual* plant or animal, owing, not to a natural cause, but to artificial treatment to that effect; or else, that large class of instances which belong to an imagination more active than trustworthy, and not unwilling to be beguiled. But not one example of a trans-

[1] Twelfth Report of the Brit. Assoc. p. 85.
[2] Dr. Buckland's B. Treatise, p. 403.
[3] See Note F.

mutation of *species*, we repeat, has ever been witnessed or proved. Now if it be said that this is a question of time, and that the evidence wanting to-day may come into existence a thousand ages hence, we have only to reply, that if we are to wait for the phenomena, we had rather wait also for the hypothesis which proposes to explain them. Meantime, we may record our wonder, that parties who, on other subjects, refuse to believe anything in the absence of facts, evidence, induction, should here so readily dispense with them all as superfluities.

9. The hypothesis proceeds on the assumption that the propensities of the animal have determined its organization; that the structural peculiarities of a species have resulted from its prolonged efforts at something for which it was not originally adapted. Now, allowing this, it only remains for the theorist to explain what it is that determined the propensities of any given species. If, according to him, the organization, so far either from being one with the propensity, or from giving direction to it, has had actually to be conformed to it, whence then this pre-supposed, organizing, creative propensity?

10. In direct opposition to the transmutation of species, all the great changes of animal conformation which come under our notice are prospective; taking place, not in consequence of a new condition, but in preparation for it. Thus, the larva of the winged insect can only walk; but, if we take it and dissect it, just before its metamorphosis is completed, we find an apparatus in progress for flight through the air. The embryonic animal has a life adapted to its condition; but this life is subordinate to the formation of organs for a life after birth; and for which, during the whole period of gestation, it is unconsciously preparing.

11. Distinct from the preceding, in particulars, but aiming at the same end, is *the embryotic hypothesis;* according to which it is affirmed that the organic germs of all animals are identical, and that the higher animals, while in the womb, pass through all the successive conditions which, in the lower grades of animals, are permanent; that the quadruped, for example, is successively a fish, a reptile, and a bird, before it attains its permanent organic form. And the assumption which professes to account for these mutations is that of "an advance under favor of peculiar conditions,"[1] by which, at some time, a fish produced a reptile; a reptile, a bird; and a bird, a beast.

---

[1] Vestiges of Creation.

12. Now here again, we might remark, that as no such an advance has ever come under human observation, we might surely wait for the hypothesis, until the phenomena which it undertakes to explain are forthcoming. But as presumptive evidence of such an "advance" is supposed to exist in the embryotic changes referred to, we must not omit to glance at the nature of these changes. And the first remark proper to the subject seems to be this; the strong antecedent probability there existed, that marked resemblances would be observable between the yet undeveloped embryos of different classes of animals. Resemblance to some extent was inevitable, for they are all to exist in the same world; and the points of analogy would be multiplied in proportion to the analogous modes of their existence after birth. But prior to their birth, and while yet their ultimate differences were only in process of formation, their apparent resemblances would be the greater, the farther back we can carry our observations — resemblances implying chiefly the imperfection of our tests.

13. It is obvious to remark also the strong likelihood there was, on subjective grounds, that embryotic resemblances would be overrated, and that mere likeness would be mistaken for identity. The tendency of the mind to generalize and conclude on insufficient data, admits of abundant illustration. It was only necessary for Marsigli to affirm certain spontaneous movements in the round apertures on the surface of sponges, and Ellis persuaded himself that he saw the same and something more; and Pallas reported, without examination, the assertion of Ellis; and, for more than half a century, it was received as an established fact in natural history. And in a similar manner, it was only necessary for certain physiologists to point out fissures improperly called bronchial, in the fœtus of the mammal, and two or three other suggestive phenomena; and forthwith others imagined that they saw the gills of the fish, the heart of the reptile, and the brain of a number of animals in succession, in the same fœtal form; and others too readily gave currency to such reports as unquestionable facts. Now it ought to be sufficient to throw suspicion on the whole hypothesis when it is known, that these resemblances only relate to some one organ or part of the fœtus at a time; that the likeness is seen only by dint of refusing to see the difference; and that the difference to be kept out of sight relates sometimes to the fœtus, and sometimes to the object with which it is compared, — thus, the primitive streak of the embryo resembles

the zoophyte in which nutrition is performed by imbibition, but no notice must be taken of the fact that this rudimentary streak extends into a membrane which becomes the vascular area; it resembles a worm, inasmuch as it is cylindrical and has no limbs for motion, but no notice must be taken of the fact, that the worm has rings and contractile bands, for its motions, while the embryo has neither;[1] and its brain may be thought to resemble the brain of different orders of animals, provided only that a sufficient variety be summoned for the comparison, and that from these a selection be made at a "certain point" of fœtal development; taking care that such point be any stage of the development at which the resemblance may be thought to be most striking. "With what shadow of reason," asks Dr. Clark, in his Memoir on Fœtal Development,[2] "can any school of anatomists pretend to say, that one order of animals can pass into another order, in the way of ordinary generation, seeing that the indispensable respiratory fœtal organs are so different in each? The fallacy which allows for a moment such an absurdity to pass, is this — that, to serve their purpose, they describe their fœtus by its central portions only, and not by its whole mass, including its organic appendages, which are essential to its continued life, and its matured structure.

14. It is to be remarked further, that many of those physiologists who have looked not unfavorably on these progressive fœtal resemblances, have yet qualified their statements with such remarks as to make them perfectly useless to the advocate of the transmutation of species by ordinary generation. Thus Fletcher, in his Rudiments of Physiology, after speaking of it as "a fact of the highest interest and moment" that the brain of every class of animals appears to pass, during its development, in succession, through the types of all those below it, adds, "it is hardly necessary to say, that all this is only an approximation to the truth; since neither is the brain of all osseous fishes, of all turtles, of all birds, nor of all the species of any one of the above order of mammals, by any means precisely the same, nor does the brain of the human fœtus at any time precisely resemble, perhaps, that of any individual

[1] See Dr. W. Clark's Report on Animal Physiology in the Fourth Report of the Brit. Association, p. 114.

[2] Read before the Cambridge Philosophical Society, (1845). See also the second volume of the Poissons Fossiles of Agassiz.

whatever among the lower animals." Even if the resemblance had been substantiated, it would not have proved the truth of the hypothesis in question; but here the inaccuracy of the resemblance itself is confessed.

15. Beyond this, the *serial* character of the supposed development fails in the most essential parts. The first set of germinal membranes laid down are those of the organs proper to animal life, the nervous system and organs of motion; but, according to the hypothesis, they ought to be some vegetable resemblances. The first indication of the embryo is, as we have said, the *primitive trace,* the rudiment of a back bone, and of a continuous spinal cord; whereas, according to the hypothesis, it should have been something assimilating the embryo to the avertebral classes; but these three entire classes — radiata, mollusca, and articulata — are passed over without any corresponding fœtal type. As to the organs of respiration; at the very time when the lower vertebrates are quitting the ovum, and "when frogs and fishes are beginning to breathe by *bronchial tufts* and *gills,* other amphibia and birds are breathing by *allantoïd,* and never for an instant breathe by gills; hot-blooded quadrupeds are breathing by *allantoïd* and *placenta* jointly; while man is breathing by *placenta* alone." As to the heart of the fœtus of a mammal, "it does not pass through the form which is permanent in the amphibia, but it does pass through a form not found permanent in any known creature. This grand correction of an old mistake we owe to the concurrent labors of Valentine, Rathké, and Bischoff, who stand in the first rank of discoverers; and no good anatomist has pretended to contradict them. The hearts of birds and mammals do not, therefore, pass through forms which are permanent in fishes and reptiles." The development of the brain also is marked by corresponding differences; and the same is true of the individuality in respect to sex.[1] Indeed, it is only during the first beginnings of life, and while the organic structure is yet in its primary elements, that we are liable to be deceived by resemblances. But who would infer that because the far-distant mountain looked uniformly green, therefore only one kind of vegetable clothed it? And yet this would be only parallel to the inference that because there is a time when, owing to our imperfect means of discrimination, the liver and the lung are indistinguishable, therefore they are identical. As

[1] Dr. Clark's Memoir on Fœtal Development.

soon as ever organs begin to be distinguishable, the distinctions are found to be specific. And, as far as we know anything on the subject, these specific differences are constant and immutable.

In the attempt, then, to advocate the transmutation of species by generation, we have phenomena adduced, the existence of which physiologists disprove; as the basis of a hypothesis whose object is to explain other phenomena which, it is admitted, no one ever saw.

16. But, as if the foregoing hypotheses were not sufficiently indefensible already, each of them has to presuppose another hypothesis, in order to account for the existence of the first species, the hypothesis of spontaneous generation or production. By which it is meant, according to Buffon and others, that plants and animalcules make their appearance under circumstances where no germs could have existed, and that they are originated by a power inherent in certain material particles.[1]

17. When it is remembered, however, that most of the instances which were formerly relied on in proof of the hypothesis, can now be explained on ordinary principles, the natural inference is that an increase of knowledge will enable us to explain the residuary phenomena on the same principles. As to tenacity of life, it is known of some vegetable seeds that they will germinate after they have been kept for many centuries, and that such minute organisms as flour-eels, and wheel-animalcules may not only be reduced to perfect dryness, so that all the functions of life shall be suspended for years, yet without the destruction of the vital principle, but that in "despite of drying *in vacuo*, along with chloride of calcium and sulphuric acid, for twenty-eight days, subjected to a heat of 248° F., some of them have been observed to recover." And as to the subtle manner in which germs thus tenacious of life obtain access to the interior of living bodies, the probability is that they can enter wherever air can penetrate. The fact that minute infusory animalcules can be raised with the watery vapor, and floated for a season in the atmosphere, deserves, as Humboldt remarks in his Cosmos, to be well considered in connection with this subject; especially, since "Ehrenberg has discovered in the kind of dust-rain frequently encountered in the neighborhood of the Cape de Verd Islands, at a distance

[1] See Note G.

of 380 sea miles from the coast of Africa, the remains of 18 species of siliceous-shelled polygastric animalcules." And if entozoa — creatures living in the interior parts of other animals — have been found in embryos and in the eggs of birds; so also, says Tiedmann, have pins and small pieces of flint.

18. Is it not enough to cast suspicion on the hypothesis, that when experimental efforts to procure spontaneous production have resulted in the appearance of anything, it should have been a *full-grown* forest of confervæ, or an *adult* infusoria? These are certainly suggestive of pre-existing germs, and seem to presuppose them. But instead of the production of the more simple seed and egg, we have the complicated and developed individual itself. And that which further assures us that the individual animalcule has, in such instances, been derived from another individual of the same species as itself, is that its body has been found to be full of eggs.

19. Indeed, the revelations of the microscope were hardly more fatal to the Brahminical doctrine, that animal life should never be destroyed for food, than they were, in skilful hands, to the hypothesis of equivocal generation. As no stomach had been previously rendered visible in the smallest species of Infusoria, such as monads, Lamarck and others hastily regarded them as consisting of a mere homogeneous substance, having neither mouth nor digestive cavity, and as nourished simply by means of absorption through the external surface of the body. And here, it was conjectured, we saw an illustration of the natural development of a particle to a mammal, at that point of the process where the organism stands between the vegetable and animal worlds. But Ehrenberg, by supplying these microscopic species with organic coloring matter as nutriment, has demonstrated that their bodies are highly organized, "provided in all cases with at least a mouth and digestive system." Accordingly his arrangement of Infusoria is "based on the structure of the digestive system, which gives rise to the two natural classes of *Polygastrica* and *Rotatoria*."[1] Besides a digestive apparatus, Ehrenberg has discovered in them a generative, and often a muscular system. Both in structure and in functions, therefore, they are placed comparatively on a level with the larger animals. The blank which they were supposed to fill in the process of transmutation is left vacant. The only legitimate conclusion is, that the small-

[1] Jenyns's Report on Zoology, British Association, 1834, p. 244.

est of them is derived from an antecedent cause, as natural and uniform as that of any other class of animated being.

20. And this conclusion harmonises with the evidence of geology. Had spontaneous production, and the transmutation of species, been among the processes of nature, we might have expected to meet with abundant indications in the bosom of the earth.[1] The subterranean fossil museum might have been expected to be crowded with monstrous malformations. The fact is, however, that amidst all the vast accumulations of animal remains, not a single abnormal specimen has yet been found. Every organic part is finished; every animal complete, — the first of his race as complete as its offspring of the present day; every species articulating with every other species, and falling into the place appointed for it in a perfect all-comprehending plan. Accordingly, the verdict returned by all the enlightened geologists of the day — some of them by no means unduly biassed in favor of the view, is "that species have a real existence, and that each was endowed at the time of its creation with the attributes and organs by which it is now distinguished."[2] The following, therefore, are to be

[1] "There are some," says Cuvier, in his Discours Preliminaire to the Ossemens Fossiles, "qui pensent qu'avec des siècles et des habitudes toutes les espèces pourraient se changer les unes dans les autres, ou résulter d'une seule d'entre elles." But he naturally inquires, "Pourquoi les entrailles de la terre n'ont-elles point conservé les monumens d'une généalogie si curieuse?"

[2] Such is the conclusion at which Mr. Lyell arrives, after occupying the first four chapters of the second volume of his Principles of Geology, in a masterly examination of the arguments which have been advanced in favor of *transmutation*. See also De la Beche's Geological Researches, p. 239. In the same view, Coneybeare and Buckland, Philips and Sedgwick, concur; and to these might be added the names of a number of eminent physiologists. *Les espèces perdues ne sont pas des variétés des espèces vivantes*, is Cuvier's first proposition. "Does the hypothesis of the transmutation of species afford any explanation of these surprising phenomena?" asks Professor Owen, referring to the facts resulting from his anatomical examination of fossil animals: "Do the speculations of Maillet, Lamarck, and Geoffroy derive any support from this department of Palæontology?" and he shows that comparative anatomy returns a decided negative. While Agassiz, at the end of his great work, Poissons Fossiles, after rejecting the scheme of natural development, affirms, "It is necessary that we recur to a cause more exalted, and recognise influences more powerful, exercising over all nature an action more direct, if we would not move eternally in a vicious circle. For myself, I have the conviction that species have been created successively at distinct intervals, and that the changes which they have undergone during a geological epoch are very secondary, relating only to their fecundity, and to migrations dependent on epochal influences."

regarded as among the first principles of physiology; that even those species which most nearly resemble each other, exhibit characteristic differences; and that these characteristic differences are constant. So that however short the interval between any two steps in an animal series may appear to be, it is still in reality an abrupt transition.

21. Classification. — We have remarked also that the indications which are traceable that animal life is formed according to a plan, were likely to give rise to a number of hypotheses respecting the principle of the classification of the animal kingdom. Accordingly, some have fancied that if all the species could be collected and arranged, they would be found to form a cone or pyramid. Oken, and a German school of zoologists, contend that the animal kingdom is analogous to the anatomy of man — each class specially representing a division of the human organs, such as the articulate representing the *viscera*, and the vertebrata the *motive* organs. Kaup, and another school, extend the fancy to the representation of the "five senses." Mac Leay propounded the theory, which Swainson and others have subsequently endeavored to develop, that all natural groups, of whatever denomination, form circles; and that each of these circular groups is resolvable into exactly five others.

22. Now the error which appeared in the transmutation hypothesis, is here repeated in another form. There, because there is evidence that relations of animal resemblance universally exist, the method by which such resemblance is produced is unphilosophically inferred without evidence. Here, because such relations render the animal kingdom susceptible of some arrangement, it is inferred that the arrangement must be one of determinate numbers, or of geometrical forms. Such a hypothesis, however, has no warrant either in reason or in observation. It assumes a regularity, if not even an actual organization, in that which is only a mere abstraction, *the system of* nature. It loses sight of the natural irregularities of the inorganic world in all geological periods; for unless the strata of the earth had been formed as regularly as the concentric coatings of an onion, the relations of their organized inhabitants could hardly be expected to be such as to presuppose the square compartments of a museum. Indeed, as long as organic nature is influenced by inorganic, certain gaps in the former cannot fail to exist. To suppose the contrary would be to infer that in many cases whole tribes of animals have

been made, not with a view "to perform certain functions in the external world, but merely in order to complete the circularity of a group, to fill a gap in a numerical arrangement, or to represent (in other words, imitate) some other group in a distant part of the system."[1] But the Divine Creator has higher ends in view; nor can his mode of operation be thus prescribed, nor its results be predicted.

23. The true system of classification in the animal kingdom, as in the preceding kingdoms, may be supposed to be that which determines the affinities of animals according to the *order* and to the relative *value* of their distinctive characters. Thus, regarding the earliest as the lowest in value, we ascend to the organs of nutrition, each organ rising in value as the order advances; then to the organs of *reproduction* in succession, as of still greater value: and then to those of sensation and volition as of the highest value, including, of course, the development of the instinctive affections. So that the relationship is to be regarded as nearest, when the resemblance lies between those characteristics which are of the highest value.

24. According to this method, 1. the classification presupposes, in order to be perfect, a knowledge of all the physiological properties of animals; of the order in which the mechanical, chemical, and symmetrical laws come into operation in their constitution; and the order in which the nutritive and reproductive organs are developed. 2. The classification is made from a calculation of all the points of resemblance; none being arbitrarily rejected as unimportant. 3. It requires that each group shall be formed of such individuals only as resemble each other more than they resemble anything else, or, as have the greatest number of important properties in common. 4. It combines the principle of the *subordination* of characters — as of the vegetable functions to the animal, with the *coincidence* of the two; for it proceeds on the principle that each system is all-related, so that the one graduates with the other. 5. It provides not only for the arrangement of animals in natural groups, but also for the arrangement of these groups in an ascending series according to the scale of animal perfection; for it recognises degrees of value or intensity in the main phenomena of the animal economy. 6. And, as we inti-

[1] Strickland's Report on Ornithology before the British Association, 1844, p. 177.

mated when treating of vegetable classification, our method has become more obvious and certain in the present department, owing to the new points of comparison and the new means of verification consequent on the additional characters of motion, sensation, and constrained volition. And it furnishes the important test which arises from successiveness, or the order in which distinctive characters are developed.

XV.

Contingent. — Innumerable illustrations exist to show that *the arrangements of animal life are contingent on the Divine appointment.*

1. In calling attention to the complex adjustments between the animal constitution and pre-existing nature, we may be reminded that such adaptations were made indispensable by the previous conditions of the system into which the new constitution came. But we have seen that these conditions themselves exhibit no original and inherent material necessity, but were primarily dependent on the Divine volition. Whether, therefore, we regard pre-existing nature as designed in anticipation of the animal constitution, or the latter as simply adapted to the former, we have a new complication of the proof of a designing will. Even if animal life could be shown to be a necessary development of previously existing elements, still, as no one who admits that the properties and laws of the mineral and vegetable kingdoms were derived from God, would deny that He foresaw all such developments, they must be held to be a new illustration of the Divine intention. No one can imagine, for example, that the air produced the ear, any more than he can that the ear produced the air; or that the two, with their complicated and refined adaptations, exist together by accident. The light could not have produced the exquisite organization of the eye, any more than the eye, as an independent organization, could have anticipated the mysterious laws of light.

2. But while the idea of a necessary development of animal life is a mere assumption, the fact of the Divine origination of matter at first, is strongly in favor of the inference of the Divine origination of every new purpose to which it is subsequently applied. In harmony with this view, we find that the fossil *Fauna* exhibits no indication of a regular development of species from the most simple up to the most complex. Of the

four divisions of the animal kingdom, indeed, the principal, or vertebral, appears last; and, of this division, the four classes appear in the order of natural importance. But among the *species* of these classes, no such order is observable. For example, of the four orders of fishes, the oldest known fossil specimen belongs, as we have seen, to the highest order, and occurs in the Silurian rocks; while the two lowest orders do not make their appearance till we reach the cretaceous system. We might notice also the manner in which whole families appear, increase, flourish for a time, then decline, and finally disappear. In the tertiary series, too, we come suddenly on an almost entire change of species; and yet so complete was the plan or outline of animal life, even at that early period, that it requires no reconstruction, or essential enlargement, for the Fauna of the present day.

3. The directness of the Divine volition is to be inferred also from the ground there is to believe that animal life is more or less independent of mere external and pre-existing influences. That it presupposes the laws of the mineral and vegetable kingdoms, and is vitally related to them, we have seen. Animals involve, in their construction, certain functional references to the length of the day, and to the seasons of the year. The weight of the earth, the density of the air, the dimensions of the solar system, have been taken into account in the plan of their constitution. But, besides this system of refined adjustments between things so widely diverse, there are numerous indications that the animal plan involves other and higher arrangements. There is, for instance, a particular period of the year in which the reproductive system of animals exercises its energies. And the complicated operations of this system "are so arranged that the young ones are produced at the time wherein the conditions of temperature are most suited to the commencement of life." Now, that the young should appear just at the season when their food appears, is itself a striking instance of adaptation; but that the time for the *commencement* of the reproductive process should have been fixed with a view to this coincidence; that this commencement for the food having been fixed, say, at two months before, the commencement for the feeder should have been fixed at seven months before that, in order that both might fall due at the same time, this must be regarded as preternatural. The striking contrast between the embryonic development of plants and animals is also deserving of attention; for, while

"the primary object of vegetable structures appears to be the establishment of the functions of nutrition," the first indication of organic development in the animal embryo is a trace of the nervous system, a rudiment of an organ destined to subserve a higher order of life, and to subordinate the mere vegetable or organic life to its use. The definite and arbitrary manner in which peculiar organic distinctions and instincts are given and confined to certain animals, is further illustrative of the contingency of the system on the Supreme will.[1] Surely no one can imagine that there was an inherent organic necessity why all animals which chew the cud should also cleave the hoof; or, any physical necessity why the cell of the bee should be hexagonal, and the bee be the only insect that builds a cell of such a form.

Then, again, the very remarkable manner in which different nerves are endowed, not with sensibility in general, but each with a different kind of sensibility, demonstrates that this property does not inhere in them necessarily. The nerve of touch is insensible to light; the eye may be fingered without pain, for the optic nerve is sensitive only to light. Each part of the nervous system is an arbitrary and special provision for a definite purpose. Indeed, so long as it is evident that the material substance is not the principle of organic life, any more than the living principle is the material substance; and so long as it appears that no one organ is universal in the animal kingdom, or essential to the phenomena of animal life, so long must we recognize in the arrangements of this kingdom the operation of the Supreme will. And the fact also that animals can be trained to changes of food, and climate, and to the acquisition of new habits, evinces that, within certain limits, they possess a constitution independent of everything but the creative appointment.

4. And the same direct dependence of animal life appears from the want of coincidence observable between the conditions of animal existence and the succession of these existences. It can hardly be necessary to repeat our settled con-

---

[1] That the power which determines these distinctions is not dependent on external physical influences, " is ascertained from the facts, that ova belonging to species the most different are all developed according to their kinds, under similar external conditions; and that ova of the same species are true to their kinds, under conditions which are not absolutely the same for any two individuals."—Dr. W. Clark's Report on Animal Physiology, Brit. Assoc. 1834.

viction that the appearance of animal life has been made to depend on certain physical and organic conditions. But it may be important to restate, that it is by no means a consequence of this arrangement, that the existence of these conditions shall be invariably followed by the existence of the life. According to the theory of natural development, indeed, this connection is invariable, inevitable; for these natural conditions are supposed to be causes, and the only causes necessary to the production of life; so that if the new creation did not follow the new condition, the law of natural development would prove a fiction. Yet such apparent irregularities abound. For example, "as to the corals of the Silurian system, the Wenlock species certainly did not make their appearance in the calcareous beds of the Caradoc series, where similar conditions prevailed."[1] Again, certain families, the Nautilus, Echinus, and Terebratula, have pervaded strata of every age; why did the physical conditions of the secondary series fail to reproduce the Trilobites, as they did the Nautilus, both of which had existed together in the preceding series? Or what was there in the fishes — say the two orders of Cycloids and Ctenoids, which make their appearance for the first time in the cretaceous system, less suited to the temperature, and other conditions, of the preceding series, than in the Cestraciont family of that series to the conditions of the second and the third, throughout which they have continued to exist together even to the present day? Evidently, the physical conditions of life are essentially distinct from its causes, and could never have been unphilosophically confounded with them, but in order to serve a hypothesis. Add to which, the facts which fossil geology supplies, if they are to be admitted as evidence at all, are directly opposed to the theory of development. For while, as we have shown, the order in which the great vertebral *classes* come into view, harmonizes with the law of creative progression, the succession in which the *orders* of these classes make their appearance is, on the whole, in the reverse direction. Now if the succession of the classes favors the theory of natural development, what is to be inferred from the succession of the orders? It will not do to accept the one as evidence, and to put the other out of court. And then it is to be observed that, while the apparently different direction taken by these classes and orders may be perfectly compatible with the ope-

[1] See Note H.

ration of Divine appointment, and even intentionally illustrative of it, a single deviation from the supposed straight line of natural development, is entirely subversive of the theory.

5. From such evidence, the only conclusion at which we can arrive is, that in the animal kingdom, as well as in the mineral and vegetable worlds, the originating cause is the Divine volition. And if so, the time of its commencement, the varieties which it should include, the order of their appearance, their instincts and habits, and the geological and geographical distribution of the entire plan, are dependent on the Sovereign will.

XVI.

Ultimata. — If animal life be thus dependent on the Divine volition, we must expect to find that it will reveal *the existence of ultimate truths.* In the last stage, we found the mystery of organic life. In the present, we find the great mystery of sensation, the medium of enjoyment, added to the mystery of life. What is the principle of a *sense?* How is it that impressions on the nerves can speak to the animal of an external world? How is it that, by the aid of its nervous system, it can become acquainted apparently not only with impressions, but with things; with the forms, and qualities, and actions of objects? And what is the underived cause of all the phenomena which we denominate instinct, affection, passion, and animal volition?

1. There are those who have set about the vain task of resolving all the phenomena of sensation into the operation of physical agents; but one of the first discoveries they have made is, that they must be allowed to indulge in the slight inconsistency of supposing a principle not physical, in order to begin even to work out their theory. For a time, the *vital principle* was the popular hypothesis; but this was a principle which, as it did not belong to the domain of physics, was the very phenomenon which required explanation. Bichat preferred *animal sensibility* and *contractility;* and these words are as descriptive, perhaps, of what we believe to take place, as any that can be employed; but still they leave us to seek for the cause of the phenomena. And, says Lamarck, one of the most extravagant speculators on the subject, "I was soon convinced that the *internal sentiment* constituted a power which it was necessary to take into account." And, hence, Lawrence, in his lectures on physiology, while affirming that the same

kind of reasoning which shows digestion to be the function of the alimentary canal, proves that sensation is the animal function of its appropriate organ, adds, "if we go beyond this, and come to inquire the manner how, the mechanism by which, these things are effected, we shall find everything around us equally mysterious, equally incomprehensible."

2. Further, "it is useful to remark, that the ultimate laws of nature cannot possibly be less numerous, than the distinguishable sensations or other feelings of our nature, — those I mean which are distinguishable from one another in quality, and not merely in quantity or degree."[1] In relation to the phenomenon of color, for example, no evidence that some chemical or mechanical action invariably preceded the phenomenon, would "explain how or why a motion, or a chemical action, should produce a sensation of color." And the same is true of every class of sensations. Point out as many intervening phenomena as we may, we sooner or later come to a point where a principle is to be presupposed. In every attempt at explanation, we have to introduce the idea of some antecedent or other which produces the sensation. In other words, the sensitive process is not caused by sensation, but by some power which exists independently of the animal in which its effects are developed.

Here, again, animal life, like organic life, is to be viewed in relation either to space or to time. Regarded in its relation to space, the question arises, how came it really and objectively to be? We may trace the phenomena which it exhibits, from the adult animal to the embryo;[2] or from the animal of to-day through fossiliferous strata of every age, and through varying generic forms, back to the first form of its existence, but at no stage can we find that it contains anything to account for its origination. And could we have investigated the first animal form that breathed, we must have felt instinctively, that the reasons of its sensational existence at all and of that existence being what it was, were grounded alike in the will of God. And then, as to its relation to time; if the first moment of ani-

[1] Mills' Logic, ii. § 2.

[2] In his work on Physiology, Tiedemann remarks, "When it is said that organic movements are occasioned by external influences, we do not admit that they are the immediate effects of the external mechanical or chemical impressions; but we assert that they are the effects of powers which the external impression, be it mechanical or be it chemical, has thus solicited to act."

mal sensation revealed a benevolent Creator, the second moment revealed a benevolent or ever acting Providence, for that sensation continued. To suppose that because we see nothing more than the organic processes, therefore there is nothing more, is to confound the means of sensational manifestation with the thing manifested. Laws are not causes. Nor do the regularity of the laws denote the absence of the Law-giver. Rather, they demonstrate His presence. Nor does the continuance of the organic processes render them less dependent than they were at first — as if they could acquire self-sufficiency by the lapse of time. They are now what they were when they were called into existence; the mere means of the manifestation of an independent and anterior power.

4. And thus we have found that everything traceable to an ultimate fact, involves a mystery which points us silently but emphatically to Him whose Nature it is calculated to illustrate. That one class of physical phenomena — for example, the inorganic — is associated with motion only; that another class — the organic — is associated with motion and life; and that another class of organized phenomena is associated with motion, life, and sensation, is, substantially, all that we can learn. Why motion and matter, life and matter, or sensation and matter, should thus be found in union, can be explained by no physical law whatever. Here all the sciences are equally and utterly at fault. They cannot show that the union is necessary; but only that, as far as observation goes, the conjunction is uniform. They cannot imitate, but only proclaim it. Our theory affirms that the sufficient reason why activity, life, and enjoyment exist in creation, is that the same properties exist in an infinitely higher respect in the Divine Creator; that one reason, at least, why He *uniformly* associates each with a certain class of phenomena, is that, as the ultimate end of each is the manifestation of His Nature, such uniformity is essential in order to our attainment of that end; and that the mystery investing the union of each with a certain class of phenomena, is just that which necessarily attends the arbitrary conjunction of things essentially different — of Creative mind with created matter. The mystery would not, could not, be diminished, were activity, life, and sensation to be associated with any other class of material phenomena. And this very fact, by proclaiming the dependence of motion, life, and enjoyment on the Will of the Creator, promotes the ultimate end of creation by disclosing the power and wisdom, the goodness and boundless resources of His exalted Nature.

XVII.

Necessary truth. — The law of ultimate facts conducts us to *the law of necessary truth.*

1. We have seen matter take possession of space, and life take possession of matter; now, we find sensibility added to life. And whether we look at the addition as an object or an event, in its relation to space or to time, we cannot but feel that the idea of, at least, a *conscious* Creator is indispensable. The sentient object contains nothing in itself to account for anything more than the manifestation of its peculiar endowments; the endowments themselves authoritatively refer us to an independent cause; for to conceive of their absolute self-origination is impossible.

Or if, tracing back the existence of animal life historically, we conceive of the first of its kind, we are compelled to presuppose an adequate cause of that life. Nor can we then conceive of that Conscious cause as not existing. We cannot but conceive of Him as existing prior to all objective revelation, and independently of it. In the objective world we behold the manifestation of an attribute, which could not but have existed subjectively from eternity. This new stage of creation brings to light another of the necessary perfections of the Creator.

XVIII.

Change. — Once more we are brought to that point in our subject which leads us to speak of *the law of change.*

1. And, again, we have to remark that, in addition to the reason for expecting such a change derivable from the fact that it is involved in the very nature of a progressive system, the introduction of animal life brings with it an entirely new ground for anticipating yet another stage. But the question with which we have now especially to do, relates to the reason that made the time of the great change which brought in the human dispensation, the right time. For even those who, as we think, erroneously adopt the hypothesis of development by natural law, must admit that the Lawgiver would prospectively regulate the development of the law, for the same reason that the law itself was appointed.

2. Admitting, then, that the successive changes of creation have not hitherto taken place either accidentally or capricious-

ly, we have to advert to the reason of the next change which ended the mere animal economy. Now the event has declared that the new stage was to be distinguished by the creation of man. The advocates of development by natural law would infer, therefore, that as soon as ever certain natural conditions were present, man would emerge into being by an inevitable necessity; that the only reason for his appearance would be the concurrence of certain favorable organic conditions, independently of any Divine interposition. Now, while we freely admit that the time of man's creation presupposes the existence of innumerable conditions, organic and inorganic, and shall hereafter have to direct our admiring attention to the inconceivable complication of these conditions, we must protest more earnestly than ever against the attempt to confound created conditions with the Creating cause. For aught that geology can show to the contrary, man might have appeared at a much earlier period than he did, had it so pleased his Creator. The origin of many of the warm-blooded species around him dates from an earlier period; and who shall say that the mere natural conditions which their appearance presupposes were not adequate for the time of his appearance, if the Deity had so pleased? Were we confidently to affirm their adequacy, we should not be so unphilosophical as they are who argue that because an event cannot take place without certain conditions, therefore it must uniformly and inevitably take place with them.

3. While it is admitted, then, that, in harmony with the law of progression, the creation of man could not be expected to take place prior to the existence of certain natural conditions, whether or not it might *then* be expected, would, we believe, depend on what we have called the law of the end; or, rather, on the coincidence of the two laws. We have to ask, then, whether the ultimate end of the present stage of creation had, in any sense, been adequately attained? Does the long succession of animal worlds, including the present, exhibit all the illustrations of all-sufficient Benevolence, which, under the circumstances, might have been expected? Now if we can be content with answering this question inferentially and approximately — the only kind of answer which, in the present instance, our mental constitution and our data render possible — we can only return one reply, and that in the affirmative. If it should appear, for example, not only that the animal economy is minutely adapted for enjoyment, but that the complica-

ted arrangements of the inorganic and vegetable worlds were prospectively constructed with a view to that enjoyment; so that where before we saw only design we now see goodness also; if it should appear, further, that animal life has been successively modified, so as to be kept in harmony with the altered character of other kingdoms of nature; that this succession of changes has been, on the whole, a succession of enlargements, so that both the domains of animal life, and the degree of animal enjoyment, have ever been on the increase; and that every element, region, and situation, where life can exist, is crowded with animated beings, as if Goodness rejoiced to find, in the endless diversity of the physical conditions, scope for its own endless resources to meet them, and to convert them into new stores of enjoyment; what more can be necessary to evince the all-sufficiency of Creative benevolence?

4. Now that all these conditions are realized, and realized in a manner the variety and degree of which is inconceivable, is beyond all question. Animal physiology shows, as we have seen, that the ways in which the inorganic and vegetable creations were preconfigured to the requirements of animal life, are literally innumerable. Complicated though the laws, even of the first of these, were, to a degree which science probably will never be able fully to explain; the addition of the second complicated them still further; and, though the complication was again repeated in the addition of the animal economy, yet every one of them all then became, for the first time, a channel of pleasure. As if every element and law of the material universe had been selected, weighed, measured, and commingled, to form a vast apparatus for animal well-being alone, the whole combined to welcome the new made sentient creation, and to bathe it in enjoyment. And "the world, once inhabited, has apparently never, for any ascertainable period, been totally despoiled of its living wonders. But there have been many changes in the individual forms; great alterations in the generic assemblages; entire revolutions in the relative number and development of the several classes. Thus the systems of life have been *varied*, from time to time, to *suit* the altered condition of the planet, but never extinguished."[1] As we ascend from the first few species of the Snowdon slates, to the hundreds of species in the Silurian formations, and number almost

---

[1] Supplementary Note to Prof. Powell's Connection, &c.; by John Phillips, Esq., p. 309.

by thousands in the oolite, and by thousands on thousands as we pass through the tertiary, till we emerge amidst the hundreds of thousands of now existing species, we are struck not merely with additions but with changes. Species, genera, whole groups of animals, come in, and die out; to be replaced and followed by others in turn. Four times, at least, do these changes take place in the course of the tertiary era; and to an extent which leaves hardly a species of the first period extant among the species now living. Of testaceous creatures, for example, the conchologist finds about seven thousand living species. But of these he finds only one or two among the four thousand fossil kinds, by the time he has descended to the chalk formation. General analogies of structure and adaptation remain, but the species are all changed.[1] Of fishes, the carboniferous, oolitic, and chalk formations, present respectively an entire change of genera. Agassiz, who enumerates seventeen hundred species of fossil fishes, and about eight thousand living species, states that, with the solitary exception of a species found in the nodules of claystone, on the coast of Greenland, and which is probably a modern concretion, he has "found no animal in all the transition, secondary, and tertiary strata, which is specifically identical with any fish now living."[2] Indeed, not a single species of fossil fishes has yet been found that is common to any two great geological formations.[3]

5. The evidence, however, that animal life, once introduced on the earth, has been continued through immeasurable periods, and not only continued, but enlarged, and not only enlarged but changed again and again for new systems of life — though sufficient of itself to establish the power of the Deity to impart unlimited sentient enjoyment — we have the means of increasing to any amount. As to the wonderful diversity of animal *sizes*, we might begin with Ehrenberg's polishing slate, formed of infusoria, of which about 41,000 millions are contained in a cubic inch; or still lower with the animalcules of the Raseneisen or iron-clod, of which a cubic inch contains about a billion; and we might show them ranging through all the intermediate degrees up to the crocodilean Megalosaurus of fifty or seventy feet in length, or to the Dinotherium giganteum, the largest of all terrestrial mammalia yet discovered. We might

---

[1] Lyell's Prin., iii. 369—373. Fifth Edit.

[2] Poissons Fossiles, Tom. i. pt. xxx., T. iii. p. 1—52.

[3] Dr. Buckland, vol. i. p. 273—277.

speak of the vast variety of animal *forms*; but, of these, the mind is apt to fix only on the more strange and striking — the heavy-armed megatherium, the large-eyed ichthyosaurian, the colossal lizard iguanodon, the long necked plesiosaurian, and the still more monstrous bat-winged pterodactyle — and to overlook the ten thousand ordinary forms of animal life; while to think of the internal structures suggested by, and answering to, all these forms, is to be absolutely overwhelmed. Adverting to *the multiplication of life* characteristic of some species, we might point to the remarkable fact that the creatures commonly referred to as the smallest in size, should be those which, by their rapid increase, present themselves in the most amazing masses. Thus the Monadæ, the smallest of infusoria, form, by accumulation, subterraneous strata many fathoms in thickness. The mountain limestone, about a thousand feet thick, and often many miles in length and breadth, consists of nothing else than the remains of coralline and testaceous forms compressed into hard masses.[1] In relation to animal *fecundity*, it is enough to refer either to parts of the Greenland seas so swarming with medusæ that, as it has been curiously calculated, in a cubic mile the number is such that, allowing one person to count a million in a week, it would have required eighty thousand persons, from the creation of the world, to complete the enumeration; or to the hotter zones of the earth, where, between the tropics, many thousand square miles of ocean teem with light-engendering life; and, of "the wide level glowing with lustrous sparks, every spark is the vital motion of an invisible animal world." Of the *universality* of animal life we shall speak again; for the present it may be sufficient to state, generally, that, from the floor of the ocean, where its depths surpass the height of our loftiest mountains, every successive stratum of waters is crowded with its own orders of life; and that from the sea-shores where the innumerable hosts of light flashing mammaria "turn each wave into luminous foam," up through every stage of ground rising to the line of eternal snow, animal life is adapted to every part, and is diffused over the whole.

6. Here, surely, is evidence more than adequate to attest

[1] There is now considerable evidence that the vast deposits spoken of here and in the preceding page, and supposed by Ehrenberg to consist of infusorial remains, should be referred to the vegetable kingdom. This circumstance, however, does not prejudice the train of thought which led to the reference. Other illustrations of it might be easily summoned.

the sufficiency of Divine benevolence for *the same kind* of sentient enjoyment to any possible extent. That the display, boundless as it is to us, is not absolutely infinite, is admitted, for such a display is an impossibility; and, if possible, would be utterly useless to man as a proof of infinite goodness. That the display, indefinite as it is to us, might be more extended still, inasmuch as the planet itself might have been more extended, is admitted, and the same might be said, and would be true, even though the enlargement should advance for ever. But the question is, whether the existing display of the Divine resources is not sufficient to warrant the conviction, that, even in the event of such enlargement, Creative Benevolence would be more than adequate to replenish the whole with enjoyment; that though the largest material area must be necessarily limited, the goodness of God could fill the whole, and show itself unlimited? Now, no one can doubt, judging from the proofs we possess, the adequacy of the divine resources for an ever increasing exercise of the same kind of benevolence to any extension of space or of time. But, if the design of the animal creation be to illustrate, in the sense explained, the all-sufficiency of the Divine goodness, we must admit, that not till the evidence of such sufficiency was complete, could the appropriate time for man's creation have arrived.

XIX.

Reason of the Method.— Respecting the *reason* of the Divine method in creation, we have again to remark that it is twofold; *relating, partly, to the constitution of the creature by whom the method is to be studied, and involving his well-being; and partly to his destiny, as a being capable of voluntarily promoting the great end of creation, and so involving, in addition, the glory of the Divine Creator.*

1. In illustration of the first part, it would be easy to show, were this the proper place, that there is not one of the laws of the method to which our attention has been directed, which is not indispensable. Thus, by placing the animal in universal relation to the inorganic and vegetable kingdoms, and by expressing this complicated relation with all the constancy and regularity of law, the Creator was but saying, in effect, in reference to man, Let his domestication of animals and their subserviency to him, be possible. And so also in constructing the animal economy according to a plan, He was, in effect, deter-

termining that comparative anatomy, and animal physiology, should be possible to man. The training and government of animals are among man's first lessons on the art of self-government, especially in the pastoral and agricultural states of society, while their habits and instincts are full of instruction, and the sights and sounds with which they enliven creation are perpetually appealing to his emotions.

But, then, if man is to be educated and benefitted by this stage of the Divine procedure, a medium must be observed between a disheartening depth and diversity in its laws, on the one hand; and a tame, unexciting superficiality and sameness, on the other. The effect of the former extreme would be, that the volume of nature would never be opened; and the result of the latter, that it would be shut almost as soon as opened. Now that such a medium is observed, is evident from the event. The zoology of nature is, ordinarily, the first book that engages the attention of childhood, and stimulates its opening efforts at comparison. It was the book from which the father of the human race received his "first lessons on objects."[1] And though from that time to this, man has been exploring its pages, yet, so far from being exhausted, it never engaged so much attention as it does at present, nor so filled the student with the conviction that it is inexhaustible. But it addresses only the attentive eye and the willing ear. For the observant and comparing eye of an Aristotle,[2] it has still unnumbered facts awaiting the right arrangement, and laws admitting of illustration to an indefinite extent. And for the listening ear, it is ever uttering new Æsopian fables, and each with a weighty moral; but only for the listening ear.

2. The second part of the reason is equally self-commending; for if animated nature is to be so construed by man as to subserve the ultimate end of creation, all the laws which we have pointed out as belonging to the method of the Divine procedure are, in one respect or another, indispensable. They have made the manifestation of the Creator possible. We cannot, indeed, conceive of his operations, except as activity according to law; for He is "the God of order." So that in embodying law, and making it visible, He is saying, in effect, Let the knowledge of the Lawgiver be possible. In imprint-

[1] Gen. ii. 19, 20.

[2] Conformity of structure is the leading principle of his classification of animals, in his work, περὶ Ζώων Ἱστορίας, as well as of Cuvier in his Le Règne Animal.

ing certain signs of dependence on animated nature, He is, in effect, leading up our minds to His own independence. The manner in which He has been pleased to add sentient enjoyment to organic life, is studiously adapted to remind us that the addition was by no means inherently necessary; but that everything relating to the mode of its manifestations, to the extent of the animal kingdom, and to its progressive filling up, are all referrible to His own purpose. So also of the selected and prepared variety of natural productions which awaited the coming of man; "till that variety was occasioned on the globe, it was not the fitting place for intellectual man that it now is. For, surely, among other uses and correlations of the visible creation, this is one—by its inexhaustible diversity, and ever-growing newness, to interest with a perpetual charm the growing mind of a rational being, and to lead him to the cultivation of the divine thing within him, which raises him above all that his senses make known; and thus to fit him for the highest contemplation of which he is capable; namely, the relation which he bears to the unseen AUTHOR of all this visible material world."[1]

3. Here again, however, the means must be measured, and the evidence balanced between two extremes. The signs of the Divine presence and agency must be sufficient for conviction, but not for compulsion. Accordingly, every law has its apparent exception; and every phenomenon its centre or circumference of difficulty and mystery. The uniformity of nature holds on its way, leaving man to infer its Divine origination and superintendence, or, if he will, to "explode the hypothesis of a God." The evidences of design are inexhaustible; but if man chooses to call certain things which his 'knowledge but of yesterday' fails at present to explain, defects, no coercive power restrains him. Proofs of the Divine goodness are lavished around him; but if he is pleased to infer that the conflicting instincts of animals, and animal death, are incompatible with goodness, though forming, in fact, a provision for securing the greatest amount of sentient enjoyment—he is at responsible liberty to do so. The laws of nature are not audibly proclaimed from Sinai; though, to the apprehensive mind, every object is a table of stone, written over with the finger of God. Nature is a volume which is "open night and day," and he that runneth may read. But while to one the

---

[1] Professor Phillips.

very first page is gloriously inscribed with the great name of the Author, to another every page is a blank; for it is written throughout as with sympathetic ink.

XX.

The ultimate end.— The laws of *the method, and the reason of it, find their end,* in relation to the present stage of the Divine procedure, *in contributing to illustrate the all-sufficiency of the goodness of God.*

1. In harmony with the view already propounded, that each preceding display of the Divine perfection may be expected to be brought forwards and enlarged in each successive stage of creation, we have to remark on the continued exercise of the power of the Deity. During the whole of the period now under consideration, the forces of inorganic nature continued, as far as we know, in full activity. The celestial mechanism was ever in motion. On our own planet, the gradual uprising of the Carpathians, the Pyrenees, the Alps, and other mountain chains, showed the unspent activity of the subterranean forces. While the regular reproduction of organic life after each geological change, and on the return of every season, went on augmenting the proofs of the all-sufficiency of the Divine Power. But here were now new displays of the same energy. It originated and sustained the new principle of animal life in all its endless varieties of organization. Life by no means necessarily results from any of these varieties. And hence it is that no organ is universal in the animal kingdom. Uniform, therefore, as the connection may be between animal organization and animal life, the former is necessary to the latter, not for its existence, but only for its exhibition. And the more complicated the organization, the richer the illustration supplied of the energy of the great originating Cause. The single property of muscular contractility, adapted and employed as it is by the Divine wisdom, converts the breathing frame into a system of animal mechanics of prodigious power and incessant activity. But in order to form an idea of the display of energy added, by this stage of creation, to all that had gone before, we should be able to multiply the average strength of each animal engine by the average number of myriads living at any one time, and these again by the myriads of ages which have elapsed since animal life commenced.

2. And here again Power is seen subservient to Wisdom;

presenting its vast resources as means for the accomplishment of important ends. In the first stage, for instance, we saw that air was the great agent in the changes of meteorology; in the second, we saw every leaf of the forest feeding on it; and now we find it discharging additional offices, as the breath of animal life, and the vehicle of sound. Thus, at every step, our views of the prospective arrangements of creation acquire a wider range, and the proofs of Design become more complicated and profound. Again: we saw that the atmosphere is composed of different kinds of air, and that these again are of different densities. What then will take place when two or more kinds of air are brought together? will not the heavier subside, and the lighter ascend, like oil floating on water? The analogy of gases to liquids would lead us to expect this. But the "principle of gaseous diffusion," as it is called, determines otherwise. Two kinds of air — say hydrogen and carbonic acid, which latter, bulk for bulk, is twenty times heavier than hydrogen — cannot be in contact without melting away into each other, and becoming uniformly mixed. Is any end to be answered by this remarkable law? Is it a provision? Now that the animal kingdom is come, if not before, we can reply to the inquiry. If the heavy carbonic acid of the atmosphere, copiously generated as it is from a variety of sources, had simply obeyed the law of gravitation, and rested on the surface of the earth, animal life would have been poisoned in its birth. If the whole were collected into a bed or layer, it is calculated that it would surround the surface of the earth with a stratum of about thirteen feet in thickness. In this irrespirable all-encircling ocean, life would be impossible. But the law of inter-diffusion is always in silent operation, obviating the evil. By it the most noxious exhalations are diluted, and made innocent. And thus — not by a chemical action of the gases on each other — but by simple mixture, by an aërial mechanism, a world of life and happiness exists, where else there would have stagnated and slept an ocean of death.

3. What is the form or figure to be given to a solid body, of certain dimensions, in order that it may move through the air or water with the least resistance? Mathematical reasoning of a very abstruse nature determines that it must be a curve. But the curve-like face or front of fishes anticipates the discovery, and shows their adaptation, on mathematical principles, for most easily moving through the element they were made to live in. The art of ship-building has reached its present per-

fection as the result of many corrections, improvements, and slowly-matured devices. They are all forestalled in nature;— the boat-like figure; the paddle-shaped levers, and their successive impulses; the rudder-like tail; the sail-like membrane, hoisted or furled, with ease, for scudding before the breeze. The valves by which the maker of a hydraulic engine prevents the retrograde motion of the fluids which are to pass through particular parts, were performing their functions in the animal economy before man was made. Long-continued mathematical and chemical experiments have led to a succession of improvements in the instruments of the optician; but on comparing each, in succession, with the eye, they are found to be all there; together with a number of provisions — exquisite refinements of provision — unknown to man's imperfect workmanship, and by which the refracting powers of the eye are instantly adjusted to the different distances of the objects viewed, the organ is rendered achromatic, is protected, kept clean, and moved in various directions. The engineer makes his axles and various parts of his machinery hollow, for it has been discovered that hollow rods and tubes, of the same length and quantity of matter, have more strength than solid ones. The bones of animals are all more or less hollow; and thus attain the end of the greatest strength with the least weight and quantity of matter. In the bones of birds, this principle is remarkably exemplified, as well as in the construction of their quills; and thus they are adapted for flight. But, in addition, in distinction from all other animals, the air vessels of their lungs communicate with the hollow parts of their bodies, enabling them to blow out their bodies as we do a bladder, and thus to rise and to regulate their flight. The air-bladders of fishes answer a similar purpose. Mathematical reasoning demonstrates that if it be proposed to fill a certain space with the greatest number of little cells, all of the same size and shape, there are only three shapes which will answer; and that, of these, that which combines the greatest convenience with the greatest strength, is the figure of six equal sides. Now this is precisely the shape of the cells of bees, by which they effect the greatest possible saving both of room and of material. But more; the higher parts of algebra enable the mathematician to prove that, to save the most room, and to give the greatest strength to the cell, the roof and the floor must be made of three square planes meeting in a point; and that there is one particular inclination of these planes to each other where they meet, which effects a greater saving of material and of labor than any other inclination could effect. Thousands of years before the mathematician had slowly and abstrusely worked his way to this conclusion — a conclusion of which Newton was ignorant, though it is one of the fruits of his most wonderful discovery — the bee was acting in harmony with it in every cell which it made. As far as we know, the beaver builds his dam on principles as mathematically correct, to give the greatest resistance to the water in its tendency to turn the dam round, as the bee its cell.[1] But the illustrations of Creative wisdom, in the animal kingdom, are endless. Every page of science teems with them.

4. The particular and proximate ends attained in the animal economy are innumerable, and yet all related. For example: there is hardly a bone which has not a constitution of its own, or a disposition of its material specifically adjusted to its place and use; there is not one of these which is not formed in relation to the whole individual structure to which it belongs; there is not an individual structure which is not formed in relation to the entire scheme of animal organization; while that scheme itself exists in close relationship to the whole circle of external nature. Still more are we impressed with the resources of Creative wisdom when we reflect, that while the admission of a single new principle into a complicated machine is attended with results which the utmost ingenuity can hardly anticipate, the indescribable variety of form and condition in which animal life seems to revel is the result of a principle endlessly diversified, as if for the sole purpose of showing that the difficulties created can be overcome. We might instance the various modes of reproduction, gemmiparous and gemmuliparous, fissiparous and oviparous, marsupial and viviparous; and the diversified kinds of locomotion. The number of distinct species of insects already known is about a hundred thousand; but while every species differs from all the rest, conformity is preserved throughout the whole to the same general plan of construction. Even when the purpose to be attained is identical, the means which are employed are inconceivably diversified, and although this diversity has to be carried through the minutest parts of the organization, yet every structure, from the most simple to the most complicated, is alike finished,

---

[1] See the admirable Preliminary Treatise of the Library of Useful Knowledge, on the Objects, Advantages, and Pleasures of Science.

and perfectly adapted to its destined condition. And when we find, in addition, that all this variety of mechanical contrivances, chemical agencies, prospective arrangements, compensations, and comprehensive inter-dependencies, is the development of a scheme which embraces the whole range of zoology; and that even when no other end appears to be answered by any part of the process, it has, at least, a direct application in filling up a place which would be otherwise unoccupied in the all-comprehending system, we almost involuntarily confess to the boundlessness of the Creative wisdom.

5. But here, both Power and Wisdom are seen in subservience to Goodness. The results of the preceding stages of creation are brought on to the present. So that on looking back from this advanced position, we can now see goodness, where before we beheld only wisdom and power; for we perceive that both the productions of power, and the arrangements of wisdom, waited to find their places in the service of Benevolence; that when Omnipotence was laying the foundations of the earth, and Infinite Wisdom was rearing the superstructure, it was only that Goodness might have a theatre in which to display its inexhaustible resources of animal enjoyment.

6. Now what are the conditions on which the conclusion — that animated nature is calculated to illustrate the all-sufficiency of the goodness of God — might be reasonably accepted? The most obvious and general of these seems to be, that the tendency of animal life should decidedly preponderate in favor of enjoyment. The monuments of power and skill are to us infinite. Had the amount of animal suffering borne any proportion to them, or had it been nearly balanced with animal enjoyment, we might have hesitated as to the Benevolence of the Creator, in this particular. But the tendency to suffering as compared with the immensity of his works, is quite as small as the proportion of cases in which design is undiscoverable is to those of acknowledged contrivance. So evidently and so designedly is the tendency of animal existence in favor of enjoyment, that it can only be accounted for by referring it to Divine Benevolence. "Contrivance proves design," says Paley,[1] "and the predominant tendency of the contrivance indicates the disposition of the designer. The world abounds with contrivances; and all the contrivances which we are acquainted with, are directed to beneficial purposes."

---

[1] Moral Phil., p. 51.

7. But if this representation be correct, we may expect that a Benevolent Being will create as great a number of animals as possible, consistently with other claims, in order that the amount of enjoyment may be the greater. And, as the same kind of animal could only exist in one condition, and yet the conditions of external nature are exceedingly diversified, we may expect, for the same reason, that different races will be created for different conditions; so that the means of happiness may be improved to the utmost. And, as the amount of animal life might be vastly increased, if a portion of the food required could be animated and happy till it is wanted as sustenance, we may expect, that, if consistent with goodness, life will be thus conditionally granted to it. Now all these conditions are found to be fulfilled on a most magnificent scale.

As to the existing *numbers* of the animal kingdom, more than a thousand species of quadrupeds, five thousand species of birds, and as many of fishes, are now known to naturalists. Of reptiles, the number and variety are immense but unknown. "The species of shell-fish or testacea, crustaceous animals, worms, radiated animals, and zoophytes, which almost cover the bottom of the vast abyss, exceed all calculation. The forms of animalcules vary in almost every infusion of vegetable or animal matter which nature presents." Nine hundred species of intestinal worms have already been extracted from the bodies of animals, and even some of these worms have parasites within them. And of insects, a hundred thousand species are known. But the number of *species* affords but a faint idea of the incalculable myriads of individuals which some of them include. Vast flocks of birds sometimes darken the heavens like an eclipse. Clouds of life float in the atmosphere. Immense tracts of the ocean are often colored by medusæ, or covered as with a sheet of fire. Every drop of the ocean, from pole to pole, teems with existence. "These all wait upon thee, O God; and thou givest them their meat in due season."

Nor is any part of the surface of the globe untenanted. The tropical desert, and the arctic sea, the stagnant marsh, and the deep sands of the ocean, the mud and the rocky strata, the subterranean cavern and the eternal hills of Polar ice, not less than the temperate clime, and the open and undulating plain, are full of animal existence. The malaria fatal to one race is the necessary condition of life to another. Where one species terminates its range of enjoyment, another begins. Desolation owns not a foot of the globe.

To increase the amount of happiness still further, not only is a large proportion of the food of animals endowed with life; some exist entirely on ova, and on the rapidly multiplied embryos of others, thus preventing their injurious increase; some on the excreted matters of the skin; and some, not only on, but *in* others, inhabiting the organs and secretions of the interior, to the mutual advantage, probably, of both kinds. One of the ends of the Divine arrangement of the animal kingdom evidently is, the production of the largest amount of life and enjoyment.

8. But if every element, region, and situation where life can exist is to be thus crowded with animated beings, the same animal conformation would be so ill adapted for many of these external conditions that life and wretchedness would mean the same thing. The benevolence of the Creator, therefore, may be expected to find scope in adapting the animal to its condition. Accordingly, these adaptations exist; and so numerous, varied, and minute are they, as to defy description. If we take only the law of gravitation, we find that to secure them from the dangers of its infraction, "the goat, which browses on the edge of precipices, has received a hoof and legs that give precision and firmness to its steps; the bird, destined to sleep on the branches of trees, is provided with a muscle in the leg and foot which makes it cling the faster the greater its liability to fall; the fly, which walks and sleeps on perpendicular walls, and the ceilings of rooms, has a hollow in its foot, from which it expels the air, and the pressure of the atmosphere on the outside of the foot holds it fast to the object on which the inside is placed; the same is true of some kinds of lizards; the walrus is provided with a similar apparatus for climbing up the sides of icebergs; and the broad and spreading hoof of the camel fits it for the loose and sandy soil of the torrid desert." And still more does the benevolence of this arrangement appear, when we remember, that each modification of a part of the animal requires the co-adjustment of the entire structure.

Buffon and others, indeed, have expressed commiseration for some species, especially for the tardigrade family, as if they were the victims of a defective organization, because their motions, *as compared with our own*, are so remarkably slow. But *our* sensations are not the standard by which to estimate their condition. The rapidity of our motions would be death to the sloth. He is made for his condition; nor does he less find security and subsistence in it, than the lion ranging the plain, or the eagle sweeping the horizon of a continent.

As an illustration of the diversity of ways by which the Creator adjusts the habits of the animal to its external condition, "let us imagine a noble forest tree, in whose luxuriant foliage the birds of the air find shelter, and whose leaves supply food to hosts of insects. In this respect, the tree may be considered a world in itself, filled with different tribes of inhabitants, differing, not only in their aspect, but even in the stations or countries they inhabit, and assimilating as little together as the inhabitants of Tartary do with those of England. . . . Some of the insects, as caterpillars, feed upon the leaves; others upon the flowers; a few will eat nothing but the bark; while many derive their nourishment from the internal substance of the trunk. . . . If we examine further, new modifications of habits are discovered. Those insects, for instance, which feed upon leaves, do not all feed in the same manner, or upon the same parts: a few devour only the bud; others spin the terminal leaves together, forming them into a sort of hut, under cover of which they regale at leisure, upon the tenderest parts; some, apparently, even more cautious, construct little compact cases, which cover their body, and make them appear like bits of stick, or the ends of broken twigs; some eat the outside of the leaf only — like the caterpillars of New Holland, mentioned by Lewin — bore themselves holes in the stem, into which they carry a few leaves; sally out during the night for a fresh supply, and feed upon them at their leisure during the day. It seems, in fact, impossible to conceive greater modifications than are actually met with, even among insects which feed only upon leaves; while other variations are equally numerous in such tribes as live upon other portions of the tree. . . . Let us now look to those tribes of the feathered creation which would frequent this same tree for the purpose of seeking food. The woodpeckers begin by ascending the main trunk; they traverse in a spiral direction, and diligently examine the bark as they ascend; wherever they discern the least external indication of that decay produced by the perforating insects, they commence a vigorous attack: with repeated strokes of their powerful wedge-shaped bill, they soon break away the shelter of the internal destroyer, who is either dragged from his hole at once, or speared by the barbed tongue of his powerful enemy. Next come the creepers and the nuthatches: they have nothing to do with the tribes of insects just mentioned; *their* food is confined to the more exposed inhabitants of the bark, the crevices of which they examine with the same assiduity, and traverse in the same tortuous course, as do the woodpeckers: the one taking what the other leaves. In temperate regions, like Europe, few insects are found on the *horizontal* branches of trees; and this seems the true reason why we have no scansorial birds which frequent such situations; but in tropical countries the case is different; and we there find the whole family of cuckows exploring such branches, and such *only*. Finally, the extreme ramifications, never visited by any of the foregoing birds, are assigned — in this country at least — to the different species of titmice, whose diminutive size and facility of clinging are so well suited for such situations."[1]

9. If the well-being of the animal depend on its conformity with the laws of its constitution, the benevolence of the Creator would be further displayed by associating that conformity with sensations of pleasure. And it is so. The legitimate exercise of every sense is accompanied with pleasure. Activity itself yields gratification. But activity so operates as to render rest peculiarly delicious. The voluptuousness of repose again is succeeded by a desire for exertion, while every appetite, properly indulged, yields a measure of enjoyment. And thus "nature resembles the law-giver, who, to make his subjects obey, should prefer holding out rewards for compliance with his commands, rather than denounce punishments for disobedience."[2]

10. But as the *constant activity* of the vital functions is essential to life, would not the Divine benevolence be shown in withdrawing their operation from the contingencies of animal volition, and in rendering it involuntary and independent? It is so. "For the continuance of life a thousand provisions are made. If the vital actions of an animal's frame were directed by its volition, they are necessarily so minute and complicated, that they would immediately fall into confusion. It cannot draw a breath, without the exercise of sensibilities as well ordered as those of the eye or ear. A tracing of nervous cords unites many organs in sympathy; and if any one filament of these were broken, pain, and spasm, and suffocation, would ensue. The action of its heart, and the circulation of its blood,

---

[1] Swainson's Discourse on Nat. History, p. 175.

[2] Lord Brougham's Illustrations of Paley's Theology, vol. ii. p. 65.

and all the vital functions, are governed through means and by laws which are not dependent on its volition, and to which its mental powers are altogether inadequate. For had they been under the influence of its volition, a doubt, a moment's pause of irresolution, a neglect of a single action at its appointed time, would have terminated its existence."[1]

11. Still, as neither of these arrangements will secure for the animal entire exemption from danger, would not Benevolence be as apparent in guarding the animal against the evil by a warning pain, as in rewarding its obedience by pleasure? Now, such an arrangement does exist. The senses have been called sentinels placed at the outposts of life, to give timely warning of approaching danger. Every sense has its own sphere of perception, ranging circle beyond circle. Every appetite, if denied the gratification necessary to animal well-being, becomes uneasy and importunate. While the skin, drawn over the entire surface of the body, becomes a robe of sensibility and protection to all the parts within.

This view affords the appropriate reply to the inconsiderate inquiry, "why is there pain at all? or, why is not every action performed at the suggestion of pleasure?" For, not only is pain the necessary alternative to pleasure, but, if pleasure were to precede the act of obedience, as well as to attend, and to follow it, where would be the inducement to activity? If the animal, while in danger of famishing, be happy, what inducement would it have to arise and eat? But, according to the existing arrangement, it is aroused to the necessary activity by a twofold stimulus — insipient hunger inciting it from within, and the desire of gratification in prospect.

Besides which, it is often of the utmost importance that the notices of the presence of objects should be transmitted instantly to the brain; for the slightest delay would be attended with serious evil, and might even lead to fatal consequences. "Could the windpipe and the interior of the lungs be protected by a pleasurable sensation, inducing a slow determination of the will — so well as by that rapid and powerful influence which the exquisite sensibility of the throat produces upon the act of respiration, or by those forcible yet regulated exertions which nothing but the instinctive apprehension of death can excite?"

---

[1] Very slightly altered, for the sake of adaptation, from Sir C. Bell's Bridgewater Treatise, p. 13.

12. But while the benevolence of the Creator is thus apparent in employing pain as a safeguard against danger, most remarkably is it displayed in the manifold contrivances adopted for economizing suffering. We have seen this illustrated in the graduated scale of sensibility, and the other alleviating arrangements, included in the system of prey. When death is the result of age, the power of feeling gradually ceases, and the last moments of departing life assume the tranquillity of approaching sleep. In the case of an injury short of death, the *vis medicatrix* is called into activity, or a power tending to remedy the evil. This is seen in the tear which flows to wash the irritating particle from the eye; and in the new bone and new flesh produced to make the parts severed by accident knit again and heal.

The vast majority of sensations intended to guard against evil, are unattended with pain. And even of those which may become painful if prolonged, many, at first, are merely calculated to excite attention: such is the insipient sensation of hunger.

The sense of danger is generally timed and proportioned according to the urgency of the case. Were the sensations always equally distressing, the animal would suffer unnecessarily; for the great majority of its dangers are trivial. Were they always equally slight, the animal would soon be destroyed; for some of its dangers require a sudden and strenuous effort, which it would not have a sufficient inducement to make. "It is provided that the more an organ is exposed, or the greater is its delicacy of organization, the more exquisitely contrived is the apparatus for its protection, and the more peremptory the call for the activity of that mechanism: and as, in such instances, the motive to action admits of no thought and no hesitation, the action is more instantaneous than the quickest suggestion or impulse of the will."[1] "The velocity with which the nerves subservient to sensation transmit the impressions they receive at one extremity, along their whole course, to their termination in the brain, exceeds all measurement, and can be compared only to that of electricity passing along a conducting wire. These nerves may, in fact, be regarded as constituting a system of electric telegraphs, established by nature as the general medium of instantaneous trans-

[1] Sir C. Bell's Bridgewater Treatise, p. 202.

missions of sensorial agencies between all, and even the most distant parts of the body."[1]

Every perception of a different kind of danger has its own distinct sensation. This is essential, in order that the kind of effort to be made may answer to the nature of the evil to be avoided. For if the sensation arising from intense heat were the same as that occasioned by intense cold, the danger might be increased in the very attempt to escape from it. But by thus varying the sensation with the danger, an important end is gained in the diminution of pain; for the same painful sensation, however trifling at first, becomes by repetition or continuance intolerable.

But that which strikingly illustrates the Divine benevolence here is, the law that each part of the body should be endowed with a susceptibility to pain from those impressions only which tend to injure its structure; while it is comparatively insensible to every injury to which it is not likely to be exposed. "The extreme sensibility of the skin to the slightest injury, conveys to every one," says Sir C. Bell, "the notion that the deeper the wound the more severe must the pain be. This is not the fact; nor would it accord with the beneficent design which shines out everywhere. The sensibility of the skin serves not only to give the sense of touch, but to be a guard upon the deeper parts; and they cannot be reached except through the skin, and pain must be suffered therefore before they can be injured, it would be superfluous to bestow such sensibility upon these deeper parts themselves. If the internal parts, which act in the motions of the body, had possessed a similar degree and kind of sensibility with the skin, so far from serving any useful purpose, it would have been a source of inconvenience and continual pain, in the common exercise of the frame." On the same principle it is that the nerve of touch is insensible to excess of light; the nerve of vision is insensible to touch; and so are also those important organs, the brain and the heart; for had they possessed such sensibility, it would have been useless as a protection, since no external injuries could reach them without a previous warning having been received through the sensibility of the skin.

What, then, is the kind of sensibility with which these various parts are endowed? In every case it is different, for it is appropriate to the function of every part. The eye may be

---

[1] Roget's Bridgewater Treatise, vol. ii. p. 330.

rudely fingured without inflicting pain; for the optic nerve is sensitive only to excess of light — its nerve of touch is distinct. The heart may be handled without feeling it; but, as the great circulatory organ, it is in the closest sympathy with all the vital powers, and keenly alive to their slightest variations. The brain is as insensible to touch "as the sole of our shoe;" but let it be diseased, and consciousness departs. The bones may be exposed and cut with impunity; but the application of a force which tends to fracture them will cause exquisite pain. The tendons and ligaments which cover them may be exposed, and cut, pricked, or even burned, without the animal suffering the slightest pain; but let them be violently stretched, and the warning pain is instantly felt. Now by this benevolent arrangement pain is reduced to a minimum. The sensibility of each part varies with the function of the part; is limited to the peculiar liabilities of that part; and is occupied in its protection.

13. But do not these facts intimate the great truth that a nerve is not necessarily sensible, but only by the Divine appointment? We have already seen that no organization, no mechanical hypothesis, no chemical process, will suffice to account for life. And here we are brought to the analogous conclusion, that the sensibilities of the living frame are not qualities necessarily arising from life; that still less are they the consequences of delicacy of texture; but that they are endowments appropriate to their assigned and respective offices. For not only have the different parts of the nervous system totally distinct endowments, there are nerves, as we have remarked, "insensible to touch and incapable of giving pain, though exquisitely alive to their proper office;" and thus showing that, in each instance, *that* office is a special provision for a definite purpose — the benevolent purpose of animal enjoyment.

"We here perceive design, because we trace adaptation. But we, at the same time, trace *Benevolent* design, because we perceive gratuitous and supererogatory enjoyment bestowed. See the care with which animals of all kinds are attended from their birth. The mother's instinct is not more certainly the means of securing and providing for her young, than her gratification in the act of maternal care is great, and is also needless for making her perform that duty. The grove is not made vocal during pairing and incubation, in order to secure the laying or the hatching of eggs; for if it were still as the grave, or were filled with the most discordant croaking, the process would be as well performed. But thus it is that nature adds more gratification than is necessary to induce the creature to obey her calls."

14. And when the complicated and minute provision necessary for this enjoyment is considered, the benevolence of the Creator is still further conspicuous. The mathematical structure of the eye alone, on which the pleasures of sight depend, and its exquisite adaptation to the physical laws of light, might well fill us with astonishment at the goodness of God. But this is only one of numberless arrangements having the same kind tendency; and when we remember that all these are parts of a prospective plan contemplated before the birth of the animal; that the foundation of the whole is laid in the germ of which its after life is only the development; that maternal care awaited its coming; that the season of its birth is adjusted to the season of the year, and to the period of the food, most conducive to its well-being, our conviction of the goodness of God is still more increased. Nor can we thoughtfully pause at any moment, and try to bring before our minds all the fulness of animal life the world contains, and the infinitely varied sounds, and motions, and signs of enjoyment which it exhibits, without saying with Paley, "it is a happy world after all;" nor recollect that every sense, of every animal, of every herd, and shoal, and swarm, and flock, which throng creation, is a gift of Sovereign goodness — a channel in which the Divine benevolence may pour forth a stream of enjoyment, and behold the reflection of its image, without gratefully exclaiming, "How great is His goodness!" And this we conceive to be pre-eminently the design of the animal creation — the manifestation of the Divine benevolence.

15. But if the animal possess not the power of apprehending the great End of its creation, it may be expected to act from an instinctive regard to that end which is relative to the great End, namely, its own happiness. And, as it can answer the end of its creation only by, and as long as it retains, its relative perfection, we may expect that a strong desire will be implanted in its nature, and form a part of it, to maintain its well-being. Accordingly, life, enjoyment, and offspring, form the objects of all the animal instincts. From its own kind, it derives higher happiness than from any other objects in creation. In obeying the highest and most important instinct of

---

[1] Lord Brougham's Illustrations, &c. vol. ii. p. 66.

its nature, it derives the highest pleasure. And in the possession of offspring, the resources and enjoyments of two distinct beings are, in a sense, imparted to each. Even the manner in which, in the higher classes of animals, nutriment has been provided for the helpless young, evinces the kindest consideration; for, besides that the nourishment itself is "the most perfect type of food in general that it is possible to give," the way in which it is imparted is a source of tranquil enjoyment both to the giver and the receiver. Indeed, the entire arrangement by which the multiplication and perpetuation of animal life is secured, appears to carry animal enjoyment to the highest point.

16. But does this great theatre of animal enjoyment demonstrate the absolute infinity of the Divine goodness? Our reply is similar to that which we have returned to the same question in relation to the displays of Divine power and wisdom. If it were a proof of goodness, metaphysically infinite, all the illustrations of benevolence subsequently exhibited in the history of *man*, and which may be hereafter displayed in the progress of the universe, would, as further evidence, be superfluous or extra-infinite. Analogous remarks were made in the preceding Parts, relative to the power and wisdom of God; and from the advanced point which we have now reached, we can see how erroneous it would have been to treat the proof as already completed, or to limit our views of those Divine perfections by the evidence then before us; inasmuch as that evidence is still in process of augmentation. And in a similar manner, the illustrations of Goodness are constantly receiving fresh accessions. To which it is to be added, that even if the objective exercise of the Divine goodness were literally infinite, it would be utterly useless for all the purposes of manifestation, since its infinity would remain unknown to us; except, indeed, on Divine testimony. But how should we know that testimony to be true, except on infinite evidence? and so on, *ad infinitum.* If we utter any complaint at all, then, relative to the limitation of our knowledge of the Divine perfections, we should begin with the complaint that our minds are limited; which would be to complain in effect, that they are created, and not uncreated. Even as it is, the actual illustrations of the goodness of God exceed our conceptions; and yet, indefinite as they are, they go on multiplying at a rate which defies all human computation.

17. The only way, then, in which an infinite proof of infinite

goodness can be presented to finite creatures, or be received by them, is by a progressive accumulation through endless duration; so that it must be always in the course of exhibition. It is easy to conceive, however, of such a display of benevolence within a space and a time not unlimited, as should furnish free agents, capable of reasoning from analogy, with ample evidence of benevolence unlimited. And such a display of goodness we believe to have been made in the animal creation. Now, in attempting to show this, it is to be borne in mind, as a fact universally admitted, that the limitations of matter in relation to space, are necessitated by the nature of matter itself; and therefore, the limitations of the uses made of it also. If, then, the material medium through which benevolence is to be displayed is itself inherently conditioned by limits, we have to determine what evidence of goodness, exhibited under such circumstances, we, as beings constituted to reason by inference, and from analogy, should be justified in deeming an adequate illustration of goodness unlimited — of the kind of goodness, that is, which is displayed in sentient enjoyment. Displays of other kinds are, hypothetically, yet in store.

18. Now, we can conceive of intelligences so superior to ourselves as to be able to recognise in the first forms of sentient life that appeared on our earth, an adequate proof of the unlimited goodness of the Creator. Their view of cause and effect might be such as to enable them to say definitively, and at once, " the Being that could *originate* these forms of happiness, must be distinguished by infinite goodness." For, be it remembered, that the full understanding of these primitive forms would include also the full understanding of the inorganic and vegetable worlds; and would evince that the production of these sentient beings had always been in the contemplation of the creative mind. But these primeval creatures were actually accompanied or followed by *a world* of animal existences. True, those early creations were not probably so diversified in their species as the later creations; but geology shows that, at a very early period, the sea-covered earth swarmed with individual life. It would have been useless for man, had he then lived, to attempt the individual enumerations of beings contained in even a section of " the great and wide sea;" and yet every being was a distinct argument for the goodness of the Creator, since every one of them all was comprehended in his Divine plan. Now surely a human specta-

tor of that scene could not have expended years and ages in the contemplation of animal enjoyment, especially as viewed in connection with the complicated provision made for it from the beginning, and with the endlessly diversified manner in which all nature ministered to it, without receiving an overwhelming impression of Creative benevolence. Long before he could have fully estimated the proofs of benevolence teeming around him, a new creation would dawn, and a new world of animate wonders come into view; and as he gradually discovered that phenomena which at first appeared at variance with goodness, only required to be understood in order to become remarkable illustrations of it; that where a liability to pain existed, the most refined and complicated means are resorted to for reducing it to the smallest amount possible, or for providing against it altogether; and that even the system of prey is resolvable into the greatest amount of animal enjoyment compatible with the existing plan of creation, he could not but feel that the benevolence to which all this was owing, must be literally past finding out. Let him revisit the earth in imagination time after time, with intervals of ages between each visit: surely he could not remark that every change of external condition was associated with a corresponding change in animal organization; that these changes were diversified to a degree designed apparently to impress him with their inexhaustibleness; that the systems of life and enjoyment were ever on the increase, and that the analogy of every part with all the rest showed the whole to be in accordance with a plan which must have ever existed in the Divine mind, without being impelled to the conclusion that for such displays of goodness to an indefinite extent, God is all-sufficient. And, beyond this, he should remark that the amount of actual life exhibited at any given time on the earth, is as nothing compared with the amount of potential life and happiness which it contains. The vegetable seeds germinating at this moment on the surface of the earth, are, probably, insignificant compared with the number concealed below to an unknown depth; and who shall calculate the superficial extent of the world, or worlds, which those seeds would be sufficient speedily to clothe with verdure? And so also of the ova of some animal species, such as the carp, the cod, or the flounder, in an individual of which more than a million have been counted, — who shall say the number of Atlantics which either of these species would fill in the course of a thousand years, if all their ova were allowed to be developed; or how many atmospheres, of the same extent as that of our planet, would, in the same time, become crowded and darkened, by the unchecked multiplication of so minute a thing as a fly? Now he could not survey the recovered fossil species of former worlds, remembering that all traces of many species have probably vanished; and then glance at the five hundred thousand species now living, remembering that the actual multiplication of some of them, prodigious as it is, is as nothing compared with their possible increase; and that this has been always true from the beginning, without yielding to the full impression, that, subjectively, the Creative goodness can know no limitation; and that, objectively, He is all-sufficient for replenishing alike a single planet, or ten thousand worlds, with sentient happiness, and for sustaining the whole for an age, or for ever. This we believe to be the impression which a world of sentient enjoyment was intended to produce on the mind of man. That it is adapted to produce this very effect is evident, for it actually produces it. And the very manner in which this end is attained — the mental effort which it demands, and the apparent moral difficulties which it involves — still farther evinces the far-reaching purpose of the Creator, in making it the means of man's intellectual and moral education. But man, " the interpreter of nature," is yet to come.

---

19. Now, suppose a being capable of appreciating the successive stages of creation as we have endeavored to describe it, to have taken a survey of the whole on the eve of that great revolution which gave occasion to the Adamic creation, what an enlarged view must it have afforded him of the power, and wisdom, and goodness of God! Could he have cast back a mental glance to the remote antiquity when the first creative fiat went forth, and then have called before his mind all the long series of creation on creation with extended intervals between, which had since then taken place, — could he have remembered how many vegetable kingdoms had successively existed and perished, only to be followed by others better adapted to the altered globe; and how every such change had been followed by a corresponding adaptation in all the indefinite varieties of animal life, so that the earth had been kept " full of His goodness," without feeling, with a depth of conviction no language can express, and long before he had ar-

rived at the close of his retrospection, the all-sufficiency of God for the indefinite enlargement and continuance of similar manifestations! He would have seen that, here, every object and event formed at least a letter in the great name of God—a symbol of the Divine perfections. Even if the creative process had been arrested at this point, never to be resumed, he would yet have felt that he was worshipping in a temple dedicated to "the eternal power and Godhead;" for the shekinah of the Divine presence was everywhere visible. But that temple had ever been enlarging and receiving fresh memorials of the Deity; and long before he had deciphered every symbol, and bowed at every altar sacred to these perfections, he would have felt prepared for the unveiling of another aspect of the Divine character.

20. Could he then have had disclosed to him the nature of man's constitution,—physical, mental, and moral,—the creation would forthwith have seemed to assume a new character. He would have seen that man was not to be made for the world, but that the world from the first had been made for man; that all its laws were mute predictions of what he would be; that all nature was pre-configured to him, and looked forwards to his coming. The earth, then, he might have said, is to be *a school for the education of the human being.* What a severe and useful discipline will it be for him, if left to his own unaided efforts, to determine the point from which his physical studies should start, the method they should observe, and the direction they should take. When the time shall come for him to try to ascertain the position of his planet in the system to which it belongs, and the disposition of the parts of that system, what prolonged and improving efforts is it likely to call forth? for he will see it "not in *plan* but in *section*;" his point of observation will lie in the general plane of the system, while the notion he will aim to form of it will be, not that of its section, but of its plan; as if he should attempt to make out the countries on a map, with his eye on a level with the map.[1] Even the size and physical geography of the planet itself are relative to the powers of the being destined to occupy it; for, while it is not so diminutive and unvaried as to promise no reward to curiosity and effort, neither is it so vast and unmanageable as to depress and forbid them. For him, the Creator has "weighed the mountains in scales and the

[1] Sir J. Herschel's Nat. Phil., p. 267.

hills in a balance." Here, objects are so formed as to call him to activity, and to give him lessons in self-government; and secrets so hid in the depths of nature as to invite his discovery, and to correct his pre-judgments; and events so intimately and universally related, as to reveal to his attentive eye the fact, that all nature is united in a close net-work of mutual connections and dependence. Here, advancing from the domain of facts, he will ascend to the region of laws. His discovery and generalization of these will constitute his natural science, his practical application of them will be his art and occupation. From this commanding point, all creation will assume the appearance of order, and be seen under law. And every onward step in this direction will bring him, by a path increasingly luminous, nearer to the throne of the Eternal, in whose hand all laws will be seen to meet.

21. The being who is supposed to be intelligently anticipating the creation of man, would foresee that the earth was designed also to be a *temple for worship*. Here—he might have said farther—wherever man may look, he willfind himself surrounded by the symbols of the Godhead. Every object on which his eye will rest, is either an "altar of memorial," or an offering to be laid on it. Even the earth itself, as it goes speeding through space, what should it be but an altar, at which he should be perpetually ministering, as the high-priest of nature?

Here, if he ask for proofs of the power, and wisdom, and goodness of God, he may ascend, by higher and higher generalizations, from phenomenal causes to the Great First Cause Himself; and from the contemplation of the uninterrupted order, the symmetry of relations, and the harmonious combination of laws observable throughout organic nature, to the conviction of universal design in the Creating Cause; and from the perception that all this exercise of wisdom is directed to the multiplication and happiness of a world of sentient life, to the conclusion that the Creator is as benevolent as He is powerful and wise.

But geology will give a range to his views of the Divine all-sufficiency beyond all admeasurement; it will admit him to a succession of departed worlds, stored with the monuments of the Creator's inexhaustible resources. Plunge as far back as he may into the past, he will still find himself in the province of the same Creator, and surrounded by evidences that "He seeth the end from the beginning."

But what impressive views of the same perfections will open on him when he shall come to perceive, that all the long series of creations by which the globe is adapted to become his habitation, has distinctly contemplated his own well-being? Were his advent among the creatures to be that of a distinguished being from some paradise above, means for developing his hidden powers, the exquisite adjustment of things to strike him with the kind forethought of the Being who had sent him here, provision for his health, and comfort, and entire well-being during his stay, could hardly have been made more obvious and abundant than they actually are. Of all the species of animated beings that have inhabited the earth, he will be the first to look upon nature with an intelligent eye. Till he comes, this glorious volume of the Creator will remain unread; and not only will he be able to interpret nature, it will be his prerogative to *employ* it for his improvement. The only use which the brute creation unconsciously make of it, is that of sustaining and perpetuating their kind. He will employ it also for the same purpose, but this very employment of it may be of a nature to call forth the exercise of his reason, and to tend to his intellectual progress. So that even in that one solitary respect, in which he and the animals will appear to be placed on a level, he will be able in reality to assert his essential superiority over them; and from it he may date his actual rise above them. They only use and only need some of the present products of the earth. Man may employ the products of every departed world. In his hands the extremes of geological duration may meet. The granite of ten thousand ages back may be made the foundation of his dwelling, or the pedestal of his image. The mountain limestone — petrified exuviæ of departed worlds — may serve to cement and beautify his abode. The wreck of the forests, that for ages waved on the surface of the ancient lands, and the ferruginous accumulations deposited in primeval waters may supply him with the principal means of his material progress and comfort. From the rich metallic veins which interlace the earth, he may derive the means of his choicest ornaments, the representatives of all his material wealth, and knowledge "more precious than rubies." Every flood which swept over the ancient continents, and every dislocating earthquake, which contributed to the formation of cultivable soils, may re-appear in man's science, and be converted to his purposes. The loadstone, in his hands, may become an instrument by which to call the stars to his aid, and to bid defiance to the apparent boundlessness of the ocean, while, in quest of scope for his enterprise, he steers to a distant region of the globe. The subterranean treasuries of the earth contain nothing which he will not be able to use; and who shall say but that the time may come in his history when its stores will prove to have been not unnecessarily great? Surely the creature who will point to little artificial contrivances of his own in proof of his sagacity and skill, will not fail to recognize in these vast prospective arrangements for his coming, convincing indications of a beneficent superintending mind! And surely as time advances, and new and more profound adaptations of nature rise to view, as man comes to find that his race have been living for ages in the midst of complicated adaptations of which they were unconscious, and which could be developed only as the result of a long series of prior discoveries, but all tending to his development and well-being, his recognition of the Creative wisdom and goodness will become more vivid and grateful, and the earth become more sacred in his eyes!

Probably, too — the supposed soliloquist might have continued — probably, as preceding changes of the earth have been followed by new and enlarged creations of animal life, the period of man's creation may be marked by some new productions of the Divine power, designed to contribute yet further to human welfare. But, whether it should be so or not, the earth, even as it is, appears to be so replete with preparations for his coming, that He alone could perceive any deficiency, whose unlimited power is able to supply it. It is only in such a world that a creature like man could live, and his character be developed. Here, every part of his nature will find its appropriate domain. The phenomena of geology alone — what lessons will they read to his intellectual and moral nature? Can he recognise in the series of organic worlds, distinct evidence of a succession of creations, without feeling as if he were reading so many proclamations of the Divine power laid up for his perusal? feeling it with a vividness which could hardly be increased even if he could reach the foundation of the earth and there find the inscription, "Laid by the Divine Hand, to be discovered and deciphered by man unnumbered ages hence." When he shall perceive that these successive creations are only the gradual filling up of a vast and harmonious outline, will he not be penetrated with wonder at the comprehensiveness of the Divine plans, and the unchangeableness of the Divine nature? Can he ever attempt a computation of the enormous periods which must have elapsed since life first moved on the globe, without being carried back in imagination to a past eternity; and without thinking, by the mere rebound of the mind, of an eternity yet to come? And, then, will it be possible for him to mark how all the stupendous miracles of the past have conspired to prepare the earth to receive him, without feeling that the adaptation must have been contemplated from the first, and without surrendering himself up to the emotions of adoration and joy?

And shall these geological records of the past furnish him with no ground of conclusion, or of rational conjecture, respecting the future? He will be able to point to an era when his race had not yet begun to exist. An age after, and man had been called into being, and had entered on his career. Every one of his posterity, therefore, traced back to his origin through the preceding generations of mankind, will carry about in his own person indubitable evidence of a miracle. And may he not justly reason that, unless the Supreme Power can be supposed to have exhausted itself in his own creation, the energy which could perform the long succession of stupendous miracles of which the production of the first man was the crowning act, must be capable of performing other miraculous acts? And unless he should suppose that he himself has been created without any object, or that God has excluded Himself from his own world, and has bound Himself in the iron chain of an everlasting mechanism, will it not be natural for him to infer that the object for which the miracle of his own creation was wrought may subsequently require the performance of other miracles in harmony with the primary one, and leading to the same result? And unless it could be shown that no beneficent provision whatever had been originally made for human happiness, the existence of such provision will surely warrant the conclusion that, if ever circumstances should arise in which it would be more for the well-being of man to modify or to enlarge that provision than not to do so, it would — all other things being equal — be worthy of Divine Goodness so to modify or enlarge it. And will not the persuasion that he stands in the midst of a system yet in progress — a system, therefore, from which God is never absent — tend to invest the earth with the hallowed character of a temple, and to convert his every inquiry respecting the past and the future into an act of worship?

22. But what if this same being who had been given to understand that the earth would be a school for man's education, and a temple for his worship, had been foretold also that it would be the sphere of human *probation;* that even its natural scenery and productions would, in a sense, be conveyed into the mind of man, and be taken up into his character; that every object and event in nature would, in a variety of ways, be wrought into the texture of man's moral history; and that every law expressed, and every truth symbolized, in nature, would sooner or later become a test of character, what a field for solemn conjecture would have been opened before him? Perversions of these truths which have become familiar to us, would doubtless have appeared to him so gross as to be next to impossible. Whatever errors man may imbibe, we may suppose him to have said — it is not to be imagined that he will ever so far discredit his reason as to mistake those created exponents of certain attributes of the Divine Nature for that Infinite Nature itself; converting the intended means of worship into objects of adoration. Man's moral freedom, if nothing else, seems to require that the period of the earth's origin should be hid in a dateless antiquity; but surely he will not therefore irrationally jump to the conclusion that it is eternal and uncreated. For the same reason, it would seem to be necessary that the successive stages of the creative process should not be so obtrusively marked and palpable as to compel the judgment to the right conclusion; but can it be that all other evidence except that of visible creative interference shall go for nothing with a being meant to reason; or that advantage will ever be taken of the absence of mere visible evidence, to affirm the non-existence of an invisible Agent? Whatever may be meant by the uniformity of the course of nature, it is evident that it must be something compatible with a succession of changes in which new races have been brought into being, differing from all previous existences. Contrary, therefore, as such a creative change may be to the course of nature for a certain period, evidently, it is by no means contrary to the great scheme to which that limited period belongs. And confidently as the permanence of nature may be relied on during a given period, with equal confidence may a change be looked for, sooner or later, to put an end to that period. The changes may be as regular on a large scale of things, as is the intervening uniformity on a smaller scale. Both are only parts of a great whole. It cannot be that man, who will actually owe his ex-

istence to one of these miraculous changes, should ever come to question their possibility; that, arguing from his own uniform experience of a few ages, he should feel himself warranted to pronounce against such changes during the vast preceding cycles compared with which his ages will be as moments; and that he should do this in the face of all the successive worlds of geological evidence to the contrary. The Divine Creator is the "God of order;" regularity is the natural characteristic of His procedure; without it, man will not be able to arrive at any knowledge respecting Him: and can it be that man will take occasion from the very order of nature to "explode the idea of a God?" shall those sequences, without which he will not be able to infer the Creative Existence, be the very reason why he denies it? shall the very laws whose existence are essential in order that he may understand anything of the Lawgiver, become, in his hands, weapons for dethroning Him?

If it shall appear from the event that one of the great reasons of the Creator for adopting the actual method of creation, was that it might be preconfigured to man's intelligent, voluntary, and moral nature, can it be that any human creature will ever come to construe the infinitely complicated coincidence of the two into a proof of its accidental origin — as if the proof of design diminished in proportion as the evidence increased. If man's free-agency is not to be overborne by the visible display of immediate Divine operation; if the evidence of creative agency is to be enough to convince, but not so much as to overwhelm, the attainment of this balance will involve relations and adjustments of infinitely diversified complication, and will form, in truth, the grand sphere for the exercise of creative wisdom and goodness; surely no human being will ever employ this freedom in questioning the existence of the agency which alone makes it possible! Without it, there would be no reasoning — no man; with it, shall there be, for him, no God?

If the ultimate end both of the creative method and of its reason in respect to man, be the unfolding of the Divine all-sufficiency, can it be that he will ever derive two directly opposite conclusions from the same creative displays? that he will at one time contend, that as his inferences can only go to the extent of his evidence, his views of the Divine perfections, derived from natural theology, are necessarily limited; and, at another, that the Being who could originate the universe must be too exalted to interest himself in any of its mere details? Is it possible that, on a survey of creation, one man should withhold from the Creator the homage involved in the recognition of His infinity; and that another, on the ground of His infinite greatness, should "compliment Him out of this world as a place too mean for His reception," and excuse Him from its government, as a care and an incumbrance unsuited to His dignity; and from its worship, as a thing beneath His regard?

Thoughts such as these — had there been a being to entertain them — might well have projected a deep shadow over the earth as the scene of man's approaching probation. But may we not suppose that the gloom would have been relieved and brightened by anticipations of a very opposite tendency? Here, the imaginary seer might have said, as he recalled the past and glanced over the present — here is a great system of argumentative appeals, for the infinite power, and wisdom, and goodness of God, appeals which predict a constitution fitted to receive and respond to them. More than one part of that constitution will be constructed to respond. Often, the response will be so sudden as to anticipate the slow conclusions of the reasoning process; so clear and distinct as to be heard by the most unwilling ear; and so authoritative and impressive as to be remembered and felt long after every opposing voice has ceased. Rightly considered, creation will be regarded as a hymn of praise to its Maker; and man will aspire to lead the song. While from the depths of the earth — from the wreck of former worlds — he will derive materials with which to erect an altar of gratitude to Him who "reneweth the face of the earth." And what even if man's moral relations to the Deity should be disturbed, and his condition should consequently become such as to require information which it is not in the power of nature to impart; even then — though some of his race, alas! owing partly to the very scantiness of their natural knowledge of God, and in proportion to it, may blindly profess to be satisfied and to desire no more, — yet the natural theology of others will, in proportion to its extent and fulness, tend to awaken a thirst for a higher and more enlarged revelation of the Divine character, and prepare them to expect it. Insufficient as the knowledge of God derivable from nature may be as a sanctuary for conscious guilt, it may yet serve as the substructions and steps of another temple, from the sacred recesses of which may be caused to issue the oracles of Holiness, Mercy, and Love. And as the vastness of the Divine resources displayed in nature, joined with the consideration that, indefinite as they must be to man, they are after all finite to

God, is the reflection which, more than any other, will impress him with the all-sufficiency of God in creation, so it may inspire him with the hope of the Divine all-scfficiency for his moral recovery, and be even employed by God to image that sufficiency forth.

23. A being placed, and informed respecting the past and the future, as we have supposed, could not have recognized the signs of approaching change — if such signs there were — symptoms of the impending revolution of a portion, at least, of the earth's surface; and then have recalled before his mind the succession of new creations, which had followed from like revolutions before, without rising to adoration, and saying, in effect, "Of old hast thou laid the foundation of the earth; and the heavens are the work of thy hands; they shall perish, but thou remainest; yea, they all shall wax old like a garment; as a vesture shalt thou roll them up, and they shall be changed: but thou art the same, and thy years shall have no end." And as he stood on the verge of the crisis, with the ominous shadows of the last evening settled around him, and all nature hushed in portentous silence, he could not picture to his mind the possibilities involved in the impending stage of the Divine procedure, without being conscious of an earnest desire to behold the creature, man, and the wondrous scenes which would signalize his eventful history.

NOTES.

Note A, p. 13.

I have been humbled at finding the view advocated in the text, spoken of by some — teachers of theology too — as an impeachment of the Divine disinterestedness; or, in other words, as an imputation of Divine selfishness. This misrepresentation might arise either from a jealousy *of* the Divine Greatness, or from a mistaken jealousy *for* it, accompanied with an indolent misconception of the subject. In the *first* of these instances, it is human self-importance entering into competition with Infinite Greatness and laboring to dethrone it, only that it might occupy the vacated seat.

In the *second* the objector appears to argue in oblivion of all the facts appropriate to the subject, and under the anthropomorphising impression that God " is altogether such an one as himself." First, he forgets that no objection can be alleged against the view that God will be his own end in the eternity to come, which does not equally lie against the view that He was his own end in the eternity past; and yet no one *can* raise a question on this point, for during the past eternity He alone existed. Secondly, the objector forgets that the view *must* be true in some high and substantial sense, for the doctrine that " of Him, and through Him, and to Him, are all things," runs through the Bible like a line of light. Thirdly, the selfishness which the view is supposed to impute or imply is purely anthropopathic, or arises from a mental transference to the infinitely blessed God of human passions, and, as such, it can have no place with God; for selfishness implies the appropriation of happiness, or of the means of happiness, belonging to others, whereas, in the present unique instance, the idea of appropriation can have no place, since all that man enjoys is of Divine impartation. Fourthly, the only alternative to *God* being the chief end of creation is, that *man* be that end. But the only reason which could be assigned for this view is (not that it is *right*, as in the case of one human being benefiting another, but) that it appears to some to be more *worthy* of God; which is only saying, in other words, that that must be the end of creation which is most worthy of God, and most glorious to him—thus, in reality, affirming the doctrine in the very act of denying it. And, fifthly, the happiness of the creature requires that the manifestation of the Divine All-sufficiency be the chief end of creation. Surely, it could not conduce to the happiness of an intelligent creature to believe that the Infinite existed for the finite, and was subordinated to it. On the contrary, the blessedness of holy beings must consist mainly in their conscious and chosen dependence on infinite excellence; in the ever-present idea of its infinity contrasted with their limitation, leaving room for progress unending. Further, I might proceed to remind the objector that if it is thought no impeachment of any Divine perfection to believe (as he himself probably believes) that animal enjoyment, though *an end* of the animal kingdom, was not the highest end contemplated by the animal creation; that the manner in which it has contributed to the enjoyment, education, and well-being of the human race, is a yet higher end; so man's creation may, consistently with the same Perfection, point to an end beyond itself; and what end can that be, but the only one which is infinite? I can hardly bring myself to confess that, in more than one instance, I have actually met with an objection to the view I am now advocating, which amounted to this, "we do not object to the *fact* that the highest end of creation should be the manifestation of the Divine excellence; perhaps this is right; perhaps it is even unavoidable, and arises necessarily from the very nature of things; we only demur to the idea of the Divine Being *designing* it!" Evidently, their conception of the Majesty of heaven is that of a great human being; of one who, (to adopt the sentiment of the poet,) having "done good by stealth," is expected to "blush when he finds it fame!" He must not accept the homage of heaven as his right, but as praise unexpected and undeserved. He, not the adoring seraphim, must veil. Their *beau-ideal* of Perfection omits prescience; for how otherwise could the Creator fail to foresee the results of his own creation; and, foreseeing, how could He do otherwise than accept, adopt, or design them? But to do this is, in their eyes, to sacrifice the *proprieties!!* "O righteous Father, the world hath not known thee!"

Note B, p. 75.

"In the beginning God created the heavens and the earth. Now the earth was without form and waste, and darkness was upon the face of the deep. And the spirit of God moved upon the face of the waters." — Genesis i. 1, 2.

From a careful consideration of the subject, it is the full conviction of the writer, that the first of the two verses just quoted was placed by the hand of Inspiration at the opening of the Bible as a distinct and independent sentence; that it was the Divine intention to affirm by it, that the material universe was primarily originated by God from elements not previously existing; and that this originating act was quite distinct from the acts included in the six natural days of the Adamic creation.[1] It should be observed that this interpretation by no means implies that Moses himself put this construction on the sentence, or intended to convey this meaning, He might; or he might not. He was only the organ for its transmission. But it is a well-known canon of Scripture interpretation, that the statements of the word of God are to be understood, not merely in that sense in which they were apprehended by the human instruments employed to make them, nor in that sense to which their hearers or readers at the time could reach, but in the sense which He himself attached to them. For example, there is ground to believe that Moses himself was not aware of the profound spiritual meaning of much of the ritual which he was employed to institute. It was an obscure text, which awaited the Divine commentary of the Christian dispensation.

Nor is it meant to be implied by this interpretation that the Bible was designed to teach astronomy, geology, or any other branch of natural science. When we are enlarging on the historical parts of Scripture, for instance, no one infers that we mean to affirm that the Bible was designed to teach either the mere facts, or the philosophy, of history. Its object, in such parts, is to teach the doctrine of God's government of the world; and all that we are supposed to mean is, that the events related in proof or illustration of the doctrine, *were matters of fact, actual occurrences*, divinely attested. So here; the obvious purpose of the inspired writer is to teach the great truth that God is the Creator of all things; and all that the nature of the case requires — and

[1] See Dr. J. P. Smith's admirable work on Scripture and Geology. Lecture VI. Part II., and Notes P. Q. Second Edition.

this it does seem to require — is, that, however anthopomorphic and *popular* the language employed may be, the events related in illustration of the truth should be *actual occurrences.* But being such, it follows that they will be found in harmony with the facts of science. The view just propounded, and which appears to the writer to be the only just construction of the verse in question, involves the following three propositions; that, by "the heavens and the earth," are *here* to be understood the material universe; that the original act of creation was the calling of the material of the universe into existence; and that this act was not included in the six days of the Adamic creation.

The *first* of the propositions — that by "the heavens and the earth," are here to be understood the material universe — hardly admits of a question. Even if the phrase, "the heavens and the earth," does not include more than the material universe — (namely, dependent sentient and intelligent beings also) — it cannot be regarded as denoting less. In proof of which, if proof be necessary, it may be alleged, that the material universe is the subject immediately taken up in the verses following; that the phrase in question became a Hebrew formula for expressing the material universe, a formula most likely adopted from this opening verse; and that such appear to be the inspired exposition of the phrase — as in Psalms cii. 25, "Thou, Lord, in the beginning hast laid the foundation of the earth: and the heavens are the work of thy hands."

The *second* proposition — that the original act of creation was the calling of matter into existence — though not, at first sight equally obvious, appears, on examination, to be equally certain. There are those, indeed, who, while they firmly believe that matter is not eternal, refuse to admit that this verse affirms its origination. Their persuasion is, that the verse takes us back only to the beginning of the Adamic creation, and affirms that God was the immediate former of the present state of things; and that the verses following unfold the process of the formation. And the chief reason which they assign for this view is, that *bara — created*, according to the *usus loquendi*, signifies, not to call a thing out of non-existence, but to re-constitute something already in existence; and is used indifferently and interchangeably in many passages with *asah — made*, and *yatsar — formed* or *fashioned;* and that there does not appear to be any word in any language which expresses the idea of creation independently of preexisting matter.

In reply, I would submit that this objection, even if it could be substantiated, does not meet the requirements of the case ; and that the only appropriate evidence is that which is derivable from the interpretations of the phrase, and of the subject, as found in other parts of Scripture. For, first, from the very nature of the subject, the *usus loquendi* never can obtain in relation to any word employed to express creation out of nothing. And the apparent singularity of the fact might have well awakened inquiry how it is that, while every language has the idea, no language has a term *exclusively* employed to express it, but adopts a phrase instead.[1] The obvious reason is, that even if a term — *bara*, for example — had been at first devised and employed to express the Divine origination of matter, man, according to a well-known and universal tendency, would soon have adopted it as the most emphatic mode of expressing his own secondary origination, or mere formation, of things. And then as, in its primary signification, it could only, in the nature of things, be applied to a single act of the Divine Being, while in its secondary sense it could be applied to all kinds of human origination of all kinds of things, the *usus loquendi* would speedily place the secondary meaning first. Let it be imagined that a new term were to be now devised to express the idea in question — let it be the term *ex*nihilate — and immediately man would adopt it to express his own production of things, just as he now speaks of annihilating them ; though he can do either only in a secondary sense. And as, in this secondary sense, he would be daily exnihilating, while the term, in its primary signification, could be predicated only of the one originating act of the Divine Being, of course the *usus loquendi* would immediately obtain in favor of the secondary sense. Now, admitting the term *bara* to have meant, when employed in the first verse of Genesis, the actual creation of matter, its secondary application would soon have acquired, in this manner, the sanc-

---

[1] When Dr. Pusey, Professor of Hebrew at Oxford, states, (Buckland's Bridgewater Treatise, note, p. 22,) that "our very addition of the words 'out of nothing,' shows that the word creation has not, in itself," the force of *absolute origination*, he appears to overlook the only point in the discussion worth remembering, namely, that this additional phrase is properly employed only when *something* is supposed already to exist, out of which the thing made might *possibly* be produced. On the other hand, when speaking of the origination of *primordial elements*, no one could say that they were created *out of nothing* without tautology; for this would be to state formally that the first has no antecedent, or that the first is not second. So that the word creation, when predicated of primordial matter — and this is the precise thing in question — does possess, without any additional words, the force of absolute origination.

tion of custom; and then, as inspired language did not differ from ordinary language, the term would subsequently come to be used, in Scripture, interchangeably with *asah* — *made* and *yatsar* — *formed.* Our only resource, therefore, is to ascertain the scriptural interpretation of the term in those passages in which the first verse of Genesis was present to the mind of the inspired writers. Or if, secondly, the verb *bara* was taken by inspiration from a prior and familiar application to a human process, and was employed metaphorically to denote a Divine act of an analogous but unique description, then also, as the thought would govern the word, and not the word the thought, we should have to look for that thought in other parts of the inspired volume.

Now, that the first verse of Genesis is to be regarded as announcing the proper creation of the matter of the visible universe, is apparent from the following passages: —

1. A comparison of the second and following verses in Gen. i. with the first verse, justifies the conclusion that the act denoted by *bara* in the first verse must have been essentially different from mere formation out of materials already existing; for after that first act had been performed, the earth still remained in a formless chaotic state. On this point, I avail myself of the critical judgment of Professor M. Stuart of America; and I do so the more readily, because he is avowedly an anti-geologist, and is therefore free from all suspicion of a bias from that quarter. "All order and arrangement plainly seem to be considered, by the writer of Gen. i. as having been effected *after* the original act of creation. * * * *The original act of creation*, as understood by the sacred writers, appears plainly to have been, *the calling of matter into being, the causing of it to exist;* and out of this the heavens and the earth were afterwards formed, *i. e.*, reduced to their present order and arrangement."[1]

2. In the opening verses of St. John's Gospel we read, "In the beginning was the Logos, and the Logos was with God, and the Logos was God. * * * All things were made by him." Here, it is evident that the design of the sacred writer is to affirm that, before anything existed *ad extra*, the Logos existed; for his object is to prove that everything was brought into existence by the Logos. If Scripture, then, is to be its own interpreter, we must infer that the phrase, *in the beginning*, as employed in the book of Genesis, takes us back to the same period. And this conclusion becomes inevitable when we observe that, in using this phrase,

---

[1] Hebrew Chrestomathy, p. 112.

the Gospel designedly, and for obvious reasons, imitates the history. If the Mosaic use of the phrase, therefore, does not take us back to a period prior to the origination of matter, it cannot be justly inferred that the apostolic sense of the phrase does; but that the "all things made by him," excepts matter, *i. e.*, that matter was not made by him, and that he did not exist before it.

3. In harmony with the view for which we are contending, and apparently conclusive of it, is Heb. xi. 3, "By faith we understand that the worlds were formed by the word of God, so that the things which are seen, were not made from those which do appear." It cannot be justly questioned that the Divine declaration, *by faith* in which we attain to this conviction, is that contained in Gen. i. 1, *for the apostle next refers to Gen.* iv. 4, *and next to Gen.* v. 24; *and so on, in orderly succession.* Now, the apostolic exposition of that declaration is, "that the worlds were formed by the word of God"—by the *commanding word*[1]—"the symbol of the Almighty and self-competent power, which requires no means exterior to itself."[2] And, still further to evolve and expound the idea of absolute origination, it is added, "so that the things which are seen, were not made from things which do appear;"[3] or, which amounts to the same, "the things visible were made from things not visible;"[4] *i. e.*, not from anything pre-existing; they were strictly originated by the creative fiat. Had the apostle meant merely that the visible creation was formed from a pre-existing invisible matter, he surely would not have made it a doctrine of faith. This is rather a doctrine of sense, in antagonism to faith; and, as such, it has been always acceptable to a sensuous philosophy.

Indeed, it does not appear that any other meaning was ever attached to the Mosaic statement, by the ancient church, than that given by the apostle. "God made them [heaven and earth] from things that do not exist;"[5] *i. e.*, from nothing previously

---

[1] Psalm xxxiii. 6; cxlviii. 5. [2] Tholuck on the Hebrews, *in loc.*

[3] Εἰς τὸ μὴ ἐκ φαινομένων τὰ βλεπόμενα γεγονέναι.

[4] Μὴ φαινομένων being here equivalent to μὴ ὄντων; for, as God alone existed to see or to know, if there was nothing visible to *Him*, there was nothing. Just as in Hebrew, *nimtsa*—that which is *found*, is a term employed to denote that which *exists;* and, with the negative particle, to denote the *not-found*, meaning the *non-existent*. See Bloomfield, *in loc.*; Stuart, Storr and Flatt, § xxxi.; Knapp's Theology, § xlvi. note; the translations of Sacy, Osterwald, Luther, Diodati, and the English versions of 1557 and 1611.

[5] Οὐκ ἐξ ὄντων ἐποίησεν αὐτὰ ὁ Θεός. 2 Macc. vii. 28. The Vulgate, *ex nihilo fecit Deus cœlum et terram.*

existing. According to the Rabbins,[1] the verse should be rendered, "God, in the beginning, created the substance of the heavens, and the substance of the earth." The Syriac translator understood the verse in the same sense.[2] It is clear, says Chrysostom, in his paraphrase of the apostolic interpretation, "that God, from things not in being, made those which are in being; from those not visible, the things which do appear; and, from things having *no* subsistence, those things which subsist." But if such is the apostolic exposition of Gen. i. 1, it follows that the same exposition must be received as the inspired interpretation of the whole of that class of parallel passages in the Old Testament, of which that verse stands at the head.

The *third* proposition is, that this absolute origination of matter was a Divine act not included in the six days of the Adamic creation. The question, here, does not respect the length of the interval between that originating act and the Adamic creation. The proposition simply affirms that *there was an interval;* and implies, that the inspired text neither asserts its brevity nor denies its length. Its duration is supposed to be indicated in indelible characters elsewhere — in the crust of the globe itself. The scriptural record is simply, but significantly, indicative of an interval.

The principal objection to this view is derived from Exod. xx. 11, wherein, as the reason for observing the Sabbath, *the entire and complete work* of creation is supposed to be described as carried on and ended in six days. To which it should be sufficient to reply, that so much of the creative process is there referred to — and only so much — as related to the law of the Sabbath, namely, the six days of the Adamic creation; or the making of the heaven and the earth as described in Gen. i. 3, &c. But, secondly, the same rule which leads one objector to rely on Exod. xx. 11, as a proof that the entire creation was comprised in six Adamic days, would justify another in insisting that it was comprised in one day, because it is said, Gen. ii. 4, "These are the generations of the heavens and the earth, in their being created, *in the day* of Jehovah God's making earth and heavens:" the obvious meaning of the original being, however, *at the time* of

---

[1] Who understand *eth*, here to denote the *substance* or *material.* Compare Gesenius, *sub voce;* Aben Ezra; Kimchi, in his Book of Roots; and Buxtorf's Talmudic Lexicon.

[2] In Walton's Polyglott, the Syriac is very properly translated, *esse* cœli et *esse* terræ — the *being* or *substance* of the heaven, and the *being* or *substance* of the earth.

their creation, or *after* they were created. And, thirdly, it is a violation of an essential rule of sound interpretation to infer the meaning of an author from a condensed sentence, introduced incidentally, instead of deriving it from his more direct, connected, and ample statements on the same subject. Now, the full and formal treatment of creation occupies the whole of the first chapter of Genesis. To affirm, without proof, that the verse in Exodus condenses the whole of the chapter, is to beg the very question at issue. That the chapter includes all that the verse relates to, I admit. But it includes more. It affirms, for example, in the second verse, the significant fact, that there was a period when " the earth was without form and void :" respecting this the verse in Exodus is silent; while, in the first verse, the chapter affirms that at some period *prior* to that state of chaos — *in the beginning* — God originated the material of the universe. And the question is, whether, according to the critical and correct rendering of the text, that period was not prior to the six days of the Adamic creation.

When it is objected to this priority, that the decision of the question might be safely left to any unbiassed mind on a perusal of the English version of the text, the objector is evidently calculating on the effect likely to be produced on the " unbiassed mind" by the mere juxtaposition of the opening verses, and by the conjunctive meaning, *and*, given to the Hebrew particle *vau*, which commences the second verse. This, however, is an appeal, not to his knowledge, but to his ignorance. It is to take advantage, not of his judgment, but of his prejudice. For unless, by an act of marvellous intuition, he could infer the Hebrew original from the English rendering, he may, for aught he knows to the contrary, be pronouncing on the meaning of a faulty translation. So that the question to be first decided, relates to the correct rendering of the original. If, for example, according to the learned and judicious Dathe, that rendering should be, " In the beginning, God created the heaven and the earth. But afterwards the earth became waste and desolate," — an unbiassed mind, in that case, could arrive only at the conclusion that a period was spoken of prior to the six natural days described in the verses following.

Now such appears to be the *true sense* of the original. The connecting particle at the beginning of the second verse leaves the question of time entirely open. It does not rule the sentence; the sentence rules it, and determines what its particular shade of meaning was intended to be. Even in our English version, it is often translated by other conjunctions: thus, in the very next chapter, verse 17, it is rendered *but.* Sometimes, it begins whole books. At other times, as in Numb. xx. 1, it spans a wide chronological interval. Indeed, as the general connective particle of the Hebrew language, it is employed as copulative, continuative, adversative, disjunctive, and for other purposes;[1] the specific purpose, in every case, being determinable by a consideration of the context alone.

To an examination of the text, then, let the question be referred. Now, that the originating act, described in the first verse, was not meant to be included in the account of the six Adamic days, is evident from the following considerations: First, the creation of the second, third, fourth, fifth, and sixth days, begins with the formula, *And God said;* it is only natural, therefore, to conclude that the creation of the first day begins with the third verse, where the same formula is employed, "*And God said,* Let there be light." But if so, it follows that the act described in the first verse, and the state of the earth spoken of in the second, must have both belonged to a period anterior to the first day. Secondly, the only adequate reason assignable for the account given in the second verse is, to prepare the reader for the description which follows of the six days' work. For it both intimates the necessity for such work, by affirming the chaotic condition of the earth; and describes the Spirit of God as hovering over the chaos, preparatory to it. Not only the originating act in the first verse, therefore, but also the *commencement* of the energizing process in the second, appears to have preceded the opening fiat of creation on the first day, and to have been introductory to it. Thirdly, if it be admitted that the regular unfolding of the six days' work begins at the third verse, it follows that the origination of the earth, in the first verse, was anterior to and independent of it; for no such an act is again adverted to in the subsequent verses. On the whole, then, my firm persuasion is, that the first verse of Genesis was designed, by the Divine Spirit, to announce the absolute origination of the material universe by the Almighty Creator; and that it is so understood in other parts of Holy Writ: that, passing by an indefinite interval, the second verse describes the state of our planet immediately prior to the

[1] Gesenius, *sub voce.* The lexicographer refers to the particle in Gen. i. 2, as an instance of its *continuative* force merely—*i. e.*, as employed for the simple purpose of connecting one part of a subject with the next which followed it in the order of the writer's design, without any reference to the length of intervening time.

Adamic creation; and that the third verse begins the account of the six days' work.

If I am reminded that I am in danger of being biassed in favor of these conclusions by the hope of harmonizing Scripture with geology, I might venture to suggest, in reply, that the danger is not all on one side. Instances of adherence to traditional interpretations, chiefly because they are traditional and popular, though in the face of all evidence of their faultiness, are by no means so rare as to render warning unnecessary. The danger of confounding the infallibility of our own interpretation with the infallibility of the sacred text, is not peculiar to a party.

If, again, I am reminded, in a tone of animadversion, that I am making science, in this instance, the interpreter of Scripture, my reply is, that I am simply making the works of God illustrate his word, in a department in which they speak with a distinct and authoritative voice; that "it is all the same whether our geological or theological investigations have been prior, if we have not *forced* the one into accordance with the other;"[1] and that it might be deserving consideration, whether or not the conduct of those is not open to just animadversion, who first undertake to pronounce on the meaning of a passage of Scripture irrespective of all the appropriate evidence, and who then, when that evidence is explored and produced, insist on their *à priori* interpretation as the only true one.

But in making these remarks, I have been conceding too much. The views which I have exhibited are *not* of yesterday. It is "important and interesting to observe, how the early fathers of the Christian church should seem to have entertained precisely similar views; for St. Gregory Nazianzen, after St. Justin Martyr, supposes an *indefinite period* between the creation and the first ordering of all things. St. Basil, St. Cæsarius, and Origen, are much more explicit."[2] To these might be added Augustine, Theodoret, Episcopius, and others, whose remarks imply the existence of a considerable interval "between the creation related in the first verse of Genesis, and that of which an account is given in the third and following verses."[3] In modern times, but long before geology became a science, the independent character of the opening sentence of Genesis was affirmed by such judi-

[1] Dr. S. Davidson's Sacred Hermeneutics, p. 672.

[2] Principal Wiseman's Lectures on the Connection between Science and Revealed Religion, vol. i. p. 297.

[3] The Note in Buckland's Bridgewater Treatise, by Dr. Pusey, who refers to Petavius, lib. c. cap. 11, § i—viii.

cious and learned men as Calvin, Bishop Patrick, and Dr. David Jennings.[1] And "in some old editions of the English Bible, where there is no division into verses, you actually find a break at the end of what is now the second verse; and in Luther's Bible (Wittemberg, 1557) you have in addition the figure (I) placed against the third verse, as being the beginning of the account of the creation on the first day." Now these views were formed independently of all geological considerations. In the entire absence of evidence from this quarter — probably even in opposition to it, as some would think — these conclusions were arrived at on biblical grounds alone. Geology only illustrates and confirms them. The works of God prove to be one with this preconceived meaning of his word. And there is ground to expect that this early interpretation will gradually come to be universally accepted as the only correct one.

Note C, p. 77.

"It has appeared to some persons that the mere aspect of order and symmetry in the works of nature — the contemplation of comprehensive and consistent law — is sufficient to lead us to the conception of a design and intelligence producing the order and carrying into effect the law. Without here attempting to decide whether this is true, we may discern that the conception of design arrived at in this manner, is altogether different from that idea of design which is suggested to us by organized bodies, and which we describe as the doctrine of Final Causes. The regular form of a crystal, whatever beautiful symmetry it may exhibit, whatever general laws it may exemplify, does not prove design in the same manner in which design is proved by the provisions for the preservation and growth of the seeds of plants, and of the young of animals. The law of universal gravitation, however wide and simple, does not impress us with the belief of a purpose, as does that propensity by which the two sexes of each animal are brought together. If it could be shown that the symmetrical structure of a flower results from laws of the same kind as those which determine the regular forms of crystals, or the motions of the planets, the discovery might be very striking and important, but it would not at all come under our idea of Final Cause." Whewell's *Phil. of the Inductive Sciences*, vol. ii. p. 87.

[1] Dr. J. Pye Smith's Scripture and Geology, pp 179, 180.

Note D, p. 131.

This note is taken, partly, from an abstract of a communication to the British Association, in 1845, by Professor E. Forbes, "On the Distribution of Endemic Plants, more especially those of the British Islands, considered with regard to Geological Changes;" and partly from his essay "On the connection between the Distribution of the existing Fauna and Flora of the British Isles, and the Geological Changes which have affected their area, especially during the epoch of the Northern Drift," in the "Memoirs of the Geological Survey of Great Britain, &c." The object of its insertion here is to illustrate the doctrine of successive creations.

"In the following remarks on the history of the indigenous Fauna and Flora of the British Islands and the neighboring sea," writes Professor Forbes, "I take for granted the existence of *specific centres* — i. e., of certain geographical points from which the individuals of each species have been diffused. This, indeed, must be taken for granted, if the idea of species (as most naturalists hold) involves the idea of the relationship of all the individuals composing it, and their consequent descent from a single progenitor, or from two, according as the sexes might be united or distinct.

"That this view is true, the following facts go far to prove. First: Species of opposite hemispheres placed under similar conditions are *representative*, and not *identical*. Secondly: Species occupying similar conditions in geological formations far apart, and which conditions are not met with in the intermediate formations, are representative and not identical. Thirdly: Wherever a given assemblage of conditions, to which, and to which only, certain species are adapted, are continuous — whether geographically or geologically — identical species range throughout.

"I offer no comments on these three great facts, which I present for the consideration of the few naturalists who doubt the doctrine of specific centres. The general and traditional belief of mankind has connected the idea of descent with that of distinct kinds, or species, of creatures; and the abandonment of this doctrine would place in a very dubious position all the evidence the palæontologist could offer to the geologist towards the comparison and identification of strata, and the determination of the epoch of their formation.

"Moreover, it is notorious that the doctrine of more than one point of origin for a single species, and consequently, more than one primogenitor for the individuals of it, sprang out of apparent anomalies and difficulties in distribution, such as those which I am about to show can be reasonably accounted for, without having recourse to such a supposition.

The hypothesis of the descent of all the individuals of a species either from a first pair or from a first individual, and the consequent theory of specific centres, being assumed, the isolation of assemblages of individuals from those centres and the existence of *endemic* or very local plants, remain to be accounted for. Natural transport, the agency of the sea, rivers, and winds, and carriage by animals, or through the agency of man, are means, in the majority of cases, insufficient. It is usual to say that the presence of many plants is determined by soil or climate, as the case may be; but if such plants be found in areas disconnected from their centres by considerable intervals, some other cause than the mere influence of soil or climate must be sought to account for their presence. This cause the author proposes to seek in an ancient connection of the outposts or isolated areas with the original centres, and the subsequent isolation of the former through geological changes and events, especially those dependent on the elevation and depression of land. Selecting the flora of the British Isles for a first illustration of this view, Professor Forbes calls attention to the fact, well known to botanists, of certain species of flowering plants being found indigenous in portions of that area at a great distance from the nearest assemblage of individuals of the same species in countries beyond it. Thus many plants peculiar in the British flora to the west of Ireland have the nearest portion of their specific centres in the north-west of Spain; others, confined with us to the south-west promontory of England, are, beyond our shores, found in the Channel Isles and the opposite coast of France; the vegetation of the south-east of England is that of the opposite part of the Continent; and the Alpine vegetation of Wales and the Scottish Highlands is intimately related to that of the Norwegian Alps. The great mass of the British flora has its most intimate relations with that of western Germany. The vegetation of the British Islands may be said to be composed of five floras: — 1st, a west Pyrenean, confined to the west of Ireland, and mostly to the mountains of that district; 2nd, a flora related to that of the south-west of France, extending from the Channel Isles, across Devon and Cornwall, to the south-east and part of the south-west of Ireland; 3rd, the flora common to the north of France and south-east of England, and especially developed in the chalk districts; 4th, an Alpine flora, developed in the mountains of Wales, north of England, and Scotland; and 5th, a Germanic flora, extending over the greater part of Great Britain and Ireland, mingling with the other floras, and diminishing, though slightly, as we proceed westwards, indicating its easterly origin and relation to the characteristic flora of northern and western Germany. Interspersed among the members of the last-named flora are a very few specific centres, peculiar to the British Isles. The author numbers these floras according to magnitude as to species, and also, in his opinion, according to their relative age and periods of introduction into the area of the British Islands. His conclusions on this point are the following: —

"1. The oldest of the floras now composing the vegetation of the British Isles is that of the mountains of the west of Ireland. Although an Alpine flora, it is southernmost in character, and quite distinct as a system from the floras of the Scottish and Welsh Alps. Its very southern character, its limitation, and its extreme isolation, are evidences of its antiquity, pointing to a period when a great mountain barrier extended across the mouth of the Bay of Biscay from Spain to Ireland.

"2. The distribution of the second flora, next in point of probable date, depended on the extension of a barrier, the traces of which still remain, from the west of France to the south-west of Britain, and thence to Ireland.

"3. The distribution of the third flora depended on the connection of the coasts of France and England towards the eastern part of the Channel. Of the former existence of this union no geologist doubts.

"4. The distribution of the fourth, or Alpine flora of Scotland and Wales, was effected during the glacial period, when the mountain summits of Britain were low islands, or members of chains of islands, extending to the area of Norway through a glacial sea, and clothed with an arctic vegetation, which, in the gradual upheaval of the land, and consequent change of climate, became limited to the summits of the new formed and still existing mountains.

"5. The distribution of the fifth, or Germanic flora, depended on the upheaval of the bed of the glacial sea, and the consequent connection of Ireland and England, and of England with Germany, by great plains, the fragments of which still exist, and upon which lived the great elk, and other quadrupeds now extinct.

"The breaking up, or submergence, of the first barrier led to the destruction of the second; that of the second to that of the third; but the well-marked epoch of the Germanic flora indicates the subsequent formation of the Straits of Dover and of the Irish Sea, as now existing.

"To determine the probable geological epoch of the first, or west Irish flora, a fragment, perhaps, with that of northwestern Spain, of the vegetation of the true Atlantic, we must seek among fossil plants for a starting-point in time. This we get in the flora of the London clay, or eocene, which is tropical in character, and far anterior to the oldest of the existing floras. The geographical relations of the miocene sea, indicated by the fossils of the coralline crag, give an after-date certainly to the second and third of the above floras, if not to the first. The epoch of the red or middle crag was probably coeval with the in-coming of the second flora; that of the mammaliferous crag with the third. The date of the fourth is too evident to be questioned; and the author regards the glacial region in which it flourished as a local climate, of which no true traces, so far as animal life is concerned, exists southwards of the second and third barriers. This was the newer pliocene epoch. The period of the fifth flora was that of the post-tertiary, when the present aspect of things was organized."

In his masterly essay, the Professor has shown that the peculiar distribution of the endemic animals, especially of the terrestrial mollusca, bears him out in these views. And among the chief conclusions which he derives from the facts and arguments there adduced, the first is, that "the flora and fauna, terrestrial and marine, of the British islands and seas, have originated, so far as that area is concerned, since the miocene epoch." And the second, that "the assemblages of animals and plants composing that fauna and flora, did not appear in the area they now inhabit simultaneously, but at several distinct points of time." These distinct periods, beginning some time after the miocene epoch and ending with that of the post-tertiary, are indicated above. And the evidence of the in-coming of each assemblage of plants and animals, in the order and at the time specified, is to be found in the fossil records which the earth contains, and which the essay clearly exhibits. It hardly need be added, that the same course of investigation is as applicable to the entire globe as to the area in question, and the relations of the ancient epochs of geology one with another, as of the present with the geological past.

Note E, p. 180.

On the subject of animal pain there are two extreme opinions. One, underrates the evil, treats it as incidental merely, and tends to ignore it. The other, morbidly luxuriates in the idea that sentient existence is one great agony; and indignantly turns away from the ten thousand mitigating proofs that there is a law of graduating sensibility pervading the animal kingdom, according to which the degree of feeling diminishes as the organization descends in the scale. It *will* have it, that "the mouse is in agonies" in the presence of the cat which is about to destroy it, even though the mouse practically affirms the contrary by quietly stopping to discuss a morsel of bread which happens to lie at the moment in its path. (A fact which I have seen). It will insist that the polypus suffers torture at the excision of one of its numerous and ever-waving tentacula, although all the other tentacula continue to wave meantime in apparently unconscious and undisturbed tranquillity.

In the text, I have maintained a medium view; endeavoring to show that, as the myriad tribes of minute organisms, in which sensibility to pain is reduced to the minimum, constitute the staple of animal food, the arrangement benevolently provides, in so far, for the least possible amount of suffering; and that as to employing them for food, it is more consistent with the greatest amount of enjoyment, that a certain proportion of that food should be animated, and be filled with pleasure until it is wanted, than that it should never have existed. One of my reviewers supposes that, in arguing thus, I must have forgotten that the food of the herbivorous animal is chemically the same with that of the carnivorous; and that, therefore, unless the stock of vegetable food failed from the superfecundity of animal life, my position is not made good. Now, I can assure him that I was led to adopt my view of the subject, not by forgetting, but by remembering the point in question, and by remembering it, in union with two or three other facts which do not appear to have ever occurred to him. He appears to satisfy himself on the subject, by erroneously limiting his view to the existence of the larger herbivorous animals. So also another writer, taking the same narrow ground, remarks, that the carnivorous animal finds nothing in the creature it devours, which it might not have derived from the vegetable food out of which the flesh of its prey was transmuted. Now, let us apply this reasoning to the ant and the aphis, or plant-louse, as an example. The numerous tribes of the aphis family of insects are most destructive to plants, of which they suck the juices with their trunk. Now, in the course of a day, an ant, whose nest is at hand, will clear a leaf of a whole colony of them. But the ant finds nothing, it is said, in the aphis, which it might not have derived from the leaf out of which the aphis was transmuted. Granted; but, according to the existing arrangement, a hundred insects lived their day of life on that leaf, which they could not have enjoyed had the leaf been pre-occupied or exhausted by the ant; while they themselves are subsequently carried off and reserved for the sustenance of other forms of life. "Consider (says Professor Owen in his Lectures on the *Invertebrata*) their incredible numbers, their universal distribution, their insatiable voracity, and that it is the particles of decaying vegetable and animal bodies which they are appointed to devour and assimilate. Surely we must in some degree be indebted to these ever-active invisible scavengers, for the salubrity of our atmosphere. Nor is this all: they perform a still more important office in preventing the gradual diminution of the present amount of organized matter upon the earth. For when this matter is dissolved or suspended in water, in that state of comminution and decay which immediately precedes its final decomposition into the elementary gases, and its consequent return from the organic to the inorganic world, these wakeful members of nature's invisible police are everywhere ready to arrest the fugitive organized particles, and turn them back into the ascending stream of animal life. Having converted the dead and decomposing particles into their own living tissues, they themselves become the food of larger Infusoria, and of numerous other small animals, which in their turn are devoured by larger animals: and thus a pabulum fit for the nourishment of the highest organized beings is brought back by a short route from the extremity of the realms of organized matter." These remarks relate especially to the processes which are ever going on in the teeming world of waters. True; the animal nourishment, in this instance, is, by supposition, already decomposed; and, therefore, does not affect the question of prey. But the view I am opposing merges this aspect of the subject, and equally denies that the consumption of animal food, whether alive, dead, or decomposed, augments the sum total of animal enjoyment; for the strength of its denial lies in the fact that the chemical elements of vegetable and animal life are the same. But who does not see that if these swarms of invisible animalcules were debarred from feeding on animal, and were confined to vegetable matter, whole tribes of them must be blotted from existence for lack of food? Nor could the process of annihilation stop here: it must extend also to whole classes of those animals whose decomposed remains they now devour; for if we are "in some degree indebted to these ever-active invisible scavengers, for the salubrity of our atmosphere," their non-existence presupposes also the non-existence of their pestilential food.

Those who argue that, because the food of the herbivorous animal is chemically the same as the carnivorous, therefore nothing is gained to the amount of animal life and enjoyment by the existence of carnivora, unless the stock of vegetable food failed from the superfecundity of animal life, appear to overlook certain facts important to a correct decision. They seem to forget that, if vegetables have a chemistry, animals have a chemistry of their own also; that, although vegetable is the ultimate solid support of animal life, yet animals drink and breathe as well as eat; and that drinking and breathing are the means of growth. The problem is not merely, Given a certain surface of earth, and a certain amount of vegetable life, to support and determine the greatest amount of animal life; but, Given both these, and an ocean of air and of water in addition. The animal draws from these latter sources as copiously as the vegetable. And the consequence is, that the quantity of animal matter in existence is incomparably greater than the amount of vegetable matter would account for. And the obvious inference is, that a far greater variety and amount of animal life is supportable by employing this vast quantity of animal substance as food, than if it were all wasted, and animal life were sustained by vegetable nourishment alone. The system of prey is only incidental to this greater question. If it be true, that the same animal seized as prey, affords a much larger quantity of nourishment than it would if it had been left to waste away in sickness and death; if the sudden and rapid multiplication of insect life would in some instance strip a district of its vegetable clothing were it not kept in check by an insectivorous provision; and if, as I have instanced in the case of the ant and the aphides, (other illustrations might be easily adduced,) their destruction for food does not cancel the previous fact of their existence and enjoyment, the conclusion is fully warranted, that it is more consistent with the greatest amount of enjoyment that a certain proportion of animal food should be animated and be filled with pleasure until it is wanted than it should never have existed.

NOTE F, p. 218,

On the presumed influences of climate, food, and hybridization, the following observations are valuable, from "Ornamental and

Domestic poultry ; their History and Management." By the Rev. E. S. Dixon, M. A.

"Some very important speculations respecting organic life, and the history of the animated races now inhabiting this planet, are closely connected with the creatures we retain in domestication, and can scarcely be studied so well in any other field. Poultry, living under our very roof, and, by the rapid succession of their generations, affording a sufficient number of instances for even the short life of man to give time to take some cognisance of their progressive succession, — poultry afford the best possible subjects for observing the transmission or interruption of hereditary forms and instincts. I shall, no doubt, at the first glance, be pronounced rash, as soon as I am perceived to quit the plain task of observing, for the more adventurous one of speculating upon what I have observed. I can only say that the conclusion to which I have arrived respecting what is called the 'origin' of our domestic races, has been, to my own mind, irresistible, having begun the investigation with a bias towards what I must call the wild theory, although so fashionable of late, that our tame breeds or varieties are the result of cross breeding between undomesticated animals, fertile *inter se*. It will be found, I imagine, on strict inquiry, that the most careful breeding will only fix and make prominent peculiar features or points that are observed in certain families of the same aboriginal species, or sub-species, — no more : and that the whole world might be challenged to bring evidence (such as would be admitted in an English court of justice) that any permanent intermediate variety of bird or animal, that would continue to reproduce offspring like itself, and not reverting to either original type, had been originated by the crossing of any two wild species. Very numerous instances of the failure of such experimental attempts might be adduced. The difficulty under which science labors in pursuing this inquiry, is much increased by the mystery in which almost all breeders have involved their proceedings even if they have not purposely misled those who have endeavored to trace the means employed. As to the great question of the Immutability of Species, so closely allied to the investigation of the different varieties of poultry, as far as my own limited researches have gone — and they have been confined almost entirely to birds under the influence of man — they have led me to the conclusion that even sub-species and varieties are much more permanent, independent, and ancient than is currently believed at the present day. This result has been to me unavoidable, as well as unexpected ; for, as above mentioned, I started with a great idea of the powerful transmuting influence of time, changed climate, and increased food. My present conviction is, that the diversities which we see in even the most nearly allied species of birds are not produced by any such influences, nor by hybridization; but that each distinct species, however nearly resembling any other, has been produced by a Creative Power: I am even disposed to adopt this view towards many forms that are usually considered as mere varieties. As far as I have been able to ascertain *facts*, hybrids that *are* fertile are even then saved from being posterity-less (to coin a word) only by their progeny rapidly reverting to the type of one parent or the other; so that no intermediate race is founded. Things very soon go on as they went before, or they cease to go on at all. This is the case with varieties also, and is well known to breeders as one of the most inflexible difficulties they have to contend with, called by them 'crying back.' This circumstance first led me to suspect the permanence and antiquity of varieties, and even of what are called 'improvements' and 'new breeds.' Half of the mongrels that one sees are only transition-forms, passing back to the type of one or other original progenitor. At least, my eye can detect such to be frequently the apparent fact in the case of Domestic Fowls. Any analogies from plants must be cautiously applied to animals; but even in the vegetable kingdom the number and reproductive power of hybrids is apparently greater than it really is, owing to the facility of propagation by extension, by which means a perfectly sterile individual can be multiplied and kept in existence for many hundred years; whereas a half-bred bird or animal would, in a short time, disappear and leave no trace. I have not met with one authenticated fact of the race of pheasants having been really and permanently incorporated with fowls, so as to originate a mixed race capable of continuation with itself; but with many that prove the extreme improbability of such a thing happening."

NOTE G, p. 223.

"Some years ago," (says Professor Schleiden, in "The Plant: a Biography,") "I was very intimate with the directing physician of a large lunatic asylum, and I used industriously to avail myself of the liberty I thus obtained, to visit at will the house and its inhabitants. One morning I entered the room of a madman, whose constantly varying hallucinations especially interested me. I found him crouching down by the stove, watching, with close attention, a saucepan, the contents of which he was carefully stirring. At the noise of my entrance, he turned round, and, with a face of the greatest importance, whispered, 'Hush, hush! don't disturb my little pigs; they will be ready directly.' Full of curiosity to know whither his diseased imagination had now led him, I approached nearer. 'You see,' said he, with the mysterious expression of an alchemist, 'here I have black-puddings, pigs' bones and bristles, in the saucepan — everything that is necessary — we only want the vital warmth, and the young pig will be ready made again.'" This is hardly a caricature of certain speculatists. "Organism" (says Oken) "is galvanism residing in a thoroughly homogeneous mass. * * * A galvanic pile pounded into atoms must become alive. In this manner, nature brings forth organic bodies"!!

Note H, p. 231.

"The geographical distribution of organic groups in space" (says Mr. Strickland in his work on "The Dodo and its Kindred") "is a no less interesting result of science than their geological succession in time. We find a special relation to exist between the structures of organized bodies and the districts of the earth's surface which they inhabit. Certain groups of animals or vegetables, often very extensive, and containing a multitude of genera or of species, are found to be confined to certain continents and their circumjacent islands. In the present state of science we must be content to admit the existence of this law, without being able to enunciate its preamble. It does *not* imply that organic distribution depends on soil and climate; for we often find a perfect identity of these conditions in opposite hemispheres and in remote continents, whose faunæ and floræ are almost wholly diverse. It does *not* imply that allied but distinct organisms have been educed by generation or spontaneous development from the same original stock; for (to pass over other objections) we find detached volcanic islets which have been ejected from beneath the ocean, (such as the Galapagos, for instance,) inhabited by terrestrial forms allied to those of the nearest continent, though hundreds of miles distant, and evidently never connected with them. But this fact *may* indicate that the Creator in forming new organisms to discharge the functions required from time to time by the ever vacillating balance of Nature, has thought fit to preserve the regularity of the System by modifying the types of structure already established in the adjacent localities, rather than to proceed *per saltum* by introducing forms of more foreign aspect."

INDEX.

END

VALUABLE WORKS

PUBLISHED BY

GOULD AND LINCOLN,

59 WASHINGTON STREET, BOSTON.

SACRED RHETORIC: Or, Composition and Delivery of Sermons. By HENRY J. RIPLEY, Prof. in Newton Theological Institution. Including Ware's Hints on Extemporaneous Preaching. Second thousand. 12mo, 75 cts.

An admirable work, clear and succint in its positions and recommendations, soundly based on good authority, and well supported by a variety of reading and illustrations. — *N. Y. Literary World.*

We have looked over this work with a lively interest. The arrangement is easy and natural, and the selection of thoughts under each topic very happy. The work is one that will command readers. It is a comprehensive manual of great practical utility. — *Phil. Ch. Chronicle.*

The author contemplates a man *preparing to compose a discourse* to promote the great ends of preaching, and unfolds to him the process through which his mind ought to pass. We commend the work to ministers, and to those preparing for the sacred office, as a book that will efficiently aid them in studying thoroughly the subject it brings before them. — *Phil. Ch. Observer.*

It presents a rich variety of rules for the practical use of the clergyman, and evinces the good sense, the large experience, and the excellent spirit of Dr. Ripley: and the whole volume is well fitted to instruct and stimulate the writer of sermons. — *Bibliotheca Sacra.*

An excellent work is here offered to theological students and clergymen. It is not a compilation, but is an original treatise, fresh, practical, and comprehensive, and adapted to the pulpit offices of the present day. It is full of valuable suggestions, and abounds with clear illustrations. — *Zion's Herald.*

It cannot be too frequently perused by those whose duty it is to *persuade* men. — *Congregationalist.*

Prof. Ripley possesses the highest qualifications for a work of this kind. His position has given him great experience in the peculiar wants of theological students. — *Providence Journal.*

His canons on selecting texts, stating the proposition, collecting and arranging materials, style, delivery, etc., are just and well stated. Every theological student to whom this volume is *accessible* will be likely to procure it. — *Christian Mirror, Portland.*

It is manifestly the fruit of mature thought and large observation; it is pervaded by a manly tone, and abounds in judicious counsels; it is compactly written and admirably arranged, both for study and reference. It will become a text book for theological students, we have no doubt: that it deserves to be read by all ministers is to us as clear. — *N. Y. Recorder.*

THE CHRISTIAN WORLD UNMASKED. By JOHN BERRIDGE, A. M., Vicar of Everton, Bedfordshire, Chaplain to the Right Hon. The Earl of Buchan, etc. *New Edition.* With Life of the Author, by the REV. THOMAS GUTHRIE, D. D., Minister of Free St. John's, Edinburgh. 16mo, cloth.

"The book," says DR. GUTHRIE, in his Introduction, "which we introduce anew to the public, has survived the test of years, and still stands towering above things of inferior growth like a cedar of Lebanon. Its subject is all important; in doctrine it is sound to the core; it glows with fervent piety; it exhibits a most skilful and unsparing dissection of the dead professor; while its style is so remarkable, that he who could *preach* as Berridge has *written*, would hold any congregation by the ears."

THE CHRISTIAN REVIEW. Edited by JAMES D. KNOWLES, BARNAS SEARS, and S. F. SMITH. 8 vols. Commencing with vol. one. Half cl., lettered, 8,00. Single volumes, (except the first,) may be had in numbers, 1,00.

These first eight volumes of the Christian Review contain valuable contributions from the leading men of the Baptist and several other denominations, and will be found a valuable acquisition to any library.

Aa

DR. WILLIAMS'S WORKS.

RELIGIOUS PROGRESS; Discourses on the Development of the Christian Character. By WILLIAM R. WILLIAMS, D. D. Third ed. 12mo, cl., 85c.

This work is from the pen of one of the brightest lights of the American pulpit. We scarcely know of any living writer who has a finer command of powerful thought and glowing, impressive language than he. The volume will advance, if possible, the author's reputation. — DR. SPRAGUE, *Alb. Atlas.*

This book is a rare phenomena in these days. It is a rich exposition of Scripture, with a fund of practical religious wisdom, conveyed in a style so strong and massive as to remind one of the English writers of two centuries ago; and yet it abounds in fresh illustrations drawn from every (even the latest opened) field of science and of literature. — *Methodist Quarterly.*

His power of apt and forcible illustration is without a parallel among modern writers. The mute pages spring into life beneath the magic of his radiant imagination. But this is never at the expense of solidity of thought or strength of argument. It is seldom, indeed, that a mind of so much poetical invention yields such a willing homage to the logical element. — *Harper's Monthly Miscellany.*

With warm and glowing language, Dr. Williams exhibits and enforces the truth; every page radiant with "thoughts that burn," leave their indelible impression upon the mind. — *N. Y. Com. Adv.*

The strength and compactness of argumentation, the correctness and beauty of style, and the importance of the animating idea of the discourses, are worthy of the high reputation of Dr. Williams, and place them among the most finished homiletic productions of the day. — *N. Y. Evangelist.*

Dr. Williams has no superior among American divines in profound and exact learning, and brilliancy of style. He seems familiar with the literature of the world, and lays his vast resources under contribution to illustrate and adorn every theme which he investigates. We wish the volume could be placed in every religious family in the country. — *Phil. Ch. Chronicle.*

LECTURES ON THE LORD'S PRAYER. Third ed. 32mo, cl., 85c.

We observe the writer's characteristic fulness and richness of language, felicity and beauty of illustration, justness of discrimination and thought. — *Watchman and Reflector.*

Dr. Williams is one of the most interesting and accomplished writers in this country. We welcome this volume as a valuable contribution to our religious literature — *Ch. Witness.*

In reading, we resolved to mark the passages which we most admired, but soon found that we should be obliged to mark nearly all of them. — *Ch. Secretary.*

It bears in every page the mark of an elegant writer and an accomplished scholar, an acute reasoner and a cogent moralist. Some passages are so decidedly eloquent that we instinctively find ourselves looking round as if upon an audience, and ready to join them with audible applause — *Ch. Inquirer.*

We are constantly reminded, in reading his eloquent pages, of the old English writers, whose vigorous thought, and gorgeous imagery, and varied learning, have made their writings an inexhaustible mine for the scholars of the present day. — *Ch. Observer.*

Their breadth of view, strength of logic, and stirring eloquence place them among the very best homiletical efforts of the age. Every page is full of suggestion as well as eloquence. — *Ch. Parlor Mag.*

MISCELLANIES. New, improved edition. *(Price reduced.)* 12mo, 1,25.

☞ This work, which has been heretofore published in octavo form at 1,75 per copy, is published by the present proprietors in one handsome 12mo volume, at the low price of 1,25.

A volume which is absolutely necessary to the completeness of a library. — *N. Y. Weekly Review.*

Dr. Williams is a profound scholar and a brilliant writer. — *N. Y. Evangelist.*

He often rises to the sphere of a glowing and impressive eloquence, because no other form of language can do justice to his thoughts and emotions. So, too, the exuberance of literary illustration, with which he clothes the driest speculative discussions, is not brought in for the sake of effect, but as the natural expression of a mind teeming with the "spoils of time" and the treasures of study in almost every department of learning. — *N. Y. Tribune.*

From the pen of one of the most able and accomplished authors of the age. — *Bap. Memorial.*

We are glad to see this volume. We wish such men abounded in every sect. — *Ch. Register.*

One of the richest volumes that has been given to the public for many years. — *N. Y. Bap. Reg.*

The author's mind is cast in no common mould. A delightful volume. — *Meth. Prot.*

THEOLOGICAL SCIENCE.

BY THE REV. JOHN HARRIS, D. D.

THE PRE-ADAMITE EARTH: Contributions to Theological Science. New and revised edition. 12mo, cloth, 85 cts.

It opens new trains of thought; puts one in a new position to survey the wonders of God's works, and compels Natural Science to bear her testimony in support of Divine Truth. — *Phil. Ch. Observer.*

If we do not greatly mistake, this long looked for volume will create and sustain a deep impression in the more intellectual circles of the religious world. — *London Evan. Mag.*

The man who finds his element among great thoughts, and is not afraid to push into the remoter regions of abstract truth, be he philosopher or theologian, or both, will read it over and over, and will find his intellect strengthened, as if from being in contact with a new creation. — *Albany Argus.*

Dr. Harris states in a lucid, succinct, and often highly eloquent manner, all the leading facts of geology, and their beautiful harmony with the teachings of Scripture. As a work of paleontology in its relation to Scripture, it will be one of the most complete and popular extant. — *N. Y. Evangelist.*

He is a sound logician and lucid reasoner, getting nearer to the groundwork of a subject generally supposed to have uncertain data, than any other writer within our knowledge. — *N. Y. Com. Adv.*

We have never seen the natural sciences, particularly geology, made to give so decided and unimpeachable testimony to revealed truth. The wonders of God's works, which he has here grouped together, convey a most magnificent, and even overpowering idea of the Great Creator. We wish that we could devote a week, uninterruptedly, to its perusal and re-perusal. — *Ch. Mirror.*

Written in the glowing and eloquent style which has won for him a universal fame, and will secure a wide circle of readers. — *N. Y. Recorder.*

The elements of things, the laws of organic nature, and those especially that lie at the foundation of the divine relations to man, are dwelt upon in a masterly manner. — *Watchman and Reflector.*

A work of theological science, not to be passed over with a glance. It applies principles or laws to the successive stages of the Pre-Adamite Earth; to the historical development of man; the family; nation; Son of God; church; the Bible revelation, and the future prospects of humanity. — *Transcript.*

MAN PRIMEVAL; Or, the Constitution and Primitive Condition of the Human Being. A Contribution to Theological Science. With a fine Portrait of the Author. 12mo, cloth, 1,25.

*** This is the second volume of a series of works on Theological Science. The first has been received with much favor; the present is a continuation of the principles which were seen holding their way through the successive kingdoms of primeval nature, and are here resumed and exhibited in their next higher application to individual man.

His copious and beautiful illustrations of the successive laws of the Divine Manifestation, have yielded us inexpressible delight. — *London Eclectic Review.*

The distribution and arrangement of thought in this volume are such as to afford ample scope for the author's remarkable powers of analysis and illustration. In a very masterly way does our author grapple with almost every difficult and perplexing subject which comes within the range of his proposed inquiry into the constitution and condition of Man Primeval. — *London Evangelical Mag.*

Reverently recognizing the Bible as the fountain and exponent of *truth*, he is as independent and fearless as he is original and forcible; and he adds to these qualities consummate skill in argument and elegance of diction. — *N. Y. Commercial.*

Dr. Harris, though a young man, has placed himself in the very front rank of scientific writers, and his essays attract the attention of the most erudite scholars of the age. — *N. Y. Ch. Observer.*

It surpasses its predecessors in interest. To students of mental and moral science, it will be a valuable contribution, and will assuredly secure their attention. — *Phil. Ch. Chron.*

It is eminently philosophical, and at the same time glowing and eloquent. It cannot fail to have a wide circle of readers, or repay richly the hours which are given to its pages. — *N. Y. Recorder.*

The work before us manifests much learning and metaphysical acumen. — *Puritan Recorder.*

THE FAMILY: Its Constitution, Probation, and History. Being the third volume of the Series. *In Preparation.*

Cc

WORKS OF JOHN HARRIS, D. D.

THE GREAT COMMISSION; Or, the Christian Church constituted and charged to convey the Gospel to the World. With an Introductory Essay, by WILLIAM R. WILLIAMS, D. D. Seventh thousand. 12mo, cloth, 1,00.

Of the several productions of Dr. Harris, — all of them of great value, — this is destined to exert the most powerful influence in forming the religious and missionary character of the coming generations. But the vast fund of argument and instruction will excite the admiration and inspire the gratitude of thousands in our own land as well as in Europe. Every clergyman and pious and reflecting layman ought to possess the volume, and make it familiar by repeated perusal. — *Puritan Recorder.*

His plan is original and comprehensive. In filling it up, the author has interwoven facts with rich and glowing illustrations, and with trains of thought that are sometimes almost resistless in their appeals to the conscience. The work is not more distinguished for its arguments and its genius than for the spirit of deep and fervent piety that pervades it. — *Day-Spring.*

This work comes forth in circumstances which give and promise extraordinary interest and value. Its general circulation will do much good. — *N. Y. Evangelist.*

To recommend this work to the friends of all denominations would be but faint praise; the author deserves, and will undoubtedly receive, the credit of having applied a new lever to that great moral machine which, by the blessing of God, is destined to evangelize the world. — *Ch. Secretary.*

"Have you read the Great Commission, by Harris?" I answer promptly, *No.* I have often attempted it, but have as often failed. Before I can go through with a single page, the book is laid down, and my mind is lost in thought; and yet so profitably and pleasantly lost, that one almost wishes to continue so. *I have* THOUGHT *it nearly through!* The book is made up *of* thought, and made *for* thought, and consequent action. — REV. A. WILLIAMS.

THE GREAT TEACHER; Or, Characteristics of our Lord's Ministry. With an Introductory Essay, by HEMAN HUMPHREY, D. D., late President of Amherst College. Twelfth thousand. 12mo, cloth, 85 cts.

Its style is, like the country which gave it birth, beautiful, varied, finished, and every where delightful. But the style of this work is its smallest excellence. It will be read; it ought to be read. It will find its way to many parlors, and add to the comforts of many a happy fireside. The writer pours forth a clear and beautiful light, like that of the evening light-house, when it sheds its rays upon the sleeping waters, and covers them with a surface of gold. We can have no sympathy with a heart which yields not to impressions delicate and holy, which the perusal of this work will naturally make. — DR. TODD, *Hampshire Gazette.*

He writes like one who has long been accustomed to "sit at the feet of Jesus," and has eminently profited under his teaching. I do not wonder at the avidity which is hastening its wide circulation in England; nor at the high terms in which it is recommended by so many of the best judges. I am sure that it deserves an equally rapid and wide circulation here. — DR. HUMPHREY'S *Introduction.*

To praise the work itself would be a work of supererogation. All Christians know it; all read and admire it. Harris is, to our view, incomparably the greatest religious writer now living — more particularly of practical works. His pages are a storehouse of "weighty and well-digested thoughts, imbued with deep Christian feeling, and clothed in perspicuous and polished language." — *Weekly Rev.*

MISCELLANIES; Consisting Principally of Sermons and Essays. With an Introductory Essay and Notes, by JOSEPH BELCHER, D. D. 12mo, cloth, 75 cts.

These essays are among the finest in the language; and the warmth and energy of religious feeling manifested will render them the treasure of the closet and the Christian fireside. — *Bangor Merc.*

DR. HARRIS is one of the best writers of the age, and this volume will not in the least detract from his well-merited reputation. — *American Pulpit.*

The contents of this volume will afford the reader an intellectual and spiritual banquet of the highest order. — *Philadelphia Ch. Observer.*

ZEBULON; Or the Moral Claims of Seamen stated and enforced. Edited by REV. W. M. ROGERS and DANIEL M. LORD. 18mo, cloth, 25 cts.

☞ A well-written and spirit-stirring appeal to Christians in behalf of that numerous, useful, generous-hearted, though long-neglected class, *seamen.*

UNIVERSITY SERMONS.

SERMONS Delivered in the Chapel of Brown University. By the Rev. Francis Wayland, D. D. Third thousand. 12mo, cloth, 1,00.

☞ Dr. Wayland has here discussed most of the prominent doctrines of the Bible in his usual clear and masterly style, viz.: Theoretical Atheism; Practical Atheism; Moral Character of Man; Love to God; Fall of Man; Justification by Works impossible; Preparation for the Advent of the Messiah; Work of the Messiah; Justification by Faith; The Fall of Peter; The Church of Christ; The Unity of the Church; The Duty of Obedience to the Civil Magistrate; also, the Recent Revolutions in Europe.

The discourses contained in this handsome volume are characterized by all that richness of thought and elegance of language for which their talented author is celebrated. The volume is worthy of the pen of the distinguished divine from whom it emanates. — Dr. Baird's *Christian Union.*

Few sermons contain so much carefully arranged thought as these. The thorough logician is apparent throughout the volume, and there is a classic purity in the diction, unsurpassed by any writer, and equalled by few. — *N. Y. Commercial.*

The author has long been before the public as one of our most popular writers in various departments of science and morals. His style is easy and fluent, and rich in illustration. — *Evan. Review.*

No thinking man can open to any portion of it without finding his attention strongly arrested, and feeling inclined to yield his assent to those self-evincing statements which appear on every page. As a writer, Dr. Wayland is distinguished by simplicity, strength, and comprehensiveness. He addresses himself directly to the intellect more than to the imagination, to the conscience more than to the passions. — *Watchman and Reflector.*

Just issued, a noble volume of noble sermons, from the distinguished President of Brown University. These discourses are fine specimens of his discriminating power of thought, and purity and vigor of style. — *Zion's Herald.*

Dr. Wayland's name and fame will cause any thing from his pen to be eagerly sought for; and those who take up this volume with the high expectations induced by his previous works, will not be disappointed. The discourses are rich in evangelical truth, profound thought, and beautiful diction; worthy at once of the theologian, the philosopher, and the rhetorician. — *Albany Argus.*

This volume adds to Dr. Wayland's fame as a writer. This is commendation enough to bestow upon any book. — *Puritan Recorder.*

Dr. Wayland is one of the prominent Christian philosophers and literary men of our country. His style is elegant and polished, and his views evangelical. — *Watchman, Cincinnati.*

His style is peculiarly adapted to arrest the attention, and his familiar illustrations serve to make plain the most abstruse principles, as well as to enstamp them upon one's memory. It is, in fact, scarcely possible to forget a discourse which we read from Wayland, and we have ever found his works to be highly suggestive. We think no minister's library complete without it. — *Dover Star.*

We must call the attention of our readers again to this attractive volume of sermons. They come from one who has attained a national reputation, and embody the views matured by the careful study of many years upon the most important topics in theology. — *Phil. Ch. Chronicle.*

It would be spending time to little purpose to attempt a eulogy on a work emanating from such a source. — *N. Y. Baptist Register.*

THE PERSON AND WORK OF CHRIST. By Ernest Sartorius, D. D., General Superintendent and Consistorial Director at Konigsberg, Prussia. Translated from the German, by the Rev. Oakman S. Stearns, A. M. 18mo, cloth, 42 cts.

A work of much ability, and presenting the argument in a style that will be new to most American readers. It will deservedly attract attention. — *N. Y. Observer.*

Dr. Sartorius is one of the most eminent and evangelical theologians in Germany. The work will be found, both from the important subjects discussed and the earnestness, beauty, and vivacity of its style, to possess the qualities which recommend it to the Christian public. — *Mich. Ch. Herald.*

A little volume on a great subject, and evidently the production of a great mind. The style and train of thought prove this. — *Southern Literary Gazette.*

Whether we consider the importance of the subjects discussed, or the perspicuous exhibition of truth in the volume before us, the chaste and elegant style used, or the devout spirit of the author, we cannot but desire that the work may meet with an extensive circulation. — *Christian Index.*

Gg

WORKS FOR BIBLE STUDENTS.

A TREATISE ON BIBLICAL CRITICISMS; Exhibiting a Systematic View of that Science. By SAMUEL DAVIESON, D. D., of the University of Halle, Author of "Ecclesiastical Polity of the New Testament," "Introduction to the New Testament," "Sacred Hermeneutics Developed and Applied. A new Revised and Enlarged Edition, in two elegant octavo volumes, cloth, 5,00.

These volumes contain a statement of *the sources* of criticism, such as the MSS. of the Hebrew Bible and Greek Testament, the principal versions of both, quotations from them in early writers, parallels, and also the internal evidence on which critics rely for obtaining a pure text. A history of the texts of the Old and New Testaments, with a description of the Hebrew and Greek languages in which the Scriptures are written. An examination of the most important passages whose readings are disputed.

Every thing, in short, is discussed, which properly belongs to *the criticism* of the text, comprehending all that comes under the title of *General Introduction* in Introductions to the Old and New Testaments.

HISTORY OF PALESTINE, from the Patriarchal Age to the Present Time; with Introductory Chapters on the Geography and Natural History of the Country, and on the Customs and Institutions of the Hebrews. By JOHN KITTO, D. D., Author of "Scripture Daily Readings," "Cyclopædia of Biblical Literature," &c. With upwards of *two hundred Illustrations*. 12mo, cloth, 1,25.

A very full compendium of the geography and history of Palestine, from the earliest era mentioned in Scripture to the present day; not merely a dry record of boundaries, and the succession of rulers, but an intelligible account of the agriculture, habits of life, literature, science, and art, with the religious, political, and judicial institutions of the inhabitants of the Holy Land in all ages. The descriptive portions of the work are increased in value by numerous wood cuts. A more useful and instructive book has rarely been published. — *N. Y. Commercial.*

Whoever will read this book till he has possessed himself thoroughly of its contents, will, we venture to say, read the Bible with far more intelligence and satisfaction during all the rest of his life. — *Puritan Recorder.*

Beyond all dispute, this is the best historical compendium of the Holy Land, from the days of Abraham to those of the late Pasha of Egypt, Mehemet Ali. — *Edinburgh Review.*

☞ In the numerous notices and reviews the work has been strongly recommended, as not only admirably adapted to the *family*, but also as a text book for *Sabbath and week day schools.*

CRUDEN'S CONDENSED CONCORDANCE; a New and Complete Concordance to the Holy Scriptures. By ALEXANDER CRUDEN. Revised and Re-edited by the Rev. DAVID KING, LL. D. Tenth thousand. Octavo, cloth backs, 1,25

This work is printed from English plates, and is a full and fair copy of all that is valuable as a Concordance in Cruden's larger work, in two volumes, which costs *five dollars*, while *this* edition is furnished at *one dollar and twenty-five cents!* The principal variation from the larger book consists in the exclusion of the Bible Dictionary, (which has always been an incumbrance,) the condensation of the quotations of Scripture, arranged under their most obvious heads, which, while it diminishes the bulk of the work, *greatly facilitates* the finding of any required passage.

We have, in this edition of Cruden, the *best* made better! That is, the present is better adapted to the purposes of a concordance, by the erasure of superfluous references, the omission of unnecessary explanations, and the contraction of quotations, etc. It is better as a manual, and better adapted by its price, to the means of many who need and ought to possess such a work, than the former large and expensive edition. — *Puritan Recorder.*

The present edition, in being relieved of some things which contributed to render all former ones unnecessarily cumbrous, without adding to the substantial value of the work, becomes an exceedingly cheap book. — *Albany Argus.*

All in the incomparable work of Cruden that is essential to a Concordance is presented in a volume much reduced both in size and price. — *Watchman and Reflector.*

Next to the Bible itself, every family should have a *concordance.* No person can study the Scriptures to advantage without one. Cruden's is the best. — *Baptist Record.*

CHAMBERS'S WORKS.

CHAMBERS'S CYCLOPEDIA OF ENGLISH LITERATURE. A Selection of the choicest productions of English Authors, from the earliest to the present time. Connected by a Critical and Biographical History. Forming two large imperial octavo volumes of 1400 pages, double column letter-press; with upwards of 300 elegant Illustrations. Edited by ROBERT CHAMBERS, embossed cloth, 5,00.

This work embraces about one thousand authors, chronologically arranged and classed as Poets, Historians, Dramatists, Philosophers, Metaphysicians, Divines, etc., with choice selections from their writings, connected by a Biographical, Historical, and Critical Narrative; thus presenting a complete view of English literature from the earliest to the present time. Let the reader open where he will, he cannot fail to find matter for profit and delight. The selections are gems – infinite riches in a little room; in the language of another, "A WHOLE ENGLISH LIBRARY FUSED DOWN INTO ONE CHEAP BOOK."

FROM W. H. PRESCOTT, AUTHOR OF "FERDINAND AND ISABELLA." The plan of the work is very judicious. It will put the reader in a proper point of view for surveying the whole ground over which he is travelling. . . . Such readers cannot fail to profit largely by the labors of the critic who has the talent and taste to separate what is really beautiful and worthy of their study from what is superfluous.

I concur in the foregoing opinion of Mr. Prescott. — EDWARD EVERETT.

A popular work, indispensable to the library of a student of English literature. — DR. WAYLAND.

We hail with peculiar pleasure the appearance of this work. — *North American Review.*

It has been fitly described as "*a whole English library fused down into one cheap book.*" The Boston edition combines neatness with cheapness, engraved portraits being given, over and above the illustrations of the English copy. – *N. Y. Commercial Advertiser.*

Welcome more than welcome It was our good fortune some months ago to obtain a glance at this work, and we have ever since looked with earnestness for its appearance in an American edition. — *N. Y. Recorder.*

☞ The American edition of this valuable work is enriched by the addition of fine steel and mezzotint engravings of the heads of SHAKSPEARE, ADDISON, BYRON; a full length portrait of DR. JOHNSON, and a beautiful scenic representation of OLIVER GOLDSMITH and DR. JOHNSON. These important and elegant additions, together with superior paper and binding, render the American far superior to the English edition. The circulation of this most valuable and popular work has been truly enormous, and its sale in this country still continues unabated.

CHAMBERS'S MISCELLANY OF USEFUL AND ENTERTAINING KNOWLEDGE. Edited by WILLIAM CHAMBERS. With Elegant Illustrative Engravings. Ten volumes, 16mo, cloth, 7,00.

This work has been highly recommended by distinguished individuals, as admirably adapted to Family, Sabbath, and District School Libraries.

It would be difficult to find any miscellany superior or even equal to it; it richly deserves the epithets "useful and entertaining," and I would recommend it very strongly as extremely well adapted to form parts of a library for the young, or of a social or circulating library in town or country. — GEORGE B. EMERSON, ESQ., CHAIRMAN BOSTON SCHOOL BOOK COMMITTEE.

I am gratified to have an opportunity to be instrumental in circulating "Chambers's Miscellany" among the schools for which I am superintendent. — J. J. CLUTE, *Town. Sup. of Castleton, N. Y.*

I am fully satisfied that it is one of the best series in our common school libraries now in circulation. – S. T. HANCE, *Town Sup. of Macedon, Wayne Co., N. Y.*

The trustees have examined the "Miscellany," and are well pleased with it. I have engaged the books to every district that has library money. — MILES CHAFFEE, *Town Sup. of Concord. N. Y.*

I am not acquainted with any similar collection in the English language that can compare with it for purposes of instruction or amusement. I should rejoice to see that set of books in every house in our country. — REV. JOHN O. CHOULES, D. D.

The information contained in this work is surprisingly great; and for the fireside, and the young, particularly, it cannot fail to prove a most valuable and entertaining companion. — *N. Y. Evangelist.*

It is an admirable compilation, distinguished by the good taste which has been shown in all the publications of the Messrs. Chambers. It unites the useful and entertaining. — *N. Y. Com. Adv.*

HUGH MILLER'S WORKS.

MY FIRST IMPRESSIONS OF ENGLAND AND ITS PEOPLE.

By Hugh Miller, author of "Old Red Sandstone," "Footprints of the Creator," etc., with a fine likeness of the author. 12mo, cloth, 1,00.

Let not the careless reader imagine, from the title of this book, that it is a common book of travels, on the contrary, it is a very remarkable one, both in design, spirit, and execution. The facts recorded, and the views advanced in this book, are so fresh, vivid, and natural, that we cannot but commend it as a treasure, both of information and entertainment. It will greatly enhance the author's reputation in this country as it already has in England. — *Willis's Home Journal.*

This is a noble book, worthy of the author of the Footprints of the Creator and the Old Red Sandstone, because it is seasoned with the same power of vivid description, the same minuteness of observation, and soundness of criticism, and the same genial piety. We have read it with deep interest, and with ardent admiration of the author's temper and genius. It is almost impossible to lay the book down, even to attend to more pressing matters. It is, without compliment or hyperbole, a most delightful volume. — *N. Y. Commercial.*

It abounds with graphic sketches of scenery and character, is full of genius, eloquence, and observation, and is well calculated to arrest the attention of the thoughtful and inquiring. — *Phil. Inquirer.*

This is a most amusing and instructive book, by a master hand. — *Democratic Review.*

The author of this work proved himself, in the Footprints of the Creator, one of the most original thinkers and powerful writers of the age. In the volume before us he adds new laurels to his reputation. Whoever wishes to understand the character of the present race of Englishmen, as contradistinguished from past generations; to comprehend the workings of political, social, and religious agitation in the minds, not of the nobility or gentry, but of the *people*, will discover that, in this volume, he has found a treasure. — *Peterson's Magazine.*

His eyes were open to see, and his ears to hear, every thing; and, as the result of what he saw and heard in "merrie" England, he has made one of the most spirited and attractive volumes of travels and observations that we have met with these many days. — *Traveller.*

It is with the feeling with which one grasps the hand of an old friend that we greet to our home and heart the author of the Old Red Sandstone and Footprints of the Creator. Hugh Miller is one of the most agreeable, entertaining, and instructive writers of the age; and, having been so delighted with him before, we open the First Impressions, and enter upon its perusal with a keen intellectual appetite. We know of no work in England so full of adaptedness to the age as this. It opens up clearly to view the condition of its various classes, sheds new light into its social, moral, and religious history, not forgetting its geological peculiarities, and draws conclusions of great value. — *Albany Spectator.*

We commend the volume to our readers as one of more than ordinary value and interest, from the pen of a writer who thinks for himself, and looks at mankind and at nature through his own spectacles. — *Transcript.*

The author, one of the most remarkable men of the age, arranged for this journey into England, expecting to "lodge in humble cottages, and wear a humble dress, and see what was to be seen by humble men only, — society without its mask." Such an observer might be expected to bring to view a thousand things unknown, or partially known before; and abundantly does he fulfil this expectation. It is one of the most absorbing books of the time. — *Portland Ch. Mirror.*

NEW WORK.

MY SCHOOLS AND SCHOOLMASTERS; OR THE STORY OF MY EDUCATION.

By Hugh Miller author of "Footprints of the Creator," "Old Red Sandstone," "First Impressions of England," etc. 12mo, cloth

This is a personal narrative of a deeply interesting and instructive character, concerning one of the most remarkable men of the age. No one who purchases this book will have occasion to regret it, our word for it!

U

THE PREACHER AND THE KING;

OR, BOURDALOUE IN THE COURT OF LOUIS XIV.

Being an Account of that distinguished Era. Translated from the French of L. BUNGENER. Paris, fourteenth edition. With an Introduction, by the REV. GEORGE POTTS, D. D., New York. 12mo, cloth, 1,25.

It combines *substantial history with the highest charm of romance;* the most rigid philosophical criticism with a thorough analysis of human character and faithful representation of the spirit and manners of the age to which it relates. We regard the book as a valuable contribution to the cause not merely of general literature, but especially of pulpit eloquence. Its attractions are so various that it can hardly fail to find readers of almost every description. — *Puritan Recorder.*

A very delightful book. It is full of interest, and equally replete with sound thought and profitable sentiment. — *N. Y. Commercial.*

It is a volume at once curious, instructive, and fascinating. The interviews of Bourdaloue, and Claude, and those of Bossuet, Fenelon, and others, are remarkably attractive, and of finished taste. Other high personages of France are brought in to figure in the narrative, while rhetorical rules are exemplified in a manner altogether new. Its extensive sale in France is evidence enough of its extraordinary merit and its peculiarly attractive qualities. — *Ch. Advocate.*

It is full of life and animation, and conveys a graphic idea of the state of morals and religion in the Augustan age of French literature. — *N. Y. Recorder.*

This book will attract by its novelty, and prove particularly engaging to those interested in the pulpit eloquence of an age characterized by the flagrant wickedness of Louis XIV. The author has exhibited singular skill in weaving into his narrative sketches of the remarkable men who flourished at that period, with original and striking remarks on the subject of preaching. — *Presbyterian.*

Its historical and biographical portions are valuable; its comments excellent, and its effect pure and benignant. A work which we recommend to all, as possessing rare interest. — *Buffalo Morn. Exp.*

A book of rare interest, not only for the singular ability with which it is written, but for the graphic account which it gives of the state of pulpit eloquence during the celebrated era of which it treats. It is perhaps the best biography extant of the distinguished and eloquent preacher, who above all others most pleased the king; while it also furnishes many interesting particulars in the lives of his professional contemporaries. We content ourself with warmly commending it. — *Savannah Journal.*

The author is a minister of the Reformed Church. In the forms of narrative and conversations, he portrays the features and character of that remarkable age, and illustrates the claims and duties of the sacred office, and the important ends to be secured by the eloquence of the pulpit. — *Phil. Ch. Obs.*

A book which unfolds to us the private conversation, the interior life and habits of study of such men as Claude, Bossuet, Bourdaloue, Massillon, and Bridaine, cannot but be a precious gift to the American church and ministers. It is a book full of historical facts of great value, sparkling with gems of thought, polished scholarship, and genuine piety. — *Cin. Ch. Advocate.*

This volume presents a phase of French life with which we have never met in any other work. The author is a minister of the Reformed Church in Paris, where his work has been received with unexampled popularity, having already gone through *fourteen* editions. The writer has studied not only the divinity and general literature of the age of Louis XIV., but also the memories of that period, until he is able to reproduce a life-like picture of society at the Court of the Grand Monarch. — *Alb. Trans.*

A work which we recommend to all, as possessing rare interest. — *Buffalo Ev. Express.*

In form it is descriptive and dramatic, presenting the reader with animated conversations between some of the most famous preachers and philosophers of the Augustan age of France. The work will be read with interest by all intelligent men; but it will be of especial service to the ministry, who cannot afford to be ignorant of the facts and suggestions of this instructive volume. — *N. Y. Ch. Intel.*

The work is very fascinating, and the lesson under its spangled robe is of the gravest moment to every pulpit and every age. — *Ch. Intelligencer.*

THE PRIEST AND THE HUGUENOT; or Persecution in the Age of Louis XV. Part I., A Sermon at Court; Part II., A Sermon in the City; Part III., A Sermon in the Desert. Translated from the French of L. BUNGENER, author of "The Preacher and the King." 2 vols. 12mo, cloth. ☞ *A new Work.*

☞ This is truly a masterly production, full of interest, and may be set down as one of the greatest Protestant works of the age.

www.ingramcontent.com/pod-product-compliance
Lightning Source LLC
LaVergne TN
LVHW020240110826
845151LV00003B/990

* 9 7 8 1 4 2 5 5 3 0 8 3 9 *